IN QUEST OF LOST WORLDS

Five Archeological Expeditions
1925-1934

By Count Byron de Prorok F.R.G.S.

THE NARRATIVE PRESS
TRUE FIRST PERSON ACCOUNTS OF HIGH ADVENTURE

COUNT BYRON DE PROROK, F.R.G.S.

Director of the Franco-American Archeological Expeditions to North Africa and Central America; Knight of the Crown of Italy; Grand Officer of the Knights of the Holy Sepulchre; Officer d'Academie, etc., etc.; Member of the International Anthropological Institute; Correspondent of the American and French Geographical Societies; Vice-President of the Atlantean Institute, etc., etc.

To my daughters,
Maureen and Denise de Prorok.

The Narrative Press
P.O. Box 2487, Santa Barbara, California 93120 U.S.A.
Telephone: (805) 884-0160 Web: www.narrativepress.com

ISBN 1-58976-048-4 (Paperback)
ISBN 1-58976-049-2 (eBook)

Produced in the United States of America

TABLE OF CONTENTS

Part I

Tin Hinan Legendary Queen of the Hoggar

PERSONNEL OF THE EXPEDITION, TO THE FRENCH
HOGGAR UNDER THE AUSPICES OF THE FRENCH AND
ALGERIAN GOVERNMENTS
COUNT BYRON DE PROROK Director

M. MAURICE REYGASSE; University of Algiers; co-Director
ALONZO POND ; Beloit College U.S.A.
BRADLEY TYRRELL ; Logan Museum U.S.A.
H. DENNY NewYork Times   ADJUTANT CHAPUIS
H. BARTH   CAID BELAID
Chauffeurs : CHAIX, MARTINI, ESCANDE

Chapter 1

It is the dead who have a tale to tell – the dead who died centuries ago – to people who still live, although, had everything gone as it seemed to be going, they also should be dead.

That I have any tale of my own to tell is lucky for me. Not once, but a dozen times it has seemed extremely unlikely that I should reach civilization again. So far I have succeeded, and sometimes have returned with material which has been of some value to scientists, and of interest to me.

Of course, it would have been cheaper, and perhaps more sensible, for me to have stayed rooted in one spot, to have pressed to the last word the tale of a particular site, to have decoded to the last comma the phraseology of one section of ancient civilization.

Honestly, I have preferred adventure. I like the greener hill, even if not always has the hill been greener. Sometimes it has not even been a hill; but I make no pretence about it all. I like the adventurous life. I like the reaction, in safety, to the thrills that have come in experience not so safe.

Probably, had it not been for the chance words of my friend Stephane Gsell, of the *Institut de France,* I should have followed calmer and easier trails to some sort of contentment. It is impossible to say.

The certainty is that, by his encouragement, I pulled away from the staid to the unstable side of archaeology, from the comfort of the well-established and well-found camp, equipped with resident scientists, papyrologists, drawers of pots, and surveyors of camp sites, where the photographers have their own staff and studio, the directors and personnel their own nice little bungalows, and their wives their tea-parties, flower-gardens, and Bridge afternoons.

That is the serious side of archaeology, possible when large endowments and almost inexhaustible funds are available for the burdening of so many shelves in the great libraries of the world. It is so serious at times that I have known one or two of the personnel to implore me to take them along on a bit of adventure, just to save their minds from cracking under the strain.

Nor, when I speak so, do I wish to leave the impression that I am being disrespectful to the very great. There is good and great work being done in these splendid homes of science. Perhaps as great work, in the long run, as is being done in the simpler, sturdier, and more courageous camps of the pioneers; the men who are working steadily and resolutely on little money, of which, even, they are not always certain.

For many years I had been working at Carthage, fighting the natives, and occasionally, the bureaucrats. The funds I had raised by means of lecture tours and interviews, largely in the United States, and by donations from American Universities and learned Societies. And I am duly sensible of the support we so obtained. We had collected a well-trained and, in every way, competent force of archaeologists. We were doing a moderately good job, to put it as modestly as may be. We were adding a little by discovery to the sum of human knowledge, an addition codified and presented by scientists of international reputation. We had opened the Punic necropolis at Carthage, and another at Utica. We had followed the same pavements that knew Cato, Scipio, Hannibal, and Caesar. We had driven through to the sanctuary of Tanit, where six thousand funerary urns spoke of the sacrificial rites. We had laughed at the curse that was supposed to lie over the city.

We had laughed, but one by one, in the last six years, those colleagues have slipped into death or into other disaster, and now only one or two remain. It is not the curse at work; only mortality.

After a few years, official jealousy and other official attributes increased. The pressure of bureaucracy grew increasingly insupportable. The cords of limitation were almost strangling. The price of permission to work became fantastic. One does not easily face the possibility of being offered as a sacrifice on the spot where the little children of Carthage made their great, but unwilling, gift of life to Tanit for the sake of the city's security. Yet it might have happened had not Professor Gsell, come from the *Institut de France* to collaborate on the proper presentation of the finds, given me the counsel of a friend and an older man, wise in the ways of intrigue and preferment.

"Why," he said, "don't you go somewhere where there is no *Service des Antiquites?* There is enough to do; there are things to be found."

The sequel came later, when I sat in his little study. Gsell, with his Socratic mien, his sandy hair turning to white, and his narrowing eyes fixed sometimes on me and sometimes on his ripe old pipe, began to tell me of ideas and researches that he had followed.

A chance word: a strange, but rather musical word, pulled me up suddenly.

"There's Antinea...Tin Hinan, for example," he said.

Tin Hinan at that moment meant nothing to me. I asked Gsell who he, she, or it might be, and learned that it was she, and that "she" was the grandmother of all the Tuaregs, their legendary queen; buried, perhaps, somewhere in the Hoggar: the secret of that warlike tribe who, last of all, submitted to the French, and then only when they were mown like ripe wheat by machine-guns which they had never seen or heard before that battle of Tit. They were strange to the hail of lead, and they fell like flies; but they charged to the very tripods, riddled and almost dead, and when they could fight no more, they snapped like wounded dogs at the guns.

They had a heritage of banditry, pillage, and murder. Ostensibly they were now subject to France, but they were not, nor are they yet, without their threat. For all their submission, during the war they took their chance throughout the whole of the North African possessions, and the country was in full revolt, needing a steady and cumulative campaign to subjugate them again. Reliable civilization is not established in one generation. The Tuareg is still the Tuareg at heart.

"You will need to be on your guard against them, for they are faithful to the memory of their grandmother," said Gsell.

To an extent, a journey into the Hoggar coincided with my own inclination; I was after the old caravan routes of the Phoenicians, and even earlier people, for caravans had been crossing the desert before Dido landed at Carthage and stretched the bull's hide.

Gsell's room was thick with tobacco smoke, mostly his; he smoked a particularly pungent brand of tobacco. Through the flood of his volcanic exhaust I saw him move to an old book on his shelf.

A few minutes later we had risen to the occasion, and were poring over an atlas, and while we worked we talked of ways and means.

Gsell suggested that it would be as well for me to get into touch with Maurice Reygasse, at that time *Controleur* of the *Commune Mixte* of Tebessa, and a known authority on the prehistoric civilizations of North Africa.

"But why not come yourself?" I asked.

"I?" he replied. "I have studied everything about North Africa for longer than I care to remember. I have made most of my expeditions in an arm-chair. I am an explorer in slippers. No, I cannot make this expedition, much as I would like to. Yet, I am not so sure that I want it made at all. I am not so sure that I approve of all this digging, all this discovery, this bringing to light of new material which alters much of what I have written and more that I still have to write. But get off with you! I will do what I can at this end."

With that he returned to a bilingual inscription that had just arrived from Constantine: returned with a smile and a little of a sigh.

In the accepted grand manner, I ought thereupon to have gone straight from his study, and with scanty stores and a few chosen companions mounted camels and made a raid across eighteen hundred miles of desert, straight to the Tomb, which would prove to be as rich and brilliant as Tutankhamen. But it was not exactly like that.

There were funds to be raised. There were permissions to be...obtained. Permits meant more bureaucrats. And there were also motor-cars to buy. They had to be built, and were built for me at the Renault works at Billancourt; six-wheelers with the back axles independently mounted, to allow passage over the dunes. Desert-going cars do not exactly grow on bushes; but it was easier and more expeditious to build motor-cars than to obtain the final permission of the French and Colonial Governments to make the journey. Signatures are delicate and difficult things to write, and there must be a certain and definite form of persuasion; the responsible authorities were desperately slow with the pen at the best of times.

Thanks to Professor Gsell and associated argument, the permit was duly delivered a little before we were ready to start, and Madame Rouvier broke a bottle of champagne over the bonnets of the cars. That was waste, perhaps, but it was a flea-bite to the waste that had preceded it.

I received more than the permit. Gsell gave me also a very broad hint. I obeyed the suggested injunction as well as I could, but could not be entirely obedient: matters were finally taken out of my hands.

Ostensibly, our journey to the Hoggar was to search for pre-historic sites and to study the origins of the Tuaregs. Of Tin Hinan, or Antinea, the less said the better; even to Reygasse.

"On your way, young man," said the Academician, "find Queen Tin Hinan for me, and I will make the report for you to the *Institut*. Then we will add a new chapter to the history of the Sahara. Good luck, and be watchful among the Tuaregs!" He went back to the library, and we went...south.

Of course, before an expedition gets under way, there is not infrequently a fair amount of window-dressing. It is good for trade, it is good for the personnel, it is good for everybody. But there are limits, easily reached.

Concessions must be made. It is politic always to be on the side of the politicians. If they will, they can facilitate one's journey, can make progress easy. They have the "open sesame." To explore in some countries this is essential, and it is necessary to submit, to a certain degree, to near-humiliations for the sake of the end in view.

But, accustomed as I was to the practices which would have delighted Bret Harte and his heathen Chinee, I was not entirely prepared for some things that happened.

The savages of the Sahara for generations had demanded "passage money" from travellers, and had accepted the cash in good faith, only later to assassinate the travellers when occasion served. The trail south is dotted with tombs – the tombs of explorers and missionaries, of French and English and other travellers. We passed a few on our way.

The Arabs! But they could learn a little from official practices. They do it better, and with the air of conferring favour – with such an air as leaves you helpless for a while and ultimately enraged. And finally, they are not entirely incapable of assuming all the credit for the work done.

Happily for me, the real interest lies in making the journey, in laying open to science new material. I should sometimes like to have a little of the credit for doing the work, but if that does not come, then it is at least consoling to know that the work has been done, and that other people have codified and arranged, and perhaps named, the results.

There were stores to buy, petrol to lay down *en route,* water to support our personnel. Much of the preparatory work had to be accepted on trust. For which reason, when it came to the stores, we found bully beef that had been left over from the war (if we found it at all), and for some other reason, at times we discovered only a part of what ought to have been there. Loss by evaporation, and from other causes, doubtless accounted for the deficiency.

In addition to material, the personnel needed to be supervised fairly rigorously, for when we made the Tin Hinan expedition, the Sahara was not exactly a pleasure-ground, whatever it may now be, thanks to the pioneers who have established the routes over which comfortable sleeping-cars run to Timbuktu.

In Algiers, having shipped the cars over, we paid a formal and pleasant visit to the Governor, and collected the real heroes of the raid, including Chapuis, the Saharan counterpart of an old salt. Believe me, we were thankful enough to have him along before we finished. For interpreter among the Berber tribes we had caid Belaid. And, as advised by Gsell, we had Maurice Reygasse, resplendent in uniform when we met him at Constantine – or rather, he met us; just a little fatigued by farewells and entertainment.

Africa is a land of politeness and officialdom; a uniform with plenty of gold-leaf goes far. Moreover, it demands attention. But it has its drawbacks. Our cars, for example, were equipped to carry water and petrol, sufficient for a stage of a thousand kilometres, but they were not designed to carry a gigantic cask of wine, which was a present from the Senator of Constantine to Reygasse.

Biskra, that tourists' Mecca, lay on our route, and has always marked a link. It is the extreme end of the chotts that stretch from the Aurés through the depression to Gabes on the Mediterranean; salt lakes that were perhaps at one time part of the inland sea, and similarly are to be found in other parts of Northern Africa; possibly of casual interest to travellers, but of considerable importance to geographers, and people with theories, such as myself.

It is the land of fable, perhaps of fable founded on fact. Possibly the Tritons sounded their horns and sailed on open water here. There are people who insist that they did, and it seems to be well authenticated that a Punic galley was discovered not far from Nefta by French officers.

At this point, the map has a distinctly significant appearance; following the course of the depressions, it would almost appear that the land of Atlantis formed an island, or at least a broad and mountainous peninsula, with the Atlantic sweeping inland from the region below Agadir in Morocco, through the valleys of the Sous and the Draa, isolating the Atlas chains, with their continuation in the Aurés and the mountains of the coast, bounded on the other side by the Mediterranean.

Absolve me from any day-dreams on Atlantis, although I have consciously and unconsciously searched for the lost continent for years. I am not alone in the search. At least here I was following in the footsteps of Belioux, and a group of German scientists later followed on my trails, coming from the universities of Munich, Hamburg, and Berlin to scour the chotts, seeking chiefly the location of the famous temple which Homer called Scheria, and Plato, Atlantis. The Arabs think of it as the "city of brass."

What these investigators succeeded in discovering was certainly of importance: Greek relics, statuettes, and the trident of Poseidon crudely sculptured on the rock face, some of which were accepted as being authentic and others as being doubtful. Imagination, of course, is necessary also to scientists, particularly in the hunt for lost continents.

One thing, however, is of supreme importance – a thing I have noted at many ancient African centres: here, in the chotts of Algeria, in Tunisia, in the Libyan desert, at Siwa, and in the Djouf, there is a distinct and definite trace of the receding tide. The desert was not always so lacking in water as it now seems to be. The water-level has steadily lowered, and with each decline there is a new or changed civilization. The Stone Age, with the foyers of primitive men, is to be found on the highest level. The palæolithic, succeeded by the neolithic, gives way, at a lower level when the water has subsided, to the Græco-Phoenician and to the Romano-Byzantine, and, at the present level, to the Arab.

This was useful to us, since we were on the way to study the origins of the Libyans.

And, occasionally, there is another evidence of the fact that water is not so unknown in the desert; but demonstration came in the shape of a raging storm which converted the depressions into temporary lakes, and we had to push our cars to their best, racing the oncoming flood. We were to an extent fortunate enough to escape disaster. The native conveyances were not so lucky!

Touggourt we reached without too much difficulty, although the trails were not so good, and there we dropped the machine-gun and ten cases of ammunition that Reygasse had deemed essential. What actually happened was that we had a little prac-tice in the sand dunes, and found the recoil or something just a little too much for the operator. Perhaps he blistered his hands on the water-jacket, or got an unexpected kick which made us incapable of regarding it with a friendly eye.

So, fully started, we left the tombs of the Sultans lonely in their sands, the early light just touching them with rose and gold, and turned south along a well-marked trail, by way of Tamelhat and Temassin.

There was mirth and real happiness among us. Denny the newspaper man, and Barth the photographer, who had been qui-etly apprehensive during the loneliness of the last few hundred kilometres, lost their doubts. This, then, was all there was to exploration! They felt that they need not really have included a fully paid-up insurance policy among their demands and pay. There was going to be neither danger nor the likelihood of dan-ger; no hardship, no trouble. There was a highway in the wilder-ness with innumerable tracks all the way along running round the high dunes and across the shaling flat stretches. We had food and water, and a cask of wine; we had guns and plenty of ammu-nition. We had a gramophone for diversion. This was the finest, the most sensible, the most delightful way of reaching the unknown. Livingstone had chosen the wrong age in which to go exploring!

And then we hit the first of our troubles.

Chapuis, who was better than expert in desert ways, had turned his face against all levity and display, although, like the rest of us, so long as that cask remained, he took his share of the luxury, and perhaps hastened its consumption, the sooner to be rid of its incubus.

On one of our cars we had mounted a winch, which was intended to haul our sand-locked cars clear should ever the occasion rise. We used it earlier than we expected, for the floods were greater when we left Touggourt. Our cars were sunk to the axles in the wet sand and the wheels got no purchase. We dismounted and took spades to release the cars, and with difficulty came free and were able to use our winch to haul the native post out of the mud also. There was the making of a good picture in it, so we sent Barth our photographer, a well-built, weighty fellow, into the stream, picking a good position for him to film the adventure. He worked steadily on, his weight telling more every second, until finally he, and the camera with him, sank nearly up to his arm-pits. The sands were quickening, and he came very near at that moment to making a claim on his insurance policy, but we passed ropes around him and hauled him clear. The stunt actors of Hollywood have very little on casual adventures of travelling cameramen, if they are on my expeditions.

Here was contrast enough for my companions, who had half expected, I am sure, that we were actually going to take a long ride on sands as monotonous and as hard as the sands of Daytona Beach.

We were in the vicinity of Temassin, and had been working for hours. We were tired and hungry, were ready enough to do justice to the fete that was in preparation for us: a civic welcome with military splendour for the *Controleur-civile,* to the glory of the caid and, as I believed, at the expense of the village.

We were wet, tired, and muddy. Our bones and muscles ached; everyone had been driving hard to make headway possible. The caid, we knew, had been preparing for our arrival ever since Reygasse wrote him, quietly amassing a banquet, and not so quietly staging it.

The only presentable member of the expedition was Reygasse himself, who had had sufficient forethought to don a burnous. His uniform was protected, and if his boots were not faultlessly shined, they were yet passable.

We were hungry, we had no idea of the size of the banquet that was being arranged for us, and we trooped into the courtyard of the caid's house, prepared to grapple with whatever was offered. First there was a thick, mealy soup laced with honey, served in large wooden platters and manipulated with wooden spoons. It looked slightly suspicious, but we had decided that whatever was offered we would accept, drowning our fears and holding our noses. Nothing deterred us; nothing could have deterred us. We saw the soup disappear and felt just a little better. The soup was followed by an enormous couscous, which also we dealt with. The next course was a sweet hash of chopped meat, dates, and raisins; good enough, and filling! We were polite with many a belch and more "Bismillahs," out of courtesy to our host, who superintended the service, but who would not partake himself until all his guests were filled.

The servants, however, as each dish was returned, cleaned the platters of all save the smell, and the dogs attended to that.

By this time we were absolutely stuffed, very thankful and pleased, but anxious to say a kindly farewell and thank you, and be on our way. But this was no banquet to offer to great generals, no gilt for gold-leaf. There followed enough to feed a small town. We had simply wolfed the food at the beginning, never dreaming of the sequel, since no menus were provided. Now politeness took its toll; there ensued a completely disguised dish – the fish. We were on a prehistoric search, anyhow, so we tried it. We were also almost four hundred miles from the sea, and I don't know how many from Yarmouth and Aberdeen; but, there, swimming in the sauce, around islands of tomatoes and pimentoes, were early kippers and fragments of neolithic haddies that had been carted up from Bone or Gabes. To the Arabs, definitely a delicacy, and of pronounced flavour; to us, just a little terrible. Still, politeness obliged. We struggled, and after we had finished, there was mirth among the servants; but not at our expense. It was the real glee of utter satisfaction; the chuckle of epicures.

After the fish, a sheep or goat, or some other animal; entire, grinning weirdly, malevolently, in baked death, with moist and pleading eyes. The sheikh, kindly and in courtesy, hooked out one eye with his thumb as a special delicacy for me. After that I lost confidence; but the banquet still went on. A dish of chickens followed.

The Americans fell casualties first. The French made an heroic stand. Were they not on historic ground? Barth, who perhaps had conserved his energy a little better, snaffled a whole bird, in the tradition of Henry VIII as interpreted by Charles Laughton, and with an impressive gesture, smashed his fist on the breastbone, ripped the wings apart, took two bites at the legs (while safeguarding the daintier portions), jettisoned the drumsticks, and shortly the chicken was no more. The Arabs, who were eating on the side, were even better technicians; from them the dogs retrieved little.

This was hospitality enough to please the most exacting. Reygasse made a formal speech to the caid, a speech of thanks and appreciation which must have made his own ears burn; and I added my little, in turn. I thought that it was we who were being entertained. Nor was I disillusioned until the whole expedition was finished and accounts were presented for payment. Then I found a neat little entry: for banquet at Temassin, and the amount inscribed in nice little figures, mostly ciphers – I paid for my own civic welcome.

We were in a state bordering on collapse after the meal; but Ouargla promised more. Occasionally, *en route,* the motion of the cars served us as other things served the Romans in similar case, and gradually we recovered from the uncomfortable stupor.

Ouargla, which looked more like a mirage when we first saw it from the distance, with its lakes and reflected minarets, its

walls glowing, rose-tinted, and palms nodding, was a jewel set
in gold.

This was the real beginning of the passage. Joy-riding was
now finally over, and we were there to tackle the crossing and
see what we should see.

The fortress stood clear in the vibrant air. The oasis shim-
mered. We seemed to be the only active people. Ouargla, like all
desert towns, was half-asleep.

In the streets the people stirred indolently if they stirred at all.
For the most part they were taking their ease propped against the
comers of the doorways, rousing a little at our approach.

Colour was beginning to spread under the slanting rays of the
sun, and such colour that all the dyers of Tunis or Fez would fail
to match.

Hueless under the full sun of day, arid and unrelieved, when
evening begins life loses its drab monotone. The shadows are
violet, the mud walls are steeped in rose and crowned with gold,
the distance flaunts a royal blue and an imperial purple.

Fittingly, perhaps, our first salute came from the White
Fathers, who trod the dusty ways, for the moment in safety,
devoted successors of those heroic pioneers whose massacre
took place not far from the oasis.

Well have the natives called them "the marabouts of the
desert." That is what they are, the saints of the Sahara who have
won the respect of the Arabs although they may not yet have
defeated Islam.

The Commandant of the post verified our permits, assured us
of our escorts in the less comfortable stretches of the trip, told us
that our camels had gone through according to schedule, laying
dumps, and then dropped all formality and invited the expedition to dinner.

After dinner, Chapuis, who was a real sand-dog and could
prick more than one bubble of Saharan exploration, took me to
the garage, to show me a decrepit old Ford, which he had used in
preparing the track across the desert to Timbuktu, for the guidance of a renowned expedition. To them was the glory; to him

the labour. I often wonder if the people of Europe give a thought to the path-finder who worked without fame to make fame possible for others. That Ford went to Timbuktu and back, and Chapuis with it, alone. It should be in a museum, as the real pioneer of desert travel.

But Chapuis would have made the desert on foot, failing camel or Ford. Hard-bitten, tough, reliable, and with no use for polite phrases, he knew neither fear nor hesitation.

Chapter 2

When day was nearing its end, and the warm magic of the sky turned the oasis into a place of enchantment, I wandered to the little chapel of the White Fathers, more like a native *koubba* than a Christian church, thinking of the journey ahead. This was not my first expedition; but in all essentials it was different.

We were running through difficult country. We were likely to make contact with tribes of whose loyalty and peaceful intentions there was considerable doubt; natural brigands of the desert, with a long roll of victims and a reputation for brutality and ferocity difficult to rival. It was quite likely that the raid would be no joke, for all the levity and inconsequence with which we affected to regard it.

At a distance, seated on a tiny hillock in the midst of a clump of palms on the outskirts of the town, I saw the lone, bent figure of one of the White Fathers, as he stared out over the limitless sand, his back to the tiny Christian cemetery with its simple crosses.

Quietly, not wishing to disturb his meditation, unless he, too, wished to speak, I approached him. The blood-red sun tinted his thick white burnous. He might have been a Knight Crusader.

"Good evening, Father," I said.

Without turning, he replied: "Good evening, young man of America!"

He indicated by a slow gesture that I should not be intruding, yet I was reluctant to break the silence.

What weight it had, that silence! It lay on the earth, and on me, like a stiffing blanket.

I sat in the sand by his side, and said how still everything was. He corrected me: not stillness, only a crouching silence.

"But there will be a more terrible silence where you are going, young man. The Hoggar! You have nerve, to try to penetrate and mix with those tribes, so soon after revolt."

I explained that it was our hope to be the first to make an extensive investigation.

"Besides," I said, "it would be less terrible to me than a life of inaction and *cafard,* such as there is here. Don't you find it terribly monotonous, Father?"

"My son," he replied, "never believe that because I am alone I lack companionship. When one has infinitude to look on, and the gift of meditation, boredom is impossible.

"Besides" – and his voice took on a strange, youthful ring – "I have memories. Perhaps I am growing a little old; but I can remember the great men who have gone..."

I looked at the tranquil old man, with his patriarchal beard: the courageous *roumi* who had tried to bring the faith to indifferent Arabs, whose adventure had been much closer to the primitive than mine, demanding greater inner resources.

"We had no wireless," he mused. "No motors, no meals of six courses carried in tins. No financial reserves. The Cardinal gave us a few thousand francs..."

He fell silent again. I had had a hint of the early struggles of the real people of the Sahara, and somehow I thought of Duveyrier with his three camels: a fabulous figure before he was twenty-five; Pere de Foucauld, who trod unbelievable miles, feet and head bare, hanging on to the tail of Laperrine's camel, by way of penitence; Douls, strangled; Laing, who died of thirst in the Djouf; Flatters, and a hundred men betrayed and murdered.

The priest's slow voice broke the silence again.

"It was in 'eighty-eight. I had been sent by Cardinal Lavigerie on a mission to the Tuaregs of the northern alliance. What I saw...

"I had reached a village called Abalessa. It was in ruins, but there was a handful of survivors, including a Targui of noble family, one Moussa Ag Tacaba. Six months previously the village had been raided by the Agouleminden of the south, while the young men were away on a raid towards Rio de Oro. Among their booty was Fati, Moussa's young wife, the loveliest girl of the Kel r'Ali. There were only old men and the women left in the village when the Agouleminden descended. The old people were massacred and the young women abducted.

"When the warriors returned, they were driven almost to insanity by what they saw, amazed by the betrayal, for they had a treaty with the Agouleminden. After burying their dead, they turned south on a quest for vengeance."

The missionary stared out to the desert, his mind working in secret. Perhaps he had it in his heart to deter me. I do not know; but there was certainly a particularly significant emphasis on the words "Tuareg revenge!"

He tapped his pipe on his low heel, and filled it again, while I waited for him to continue.

"You must understand," he said, taking his own time, "that Moussa had succeeded to the titular headship of his tribe, and that he had only one idea: to recover Fati and take his revenge."

His voice was sinister; cold. Perhaps for a moment he had forgotten his peaceful mission. A jackal cried in the distance, prowling among the shallow graves of the Muhammedan cemetery, sending a shiver down my spine.

"For weeks Moussa and his warriors patrolled the trails of the desert, seeking the encampments of the Agouleminden. Sometimes they would cover a hundred kilometres in a day, their only food a handful of dates; and, ultimately, near Tafasasset they came upon their quarry, who still believed that the young warriors of Abalessa were well away on their *razzia* towards Rio de Oro. But, according to their custom, the Tuaregs attacked at dawn, creeping across the sands, and the battle was fought without mercy. No quarter was given. The Kel r'Ali took no prisoners, and left none alive; but Moussa found no trace of Fati, save that one of the Agouleminden had fled the battle, escaping towards the west.

"Moussa followed alone, riding one camel and leading two in reserve, carrying only food and water."

Again the White Father paused, grew reminiscent.

"I, too, have tramped the desert," he said. "And I have known the terrible thirst. The first hours of the night are demoniacal. When the moon rises, it seems as though an acrid dust fills the air; blinding and suffocating. Imagine a man, hunted and athirst. You move mechanically, steadily, in an attempt to escape the dust that hits the throat like fire. Then, perhaps because nature can stand no more, there comes a sort of relief, a certain stupefaction; but you keep on without stopping, forgetting even that you are on the march. The night goes, and the bitterest hour comes when you seem to be dying of thirst and chilled through with the cold. Weariness is overwhelming: that terrible breeze, forerunner of the dawn, is no solace. On the contrary!

"It is a strange sensation, to be dying of thirst. At first the suffering is beyond belief; but then it softens a little. Insensibility creeps on. Little events out of the past creep back to your mind. Your brain burns..."

The moon began to show over the fronds of the palms. The old brother of the fraternity of the sands was silent; thinking. He seemed no more than a ghost; unsubstantial, other-worldly. He came out of his reverie with a start.

"After five days, Moussa found his adversary's camel, spent on the sand; but the abductor was gone, seeking to escape on foot. Then there were hopes of saving Fati; but it was too late. Among the scared rocks which the Agouleminden had followed, hoping to make pursuit by camel impossible, Moussa found the dead body of his bride, mutilated by the terrible incision of the Berber races.

"He stayed only long enough to give one last look at her, and to dig a hurried grave. Then he pressed on along the trail, death in his heart, following the track of his enemy with a relentless fury that is impossible to imagine...for you."

The dull glow of the padre's smouldering pipe was the only light in the oasis. He had chosen a dramatic enough setting for this tale of encouragement to a man whose objective was no other than the village of that same Moussa. The moon was hidden behind a thick veil of the palms of the plantation.

"So the end came. The tragedy unfolded. The Agouleminden was found, nearly dead from thirst, crawling on all-fours, his purple tongue hanging like a dog's from his mouth. When he could move no more, he lay on the ground and Moussa taunted him with a full flask of water, withdrawing it when the hands of his enemy had almost closed on it. Impossible to describe that torture! When his victim could no longer stir, Moussa spat in his face, to show that he was not thirsty. Then binding his wrists, he carried him to his camels and bore him to Abalessa. It was the end of the tale...

"There, Moussa buried him up to the neck in the sand, leaving his head bared to the sun. The first day he cut off his eyelids, so that the sun-glare could not be escaped. In a few hours the Agouleminden was blind and half mad; but he was still thirsty.

"The second day..."

As though it was too much to tell, the peaceful old priest hesitated a moment.

"The second day he cut off nose and ears, and with his own hands carried red ants to the murderer of Fati. When I heard of it, I hurried to the place, but it was already too late. The maniacal shrieks ceased when I was yet afar off. There remained little more than a grinning skull, with a stream of ants passing through nostrils and mouth to the brain...

"That, my son, is Tuareg revenge..."

There was a moment of silence. The old man took up his reverie once more.

"So you see, young man, there is no absence of incident in the desert. One sees things...one sees many things! And now good-bye! I shall be there when you start to-morrow, You, too, will see things. There are things to be seen..."

Not for a long time after he had withdrawn to his little hermitage did I stir, and when I rose I was stiff with cold.

I looked to the horizon to the south, towards that unknown, and as I went back to the camp I could hear those terrible cries of Moussa's victim; but it was only a jackal. I wondered, should we really see things down there.

Immediately after leaving Ouargla we pitched our tents under the lee of Gara Krima, "the Earth Sister of the Rainbow," which was in striking-distance of the town. It is a mountain of eerie beauty; the stones are of every colour and shade; but we were not there to admire the scene. There were traces of the old Libyan fortresses on the summit of the hill: prehistoric walls and a number of flint instruments, which showed that it had been a human outpost from earliest times.

The view from the height was immense. The eye commanded the entire stretch of desert to the far horizon. It was a natural, almost impregnable stronghold, only to be brought into subjection by starvation or by modern machines of war. On the top was a well, sunk through the living rock.

Here we camped, and began our first research along the Oued Mya for prehistoric remains, our earliest discoveries being of the Chellean period, including some rare and finely-worked flints, which inspired certain jealousies.

Let no one believe that scientific expeditions, with mixed personnel, can be carried through from beginning to end without trouble. Science may be an international affair. There may be a freemasonry as regards published results; but there is considerable jealousy as to the possession of the objects found. Museums like to add to their store of treasures, and people love to see their names on little tablets: sometimes their only link with posterity; their sole memorial.

So a battle royal was staged between the Logan Museum, represented by Alonzo Pond, and the Museum of the Bardo, represented by Reygasse. Each was making a collection for his own museum, and whenever a particularly juicy find was brought to light the argument of ownership broke out afresh; but the issue was postponed, for we had to keep our load as light as possible, and it was agreed that the finds should be cached, to be picked up on our return.

We had only two tents with us; which was another source of trouble. Prestige and precedence, you might expect, would gladly be left behind on such an expedition; but first the mechanics and chauffeurs claimed the right to the tents, as being the only people who really worked on the trip. Reygasse then advanced his importance, and Denny demanded protection for his typewriter, since he had to prepare dispatches for sending from any and every military post in the desert that had either camel-courier or wireless. Barth, not to be outdone, insisted that as an overworked photographer he needed proper rest at night.

Chapuis and Belaid, with a sarcastic grin, took no part in the discussion. They simply scooped out holes for themselves in the sand and went to sleep. I stretched myself out on one of the seats – actually a far more comfortable berth than was possible in the tents.

Above, the stars glittered in a hard, dry sky that curved like a steel bowl inverted over our heads. There was peace and a little respite from the torrid heat of the day; a respite that soon became something of a menace as the night advanced and the temperature fell. Rocks that had borne the heat of the day, but could not withstand the cold, split and whistled. The sand began to speak in strange, sibilant whispers.

The camp was still for a while, although the final compromise had not yet been reached. No question of uninterrupted sleep had been discussed; but it was soon obvious that we were divided into two parties; the snorers and the silent. Some members were excellent performers, and woke each other. Little by little, they drew apart and slept at a safe distance.

That was the last time discussion arose concerning the tents. They were abandoned to the mechanics and the Arab cook...If only everything could have been settled as amiably!

The Mya is a dead Nile of the Sahara. At one time, fed by streams from the Hoggar Mountains, it must have been a fine river. Even now, it was a strange comment on human nature,

that petty squabbles could continue in such grandiose surroundings. The dried bed and strange banks of the river rose in multi-
coloured terraces from the white sand. In the distance a clear
blue sky, innocent of cloud, joined the horizon. The crested
dunes were tinged with rose and amber; deep purple shadows
and crimson flanks. Stretching the length of the stream were the
foyers of migratory neolithic tribes. The traces of their fires
were still there, visible as soon as we swept the sand from their
sites.

It fell to Chapuis – no scientist, but a great hunter – to unearth
the first *coup de poing,* which sent Pond and Reygasse into
antiphonal chants of delight. We were in a prehistoric paradise;
fossil bones of long-vanished animals were there, evidence of
the truth that at one time this had been verdant and well-watered
country.

Of course, it was seen that the specimens could not be carried
with us and peace was concluded between the rivals, only to be
broken as other pacts have been broken before and since; for,
with the keen and exclusive pride of the collector, Reygasse
continued with his great sack, examining every find, and, fearful
that they might have disappeared by the time of our return,
selected the choicest for his collection, which he deposited in the
cases.

Pond naturally, not to be outdone (and Pond was as persistent
as ever man could be), followed suit, and there was a serious
possibility that we should be swamped with treasures of flint.
Other sanctions were invoked, and the zealots cooled off, as collections were separated and piled in accessible places against
our return: grinders, lances, axes, hammers, and arrowheads.

The importance of travelling as light as we could was soon
impressed on us, for the Mya, beautiful as it undoubtedly is, had
laid up a store of difficulty for us. The giant dunes stretched on
either side, and there was no way round: we had to go through.

We were in the sand Alps, the mass sometimes rising to a
total height of a thousand feet, with steep-sided peaks, crested
and sheer to leeward. For the smaller dunes, the trick was to get

enough leeway to charge at them, and take them like a switch-back (if the wheels continued to grip), and then to take a strong hold on whatever was handy to receive the blow in the middle of the back as the car stood for a moment on its radiator cap before sliding precipitously down.

That was not always possible. We would, and did, charge, and suddenly throw in low gear, while the six wheels churned up a cloud of sand as we toiled, hot and blistered, to the loose and treacherous crest.

Day after day we were plunging, fighting, sweating, and swearing, to cover a few miles, with scouts on either side look-ing for any traces that might have interest. Not infrequently we would go axle deep into the sand, and the full crowd, with some-times one exception, would help to unload, or keep running like ants round the cars, laying and taking up strips of matting and rolls of chicken-wire, to give purchase to the wheels.

Early optimism began to fade a little. Exploration was not altogether a peaceful, leisurely progress in an arm-chair to sites never before seen by the eye of man.

Sweat meant water, and water was rationed. One of the crowd developed kleptomania. Unobserved, he would steal back to the cars while the rest of us were preparing a way through the sand, and drink his fill; not once, but a dozen times as day drew on.

When we came to our bottles, they were empty. His was the only full one, and we were terrified by the loss, as we thought, by evaporation or accident. But finally we caught him – luckily before the reserve tank was exhausted, and this was measured and protected. Then, rations were rations, and he could drink his as and when he liked; but ours were ours. Finally, we were able to impress him with the truth; but never quite completely. He still found ways and means of getting a little extra, nor could he help it entirely. He was more to be pitied; for working with spade and bare hands in the sand, under a broiling sun, flayed by a hot, dry, desiccating wind, was no sinecure, and at that time we were traveling three to cover one mile of trail. How the cars stood up to the grueling was a miracle.

Nor was the sand all. We left the dunes with more than a sigh of relief, to come out upon rocks and flints piled inches deep; flints cracked by the heat and sudden cold, as sharp as knives; flints which ripped our tyres to pieces and exploded them like heavy artillery.

Among the flints we made camp. We were in a stone meadow, and there seemed to be possibility of other than naturally chipped specimens.

In the earliest glimmer of dawn, while coffee was being made, I scoured the deposit, and was lucky enough to stumble early on a workshop of primitive man, which contained flints corresponding very closely to those of the Fayum.

Later, we spread out like beaters; even the chauffeurs were given a little instruction so that they could recognize worked stone, and on hands and knees we covered a large part of the field; linked, and keeping regular distance.

This discovery was one of a series I made in that belt of the Sahara that stretches roughly along the tropic of Capricorn; the commencement of a series of seven expeditions which curiously linked the civilizations of many countries.

The flints were of extraordinarily fine workmanship, impossible to be copied to-day, the product of an unknown race of flint artists.

My later investigations seemed to lead to the idea of a vast prehistoric migration, for the handiwork seemed clearly identifiable with specimens found along a stretch of country east and west of this point; in the Libyan desert, at Siwa, in the Fayum, in the Tripolitan Sahara, and even so far as the Red Sea to the east and the Atlas Mountains and the Atlantic to the west. And in later years we picked up the same chain when we crossed to Yucatan and Central America.

To the north and south of the line so marked, the workmanship had different characteristics; but we found similar specimens, and traces of this highly individualized prehistoric folk by hundreds of thousands, stretching to Ethiopia and the British Sudan.

I wondered, and still wonder, if ultimately there may be a definite link with the Atlanteans along this line; the wonder has at least stirred me to make succeeding expeditions.

From time to time on our trail we would discover strange mounds of stones that occasionally we excavated, hoping to find some evidence of sorts; but they were only signal mounds, perhaps marking the caravan routes of historic times, but certainly not of modern times.

At night, around the camp fires, our minds naturally tried to retrace the centuries. We wondered how the early caravanners had done it: we were having enough difficulty, although we had every advantage that civilization and invention could give. Those old travelers did have elephants. They had buffaloes. But they did not have camels. Certainly there was more water than there is now; so, perhaps, it was not so arduous a trip as the present Sahara suggests; but many thousands of slaves must have perished on the trail to Carthage with their loads of gold dust, ivory, and precious stones from the land of the Garamantes.

Side-trips, and the unexpected enmity of the desert, added two days to our journey. They also took two days off our reserve of water, and we were running very near to the danger point when we were forty-eight hours away from Hassi Inifel, where we expected our first dump.

Save for one bottle per man, the last thirty-six hours of the run were dry, and by the time we reached the well at Hassi Inifel we were bone-dry. So far, we had squandered our water a little carelessly, counting on arriving in time.

If the experience was unpleasant, it was ultimately healthy, for we were acquiring desert lore. There is no torture quite so real as thirst, and luckily we had not yet got so far as that. We were dry without being hopelessly parched, and we had hope with us, the certainty of a supply near at hand.

Hassi Inifel was deserted. The Foreign Legion had done all that was demanded of it, and was gone. The mud fort, with its white-plastered walls failing into ruins, stood as a terrible monument, half-covered by sand.

The first thing we saw was the abandoned fuselage of General Laperrine's plane, in which he was making the first flight across the Sahara; Laperrine, friend of de Foucauld and conqueror of the Sahara, who, on his flight, was caught in a sandstorm and separated from his companions, to be blown against the rocks, a hundred miles away. His machine was ultimately recovered, and had been transported so far on its way back to France.

Chapuis had been one of the searchers for the general, and around the camp-fire that night we heard the story of his death; the last in the long line of martyrs of the Sahara.

When his plane crashed, Laperrine's ribs were caved in. He knew that he was bleeding internally, and that his case was probably hopeless. His companions were bruised; but not otherwise too grievously damaged. They had a chance, although there seemed little hope of early rescue. The great necessity was the close rationing of water and the scanty provisions they carried.

At every allotment, the general accepted his allowance of water and chocolate; but, when night had fallen, and his comrades snatched a few hours' sleep, he crept on hands and knees to pour the major part of his water back into their bottles, and to return the chocolate to the general fund.

Scouting parties were abroad, dispatched from every post. Planes swept the desert. The tribes were roused, and many of them worked out of real affection for the general. Lights burned on the high dunes.

Eight days after the crash, the Tuaregs found the wreckage. Laperrine was dead. His two companions were barely alive. They were carried back to Tamenrasset, where the general was buried beside his friend de Foucauld. His last words, committed to his companions, were a caution to all Saharan explorers.

"Tell them," he said, "that they may conquer the Sahara by caravan and motor; but it will always remain the Sahara, and it will still claim its victims."

To hear Chapuis describing the search was stupendous. Even he, case-hardened as he was, was moved. He still showed the unquiet spirit that pervaded every post in the desert. Villages and oases sent out their contingents of men to scour every inch of the way. Tuaregs, Chambaa, and men of all the tribal confederations were abroad, with instructions to find their general, or never return. And, in fact, many did not return until months later, after the general had been found and carried to his grave. Time meant nothing to them, and they had had no news.

From Hassi Inifel, our next water-hole was Ain Guettara, across the sun-scorched region of Tadmait. The stones that littered the desert were as black as ebony from the heat, as though they had been charred in a furnace, and it was on our way to this well that we found the "Love Mountain" of the Sahara, rising from the course of the Oued Mya.

While the others searched the bed of the stream for possible traces of prehistoric man, I climbed, and was amazed to find terrace after terrace of inscriptions in Tifinar, and curious engravings of pairs of feet, standing together on the edge of the precipice. When Belaid joined me, with the others, he read the inscriptions, which went back many generations. Some were understandable, others demanded laboured study by savants, to whom we took photographs and tracings.

It was probably the Gretna Green of that part of the Sahara, in times of greater productivity and greater population; the spot where the marriage ceremony of the lineal descendants of the ancient Libyans took place; one of the last links with them.

From the modern Tifinar, Belaid deduced that the practice had been continued, and that the pairs of feet outlined were the marriage signature, the feet being means of identification.

What was noticeable, and perhaps significant, was that the feet were always to the edge of the precipice, the man's to the right, the woman's to the left, and round the feet were written names and a proclamation of eternal love. Some, it was found, went back nearly two thousand years. The date is fixed within a century or two of the beginning of the Christian era. Others could not be deciphered, and may be older still.

A circle round the inscriptions denoted that an unfaithful individual had been brought back to the place of his vows and thrown over. Infidelity was punishable by death among the ancient Libyans; unlike the Tuaregs of to-day, their probable descendants.

The Libyans were the common progenitors of the Berbers, and in this connection we discovered some peculiar coincidences before the expedition was finished, coincidences borne out by later exploration.

Tin Hinan, to whose place of burial we were traveling, proved to be of the third or fourth century of our era, and had cranial measurements, and other ethnological peculiarities, precisely the same as are to be encountered among the existing Tuaregs, the Berbers of the Rift, the Kabyles, the Maures of Mauretania, the Guanches of the Canary Islands, and the Mayas of Yucatan, as well as the people of Siwa.

"Love Mountain" was so interesting that we filmed the whole of the inscriptions. It is not often that one has the luck to come across so romantic a place, a thousand miles from civilization, across an almost trackless waste.

Chapter 3

Ain Guettara was a little fortress, with one lone watchman, deserted now by the military; but it served as our dump, and the watchman was there to see that no looting happened, although how he could have prevented it, had the Tuaregs or others come in force, I could never understand.

The water-hole was cleared. We filled up our supplies, and then drew lots for precedence, to take our first baths for a week, and I got the last place. The old guardian watched us in amazement. He had never had a bath for so long as he could remember, and now he never would have one.

We asked him what he thought of life, and he told us. Until the Citroen Expedition, three years previously, there had been little traffic, and now we had arrived. It seemed that he began to esteem himself the forerunner of all Saharan police on point duty.

Yet not everything was so quiet. A patrol met us, sent out from In Salah, to warn us of a *djich,* or company of raiders, loose on the trail somewhere, striking up from Rio de Oro, three hundred guns strong and making in our direction; probably on a predatory *razzia* to the Tuareg settlements north-east of Tamenrasset. We were advised to make the best speed we could through the intervening territory.

A trail led from the plateau to the valley below, roughly cut during the war by army engineers, without which we should have been unable to take the cars down, since the drop was almost sheer for about a thousand feet.

In the terraces of the wall of the plateau were caves, many with prehistoric remains; but our investigation was slight. We were ordered to drive on, and our way was through the ghastliest part of the desert. On this trail, three years earlier, Chapuis had picked up the bodies of a few wanderers who had succumbed to thirst before reaching the well: father, mother, and child.

The child had died first. The mother had made a few kilometers more. The father was actually within two hundred yards of the well, trying to get water.

Nor was that the only sign of tragedy. Chapuis pointed out to us the scene of an ambush in 1917, which marked one of the bitterest little actions of the revolt. We were passing after ten years; but the scene was almost unchanged.

A convoy of six cars had been ambushed by a *djich* of Senussi and Tuareg warriors, perhaps the same company that had massacred Pere de Foucauld and his companions. As the cars had filed along the narrow path, the raiders, hidden in the rocks, had opened fire. There were about thirty men in the convoy, sent to prepare an aviation outpost against the Senussi; Chapuis, gaunt, gray, gnarled, took us to the point of the last stand, where an officer and one or two of his men, who alone had escaped the first onslaught, made their last stand. Two hundred spent cartridges told the tale.

Every one of the soldiers had been killed, and the bodies were mutilated in the Tuareg fashion: the abdomen slashed open with a knife.

Relics remained, just as they had fallen: bits of burned uniform, broken glasses, and cartridge cases. Great grease-spots stained the sand. The guns, of course, had been looted.

Chapuis had been in charge of part of the punitive force, and spent months blasting them out of their refuges. That force took no prisoners. The sand-dog followed, tracing them by their wounded; found their graves, identified the tribes, and stayed on the trail till it was all over. A man to have with us, even though, in the heat of the tale, he said that he had dispatched some of them, joyfully, with his own hands. I could well believe it.

We kept a close watch, nervous of the *djich*. News travels fast in the desert; how, nobody seems to know. Chapuis was certain that they had been advised of our mission, and were making for whatever plunder was available. So there was never a guard lacking in camp. Some slept while others watched, and, if we needed any stimulus, the thought of the massacre whose site we had just left served admirably.

We obeyed orders and made for In Salah with all speed, driving as late into the night as was possible, and resting as little.

The territory was absolutely without sign of life; nothing but a flat, featureless place, except for the terrible sign of the toll of the desert, lines of camel bones, and occasional human bones, marking the waterless trail.

A few things stand out still in my memory, accentuating this road through hell. There was one palm bole, which had been raised to mark the military trail to In Salah. It stood boldly out, visible for miles around, above the flat, pebbled stretch that looked like the bed of a waterless sea. At its base, when we reached it, was the body of a lost camel, dead and mummified, its teeth sunk into the hard, dry base of the sign-post, as though it had sought some little moisture.

About fifty miles farther on, we came to one of the tragedies of the Citroen Expedition, one of the caterpillar cars burned out, and left in this blasted region; the skeleton lying there to be excavated in subsequent eras, and carried to a museum as a prehistoric remainder. Some of our passengers took what they could as souvenirs, the radiator cap and bits of the chassis.

And, after traveling another fifty kilometers, we found an old water-dump, and a desert bustard lying alongside, with its beak smashed in an attempt to puncture the can for the water it contained.

At the end of two days in this hell, we knew we were in the region of In Salah, but the dunes had returned. We had caught sight of the fort, before sunset, with the sun plainly outlining its walls, and we had taken our bearings, thinking that we should make a good and direct entry, but we lost our direction. The cars were separated, and we circled round and round, interminably.

Dinner must have been waiting for hours. All the glory was spoiled.

The officers, seeing our headlights moving round in circles, mounted their searchlight on the flat roof of the fort and gave us a signal. It was one o'clock in the morning before we arrived, escorted by search parties of camel corps that had been sent out to lead us in; and, instead of arriving in order of line ahead, we came in singly, very bedraggled and weary.

A good picture was lost, but we made up the deficiency in the morning, when we were rested. Barth took his place on the roof with his cameras, and the cars were sent back into the desert, to make their entry in good order, as the world demands. Reygasse found some use for his medals, as they flashed quite impressively in the sun, and a formal reception was staged. The speech of greeting flowed in sonorous and official French, and damage was repaired in time for a review of two hundred men; the natives with their tom-toms beating a hilarious welcome, which they, at least, thoroughly enjoyed.

We were quite in the tradition, apparently, for we saw Chapuis roaring with laughter. Reminiscence was at work. He had brought in the Citroen Expedition, and our little echo had set him off again.

The expedition had rehearsed the entry half a dozen times, and was filmed from every angle; but when they got back they found that their labour was much in vain, and they used the first shot which was fairly lively. Slow fatigue appeared in the others; the soldiers were beginning to droop. The natives simply melted away.

Our rehearsal over, we celebrated the occasion with a few bottles of champagne which we had brought for the garrison, and I shall not easily forget the enthusiasm of those marooned frontiersmen of France.

The next day we took things easily, and had a little fun, because the officers, doctor, and wireless operator of the post had awaited our arrival before inaugurating what must be the greatest Saharan development: a swimming-pool in an oasis some distance away, where they had erected a springboard and pavilion.

For that journey, we were provided with camels. Barth had never been on a camel before, and was mounted, with his cameras strapped to the saddle, on a giant *mehari*. We lined up, and raced for the hole.

Our own clothes were in rags, so the officers lent us white pyjamas, while the one German member of the Foreign Legion attended to the rents and holes of our kit. I remember him well, with his long, white, patriarchal beard and his horny, but surprisingly delicate hands.

Off we went at a good lick; but somehow the rattling of the camera spurred Barth's mount unduly, and instead of trotting, he started to sprint. There were great boulders in the way, to right and left, and we held our sides, and our saddles, at the sight of Barth's *mehari* traveling like a kangaroo among the rocks. Poor chap, as his steed veered suddenly, he would lean out at an angle of forty-five degrees, to receive a clout on the head from his tripod. As abruptly, he would crash from port to starboard, and we saw the light of day between him and his mount, while he cried for a more expert performer to come and control his camel.

Finally, with us all tearing after him, to overtake and control the *mehari*, he took a giant leap over a rock, and when Barth came down his camel was yards away. His first lesson was over! One trooper caught the camel, and we turned about, following the trail, to pick up bits of equipment that he had dropped. It was hard luck on Barth; but, after all, it was worth his momentary discomfort to hear the officers in unrestrained laughter; the first unalloyed mirth that had sounded in In Salah for months.

After In Salah, little of interest came our way for nearly a week, save that at Meniet when we arrived we found our stores gone. Petrol had been brought across the desert by camel, and all we found were empty tins. Nor was there any water.

This was serious, for it meant that the supplies for the return journey simply did not exist. We looked like reaching the Hoggar – and staying there.

The well had been fouled, either by a caravan or by Tuaregs, purposely or otherwise. It was impossible to say what had happened; but the well had been trampled until it was nothing but a slimy mass, useless to us and the cars, and we were miserably disappointed.

Chapuis, however, was by no means beaten. We collected all the water we had, and filled up one of the cars, when he took us about fifteen miles off the trail, into the region of the Moudir, where great precipices form a wall of rock, believed by the Tuaregs to be the fortress of the Amazons, ruled by a white goddess: the old fable of Atlantis. There was no way up, which perplexed us considerably. Whatever foundation there was for the superstition, it seemed not unlikely that there would be some sort of ruin up there worth investigating; but, though we tried consistently, it was impossible for us to scale that sheer wall.

We followed under it, and Chapuis, who was seldom without a joke, suddenly disappeared. How he, or anyone else, had discovered the fissure it is impossible to imagine. The opening was hardly wide enough to admit a man. One minute he was there; the next he had vanished.

He left us to guess for a moment, and then returned, to call us after him. We threaded our way down a narrow corridor, which speedily darkened, so that we had to use our torches, and were surprised to come upon a clear, transparent pool, with a fine sandy beach. The walls around were covered with inscriptions and rock drawings of elephants, buffaloes, antelopes, and ostriches. Not one or two; but scores of drawings were there, and we knew that we were definitely on the trail of the old caravan routes to the gold and ivory lands of the ancients.

The copying of the drawings waited until we had flung ourselves flat and taken our fill of the clear water. Then, our one car was loaded up and sent back with supplies for the others, which later joined us, and all our tanks were then filled to capacity.

Reygasse and I copied the drawings, and the cook immediately set about preparing a meal. We pledged ourselves not to take a dip in the pool until every last drop of water necessary for use had been drawn.

How Chapuis knew of the lake, I never learned. Probably he had news of it from the Tuaregs. If that is so, then Tuareg mischief at Meniet had been offset by their pride of possession in boasting to the cunning old guide. Without it, we should have been in a terrible plight before we got through the *Bled es Khouf.*

Now we got our first sight of game. As we traveled along the rock face, we saw a group of eight or ten gazelles, and the rocks echoed to the roar of the cars as we speeded them up in the chase; perhaps a little unfair, since it offered no hope of escape. We were not sportsmen at that moment; we were hunting for the pot, and had had no fresh food for weeks.

Camp that night was a feast, as we halted at the entrance to the gorges, and the following morning we were away before dawn, in the hope of pushing through on a single stage, due to the superstitions of Belaid and the terror of the Arab cook, who knew the reputation of the *Bled es Khouf:* land of fear, and gateway to the Hoggar.

These gorges, called the Gorges of Arak, are reputed to be the abode of evil spirits, who prowl and talk at night. They are also the scene of many a vicious Tuareg raid, for, with the mountains behind us, the sudden cleft wound slowly through a narrow defile; tremendous, unreal, and awe-inspiring.

It was a valley of massacre, only a few years previously the true hunting ground of raiders who suffered none to pass without toll, and repaid resistance with death.

We had fifty kilometers of this land to race through, and Chapuis was of opinion that if we started by three o'clock in the morning we could do it in one day.

After covering one kilometer we came to a full stop. Belaid and the cook were certain, and even Chapuis was almost persuaded, that the trouble had been arranged. The rough trail was blocked by a pile of stones. We felt already that we were not wanted in the mountains of the Hoggar. No word had come through to us that there was trouble on the way, or that the trail had suffered damage; but Belaid was positive that the Tuaregs had thrown down the rocks to hold us in the gorges until nightfall. And then...

And then there was nothing for it but to get the whole of the expedition to work, stripped to the waist, and from four o'clock in the morning until well in the afternoon we were removing the rocks, and building a new trail. We must have shifted tons of rock, to make an opening just wide enough for the cars to thread their way through. The heat was frightful. The sun beat straight down. The walls of the canyon threw back every particle of heat. We worked in an oven, whose fires were constantly stoked.

When we did move it was to travel another kilometer; but this time the trouble certainly could not have been caused by human agency. At some time or other there must have been a deluge which had washed the trail away, and our trouble now was not to clear boulders from the path; but to find them, and build a trail across the hollows.

That night, we were so exhausted that as soon as the sun went down we slept, to be roused later by the sound of a sharp explosion, and a cry, when the echoes filled the gorge.

Reygasse and Barth made a dive for their guns, shooting wildly up the walls, shouting that we were ambushed.

Chapuis, cool, but violent of tongue, told them to stop shooting – he never was careful of his words – lest they bring worse on our heads.

I thought there would be war in the camp; but Chapuis brought us to an even keel, and just in time. A slow avalanche of pebble and rock slid down the side of the precipice, and cut off our trail again. It might as easily have fallen on us.

When we were settled, Chapuis explained his violence, and, incidentally, the terror these gorges have for the tribes.

The heat of the Saharan day, which rose to 130 degrees in the defile, followed by the icy chill of night, explodes small rocks from time to time, which go off with a report not unlike the shot of a rifle. Sometimes the sound is not easily distinguishable from a burst of machine-gun fire, the echoes reverberating through the passes.

The natives ascribe the tumult to the agency of evil spirits, and will never camp in the gorges. It is a real land of fear.

"And," continued Chapuis, driving home a little understanding of desert warfare, "if it had been an ambush, that was the worst possible thing to do, to stand out in the open and fire up at the rocks. The Tuareg would only have to aim at the flash, and where would you be? Don't forget that they have guns, and can use them."

Fortunately, this was about the last time we had to clear the trail, and the Gorges of Arak, which we had hoped to cover in one day, took us only three. We came out like a snarling pack of wolves, on edge with each other, and finding refuge either in strong language or stronger silence.

Chapuis saved our tempers again when we emerged into the Valley of the Giants, by leading us off the trail to a place where, on one of his raid-cutting expeditions years previously, he had secreted the fossilized skeleton of a man, which he had stored in petrol tins.

We did not take it up, but measured the skull, then resealed the boxes to be collected on the way back. Fossilization did not necessarily mean extreme antiquity; but close examination later at the Anthropological Institute placed this particular individual in the Neolithic age, and was of considerable importance in the placing of man in the Sahara. The skull was thicker than that of Tin Hinan, and Tin Hinan was thicker than the skull of a modern Tuareg which we (secretly) lifted at Tamenrasset.

Chapuis continued to be amazing. He had caches all over the place. At another camp he took us along and produced the hip bone of a prehistoric animal; but sometimes he was disappointed. The ants had found his store. It seemed strange to think that he had been scouring the Sahara ever since the battle of Tit in 1903, making his own discoveries; but never receiving any credit for his finds.

He began with us as Adjutant Chapuis; but we promptly pro-
moted him Captain, and that night in the Gorges we made him a
Colonel; whatever the Army authorities might have left undone.

The Valley of the Giants, which we now entered, is a region
of sandstone, tortured by the wind into fantastic shapes. Sometimes the wind had worked away at the base, using grains of
sand as chisels, so that the stones appeared now in the form of
giant mushrooms, now in the shapes of groups of hippopotami
or elephants. Belaid said that the Tuaregs regarded it as the site
of a gigantic battle between monsters.

Their appearance in the moonlight is indescribable. Then,
they did take on a cloak of reality; the light was not too sharp.
We seemed to be passing through an infernal Zoo, especially
just after sundown, for a little while, when the heat waves from
the sands, still shimmering slightly round the bases, gave a semblance of slow and ponderous motion to the brutes. It was not
difficult to imagine the effect such an illusion would have on
superstitious minds.

The next day, as we climbed from the valley to a high plateau, we had our greatest thrill. Ahead of us lay the volcanic
peaks of the Hoggar, clustered together like a hundred purple
needles thrusting thousands of feet up to reach a burning sky,
their bases cut off by mirage. It was the tabular land of the
Atlanteans, and a worthy setting to the fable that may perhaps be
not so entirely ill-founded.

We camped within sight of the range, already five or six
thousand feet up, and it was shivering cold, even round the camp
fire. We crept into our sleeping-bags, trying to make ourselves
warm by putting on all our socks and sweaters, and still we
trembled with the cold.

Suddenly, a voice broke the silence.

"My God! What's that?"

We looked. Outlined against the night sky, like an apparition
from another world, were five or six giant camels, ridden by
huge men in long veils: our first glimpse of the Tuaregs. They
had appeared out of nowhere and, on the brow of a hill over-

looking the camp, monstrous in the moonlight, they had the effect of being ten times their actual size.

They stared, motionless on their mounts, as we sat up, like folded cocoons, still helpless in the bonds of our sleeping-bags. For a few moments they gazed at us, and disappeared as silently as they had arrived.

When we had crawled out of our bags to follow them, we could find no sign. Were they outriders, we wondered, measuring our strength?

The next day we discovered their tracks. They had come from a village that lay on our trail.

That day we came upon the first settlement of the Hoggar, inhabited by the Hartani, or slave caste of the Tuaregs, who were black, but not Negroid. They have nothing to do ethnically with the Negroes of the south, of Senegal, or the Congo, it would appear; but are a people entirely separate, more like the North American Redskins, with straight noses and thin lips, and are subject to, but now moderately independent of, the white Tuaregs or Targui: the noble caste. Some say they are black Antineans. It is a nice theory.

The village was surrounded by swamps for protection; swamps cunningly devised by diverting a small stream so that it trickled among the loose, fine sand, making it almost impassable, and always laborious. We had a miserable time getting through, when the time came. Chapuis warned us against the marsh, which was actually a bed of quicksands.

At our approach, tom-toms began to beat, and we proceeded with due care. The village lay in a grove of bamboo – unexpected stuff to find in the desert – and was further protected by a stockade of interlaced canes with sharp points protruding. Evidently the Hartani were not nomadic. They had hutments of a sort, all made of bamboo, and thatched with bundles of leaves.

The chief, riding on a zebu, its enormous hump flopping from side to side, came out of the solid wall of bamboo to ask us what it was all about. He was frankly antagonistic, and in no humour to treat with us.

One of the cars had gone a little too far, and was beginning to sink into the sands. We anchored it, and Chapuis strode forward to negotiate, while behind the chief gathered a crowd of his tribe.

No! He would not help us. We had come unbidden. Our plight was our own affair.

Chapuis threatened him with a visit from the military if he refused us labourers, and finally he won. The whole population of the village was enrolled, and began to cut bamboo to make a safe trail through the marsh.

When we had reached good ground, we halted and made camp; but that night we were treated to a spectacle that was distinctly unnerving, and not in the least propitious.

The whole village, rested from its labour, and perhaps having gained courage because there was no sight of the threatened military patrol, rose in a body, and the natives began to dance round the cars, drawing steadily nearer.

The blacks arrived in a compact mass, armed with spears and lances, swords and sticks, their women beating the *toboles* which spurred the dancers to excitement; who waved their weapons in scenes that were Dantesque in their ferocity, with a background of mountains and dry, whispering bamboos. Some of us, by accident or design, received a stout flick with the sticks, and Reygasse was distinctly uneasy, while Chapuis tried to argue with the chief, telling him that we were neither invaders nor robbers.

Barth, fortunately, intent on his own job and not to be denied a good picture, had hauled himself to safety on the top of one of the cars and had mounted his camera, preparing his magnesium flares methodically. Automatically, when he was ready, he set one going. The light burned slowly to its maximum, and the dancers began to melt away as though by magic, now thoroughly scared in their turn.

At the first burst of flame they had stood, petrified, and very soon the whole village was illuminated. The warriors saw Barth turning the handle steadily: perhaps they had memories of machine-guns, I do not know; but they turned in their tracks, and in a moment the plain was deserted. White magic had saved us further trouble, and Barth had recorded a marvelous shot. After that we got some peace, although the tom-toms talked through the night. We slept with our guns handy.

The next day we reached Tamenrasset, after winding our way across a rocky stretch to a plateau, called the Koudia, and saw the fort with its tricolour in the distance.

Tearing across the plain, raising a cloud of dust in a mad race to be first, we completed the first half of our journey.

The guns gave us the salute. A cheer went up from the legionaries as they saw the mail-bag in my hand.

The greeting was at least understandable. It was shouted in enough languages German, Arabic, Irish, Portuguese, and French mingled in one common hail. Adjutant Murphy calmly informed me that we were late with the mails, although we were six weeks ahead of their regular camel caravan.

Thanks to the Gorges of Arak we were nearly a week behind schedule, and the post had intended to wait one more day before sending out search parties, wondering if we had been caught by the raiders.

Our first two thousand miles had been accomplished by reaching our immediate objective, and we were formally welcomed to the Hoggar by Commandant Count de Beaumont, officer commanding the post at Tamenrasset.

The following morning we were presented to the Sultan of the confederation of Tuareg tribes, after we had placed a wreath on the monument erected to the memory of Pere de Foucauld, the hermit saint of the Sahara, and General Laperrine, the French Kitchener.

Pere de Foucauld was murdered by the Tuaregs and Senussi during the war. There was a probability that the actual assassins were standing by at the memorial service. Chapuis said that a couple of ruffians at my elbow were quite likely to have been the culprits; but that could not be established.

De Foucauld and his servants were surprised and shot before they could offer resistance, and after the massacre their bodies could not be found for some time. Finally the skeletons of the servants were discovered, and de Foucauld's body at some little distance from his chapel-fort. The murderers had taken every means they could to escape detection.

The singular thing was that although the servants' bodies were completely decomposed, de Foucauld was found mummified, buried in a kneeling position, with his hands tied behind his back, and a bullet-wound in his head. His blue eyes were wide open, peacefully regarding the infinity to which he had so quickly sped.

Such preservation was miraculous, fit token of the canonization that awaits him.

His body has now been removed to Ouargla, for fear of desecration and the threat of revolt that is never quite absent, and now he awaits elevation to the position that he already holds: the saint of the Sahara.

The tribal confederation was a sight never to be forgotten, and after Reygasse had made his usual speech, which by now we knew by heart and could have made for him, an old German Legionary fastened our bronze wreath to the monument.

Then the Sultan appeared: the Amenokhal Akhamouk, with his magnificent escort, and our presentation was made on the open plain, outside the walls of the fort, for he would not enter, being of a suspicious nature and fearing possible betrayal.

It seemed to me that we had come into the presence of a race of giants. I myself am no dwarf, topping six feet, but these were men to make me seem small. Some were nearly seven feet high, and they looked like a prehistoric race which had been marooned and left to survive unchanged. They were actually as big as the Grimaldi man, and, clothed in their flowing, majestic robes, with the mysterious veil over their faces, their eyes brilliant with kohl, they looked what they were, the dreaded gangsters of the desert.

Naturally, expecting the Amenokhal, we had brought him a variety of presents, including a magnificent gun, and when he handled it, it was no small entertainment to see the glint of his eye, and the enigmatic turn of his lips; just a flash of expression, the vestige of a grimace; but what volumes it spoke!

For the others, there were alarm clocks and sugar loaves, salt and tea. So were good relationships established between us and "the abandoned of God," for the time being at least.

Our great interest, of course, was to get into closer contact with their life, and in this we succeeded so that before we finished, Barth, whom I lent to Reygasse for the purpose, made a completely documented film of all their habits and pursuits, amiable and otherwise, from war manoeuvres to the building and erecting of their tents, and their frenetic love affairs.

We had to angle, however, for an invitation to the Sultan's camp, fifteen kilometers away from the fort, where the full confederation of tribes was halted. We got that invitation, and the expedition lived among the Tuaregs for a fortnight, in the heart of the Koudia, or Attakor, the very focus of the Hoggar.

Fine tents were allotted to us, pitched slightly apart from the rest of the encampment, which looked like spots of blood on the silver sand of the white plateau. Three hundred tents were there, with fires burning before the low, sombre openings.

Chapter 4

Naturally, there was a banquet in our honour, and in the great tent of the Sultan we presented the surprise gift: a beautiful carpet that we had carried with us all the way.

To say that we ate would be to exaggerate, for if the food at Temassin had been dubious-looking, the dishes in this camp of the desert Sultan were distinctly suspect.

Perhaps the most amusing course was made of dates stuffed with locusts, their legs cut off, swimming in thin honey with the tails of snakes and lizards. This was washed down with the milk of desert camels, tolerably strong and with a taste that was also a smell. But the platters, carved with Tifinar inscriptions, were real curios, and a definite link with the past.

As a mark of courtesy, the Sultan appropriated to me three of the most charming young ladies of the confederation: Dassine the younger, Yemma, and Yehali. Before I had completed my stay, these delightfully unsophisticated beauties occasioned me a little anxiety, for the next day we were invited to the great "salon" of the Queen.

The ladies arrived, Queen and court and attendants, quite early in the morning and, to show their importance and the magnitude of the honour that was being paid, did not approach the camp immediately, but circled round for an hour, slowly filing past our tents at a distance.

They were beautifully made, those Tuareg women, with their faces unveiled and their shoulders square, their feet in fine sandals; women without a blemish, in purple robes worn Egyptian fashion to leave the right shoulder bare.

The ceremonial approach ended and we were presented to the Queen and her ladies-in-waiting with a pomp and ceremony that would not have disgraced a European court. Here were the real masters of the land!

I was astonished to discover the matriarchate still potent in the world; more potent here, even, than it is in the United States, which, until that moment, more closely approached absolute domination by women than any country I had seen.

The women, with their clear, open faces, were worthy of their dignity; they were open, frank, really beautiful; obviously noble both by inheritance and character. The men were haughty, inclined to reserve; the women, friendly. And they promptly invited us to their Ahal.

The Ahal was timed for the evening, as the moon rose; but in the meantime the tribes had prepared a pageant which would have been a credit to the court of Arthur, or the displays of Charles the Bold.

We, of the expedition, sat in places of honour, on antelope and other skins, while the veiled knights performed on giant camels, attacking in formation with all the glitter of horsemen competing at Olympia. We were the spectators; but everything was in honour of the ladies, who, by the way, are all called Tukalinden, which means "Little Queen."

Fighting with lance and great, double-edged broadswords, whose hafts were Christian crosses, they attacked, parried, and thrust, taking the blows on tough antelope-hide shields. We rubbed our eyes, wondering if the time-machine had carried us back to the Crusades.

It was a country upside-down. The men, as I have said, were painted and veiled. The women were not.

Inheritance is by the maternal line. The councils are really dominated by the women. The Sultan is only the nominal ruler, chosen by the tribes for leadership in war, actually only a representative of the Queen.

The name of the family is taken from the mother. She is supreme in councils of war, and the women accompany their men on the great trails, riding side by side, taunting the weak and the cowards, spurring them to their greatest bravery.

It was amusing to see the men painting their eyes with kohl and having their long hair braided – the women are quite modern, and are bobbed – preparatory to the meeting with the ladies; women who, incidentally, make the lover-like advances and are not dismayed by a ride of a hundred kilometers to visit the chosen lover. It is the women who demand the hands of the men in marriage. It is the women who take what lovers they will, and when. It is the man who is ridiculed should he so far forget himself as to show jealousy within the tribe. Without the tribe: that is another story! For it must not be thought that these veiled devils are effeminate or unwarlike. They are bitter, remorseless, unwavering in their loyalties and, their word given, will go to unbelievable extremes to keep their vows.

Chapuis told us of one Tuareg messenger who, when Fort Zinder was attacked, ran three hundred kilometers to Tamenrasset to give the alarm. Three hundred kilometers, dragging one foot after another, without stopping on his way and, the message delivered and understood, death without complaint.

The Ahal, to which we were invited, was held in a lonely spot some distance from camp. How closely I may describe it, I do not know; but take imagination with you. Let it run as it will, it cannot pass the bounds of actuality.

The elder Dassine presided, poetess and literary leader of the three tribes of the confederation, and around her were assembled all the younger members of the tribes.

My three ladies of honour escorted me thither. It was the night of the full moon. There were musicians sitting around in a circle, playing the *amzad* or native violin.

In America, and perhaps by now in England, it would have been known as a petting party, and there were no restrictions, save the willingness of the lady and the taste and ability of the escort.

Rightfully, the privilege of admission should be earned by poetic ability. Whatever the equivalent of rhyme may be among

them, the young men needed to be proficient. Should they be
unable to rise to the heights, they were escorted to the outskirts
of the party amid roars of laughter, and it was undignified to
protest, or show chagrin.

We had taken our own drinks – a little whisky and gin that
remained; but they had *lubki,* a potent fermentation of palm
wine.

The music was plaintive and melancholy at the beginning,
but slowly the girls began more ardently to court the men, with
little subtlety and considerable charm. I was somewhat troubled
by the warmth of the advances made by my three companions,
who expected much from the leader of an expedition.

The music increased in fervour, melancholy gone, and gaiety
present. All limits were off; those interlaced figures under the
moon had a certain grace in their stupendous vigour.

I called to Belaid, that he might explain to my three damsels,
when they began to chide me for indifference, that I was a serious gentleman, and married, and that it would be against all my
tribal customs to succumb to the blandishments of the now completely naked young ladies.

They too, however, had their tribal customs, and what was
more, they had definite orders from the Sultan to entertain me. It
seemed to them that entertainment must be mutual.

As I left the love-arena, they followed me like three clouded
Graces, and Belaid said that the only thing to do in such a case
was to enter into a little conspiracy with them.

I could not openly refuse their attentions without offering
some slight to the Sultan, who would believe that his gift was
not appreciated, that the ladies were lacking in beauty, or that I
was a weak and inconsiderable person.

Therefore we did enter into the conspiracy, and all retired to
my tent, whither were summoned their languishing sweethearts,
to take the gifts off my hands, an arrangement received with
complete and mutual satisfaction. What followed is perhaps
nobody's business; but the girls, through Belaid, made me understand that they were thoroughly happy in the arrangement, and

promised to sing my praises to the Sultan, and to tell him what a wonderful man I was, to have entertained them all so well.

The following morning we progressed in state, to conversation with the Amenokhal, our interpreter alert for any suggestion of folk lore which might indicate the whereabouts of the sacred tomb, if, in fact, it proved to exist.

Reygasse and Pond were busy collecting souvenirs for their museums. We, Belaid, Chapuis, and I, went to court, to listen to the official teller-of-tales.

Audience was given by the Amenokhal, who had his master of ceremonies by his side and, for entertainment, the historian with his bag of pebbles.

The teller-of-tales was the living volume of superstition and history, and he was our great hope. There was no use whatever in seeking information concerning the tomb, openly. Our only chance was that he would drop a hint at some time or other, indicating which of the many known mounds was the tomb of the legendary Queen.

I suppose that Chapuis knew most of the mounds; he had been wandering about the desert for years enough, and if we could get him a lead, he would do most of the rest.

There before us was the story-teller with his bag of pebbles. Each pebble, he said, was a different tale. As he drew them out, haphazard, he told us of the great heroes of the Tuareg confederation; of loves and battles, of raids and counter-raids; and when it seemed that there would be no information coming that day, he let the cat out of the bag.

On a blind draw, he took a pebble and looked at it, Belaid nudging me and interpreting what followed in quick, quiet sentences.

"This," said the historian, "is the Tale of Tin Hinan, our goddess, queen-ancestress, and her venerated tomb..."

His hand was raised in salutation, and he bowed in obeisance, turning a little to get the right direction, which Belaid and I marked carefully.

There was our indication. With Chapuis's knowledge, it might be enough. We had the direction: not north, a little south. A great tomb, perhaps on the trail towards Timbuktu.

"I know where there's a tomb that might be it," said Chapuis when we were free. "There is a big mound lying off the trail."

The next morning, Reygasse not having returned from some private mission of his own, Chapuis, Belaid, Tyrrell, Denny, and I, with our leading chauffeur, took one of the cars, ostensibly to visit other Tuareg settlements in the mountains.

I left a note for Reygasse and Pond, asking them to follow when they had finished their own investigations, and to come to the village of Abalessa, about eighty miles away, and to send on supplies as soon as our camel caravan arrived. It was already late; but we knew it was on the way.

Then we got under way, and Chapuis scanned the mountains to right and left, trying to pick up his landmarks.

At the confluence of two rivers, now only dry courses, there was a large circular structure, standing high, at the sight of which Chapuis let out a cry of satisfaction. That was it! There was a chance that we had found the secret of the Hoggar.

We kept on our way, while Chapuis went to the village of Abalessa, some kilometers from the mound, to work with the Harratin chief, by persuasion and bribe, to get a score of labourers. Nearly everything presentable that we had went in the bargaining; but after we had made our camp in the river-bed below the monument, the blacks came, with obvious reluctance, to await instructions.

Chapuis wanted to begin with the central court, for the edifice was circular, with eleven rooms, and he believed that that was the more logical spot; but, for some reason or other I chose the highest point, and there we began.

The Hartani, perhaps remembering their serfdom and dreading the wrath of their Tuareg overlords, were nervous from the outset, and we had to reassure them in every way that there was no desecration, that the tomb had actually nothing to do with their history, legends, or faith; but was just a pile of stones in the way.

The curses on that work were manifold, our principal misery being the millions of flies that were attracted by the sweating, naked bodies of the blacks, and covered us from head to foot; but we carried on without casualty, and succeeded in clearing many of the fallen stones from the top of the mound.

These stones had obviously been worked, and well worked, in a fashion beyond the patience or ability of the Tuaregs...beyond the imagination of any Muhammedan tribe at the time of the Arab invasion. They were somewhat reminiscent to me of the work of Roman soldiers. I wondered if, by chance, there were any possibility of our having discovered something even more significant than the tomb of a legendary queen: a far outpost of Rome's legions. Even the amount of excavation our small party was able to do revealed the fact that this was more than a burial-place. The walls were enormously thick, and capable of offering stout resistance to any attack, being from four to twelve feet in cross-section.

The upper walls had fallen in, piling masonry on the inner chambers, which gave the mound an illusory architecture. When we attacked it, it looked to have been rounded off, and made conical; but the walls must originally have risen straight from their bases.

A scorpion emerging from its crevice put a halt to the effort of the blacks. They were ever watchful for an excuse to stop, anyway, so five whites tried to do all the work, and had to, for a while, until Chapuis had the Hartani back again, threatening the men with all the furies he could imagine.

On the third day, however, work was completely stopped by the appearance of a storm breaking over the Attakor. This threw the fear of God into the slaves, who believe that each time a storm so gathers it is a sign that something has offended God, and that He sends His vengeance, in the form of lightning, to punish evil-doers.

That we calmed, ultimately, and carried on; but our food was dwindling rapidly, despite our short rationing. The supply caravan had not appeared, our car was immobilized for want of petrol, and we did not dare to send a messenger from Abalessa to Tamenrasset, lest he should report our work to the Tuareg confederation, and let trouble loose on us. We had to subsist on coffee and beans, eked out with a little cornmeal which we managed to obtain in Abalessa. Even that supply ceased very shortly, and beans and coffee were all we had. Water, too, was a difficulty, although we scooped a shallow well in the bed of the river, and waited for a slow trickle to fill a glass, when the chauffeur made one of us coffee, repeating the process until we were all served, and then beginning afresh.

On the fifth day we were getting fight inside, and small objects began to appear, which indicated the likelihood of a discovery which would send a thrill over the wires when we could report it. There were cornelian and turquoise beads in the sieves as we riddled the sand, and we reached a chamber which contained ancient pottery – provisions in the jars were for the voyage of the dead to the other world. Thousands of date-stones bespoke the work of ants, and Chapuis was sure that everything would be destroyed; but we continued, and came to a stone-lined room, whose floor was covered with the skins of wild animals, dried hard, with fine fringes, which pointed to something still more important down below.

By this time we calculated that we had removed, in all, some twenty thousand pieces of stone, and the work was hard; harder because of our food shortage. As yet, there was no sign, no rumour even, of the approach of our caravan or the other cars. The Hartani refused to sell us anything else, because we had no tangible goods to exchange, and they were giving nothing for nothing. The beans and coffee were quickly going. We saw the end in sight, but worked to the last moment.

Actually, we worked beyond the last moment, for we were stripped clean of food before relief came. Excitement sustained us; but, to add to our discomfiture, a sandstorm broke, and swept over us like a cloud-burst. We worked through it for a while, with our faces swathed; but progress was pitifully slow, although traces of ultimate discovery were more abundant.

Three great stones, each half a ton in weight, sealed the chamber. I believed they marked the final stage, so we robbed the village of its best pieces of wood, and took levers and jacks from the car, driving the blacks to their work again.

They got a good purchase, and slowly the first slab gave, making an aperture just large enough to permit the egress of a huge black snake, which marked the end of the blacks. We never saw them again after that, as labourers. They were sure the snake was the guardian of the tomb, and fled.

During the night, we heard the beating of tom-toms in Abalessa, and had a feeling that the Hartani were encircling the camp. In the darkness, Chapuis fired across me into the bamboo, at what he took to be the figure of a man, with a lance in his hand. Next day, sure enough, we saw his tracks.

The beating of the *toboles* became more and more insistent, and less peaceful. We sensed a growing excitement; but we got the stones up and at last were in the tomb, to meet disappointment on first sight, for sand had filtered in and choked the chamber. We were faced with hours of slow work and careful sieving as the sand was raised in handfuls and passed outside. Every now and then a scout would climb up to the top of the mound, to see if there were signs of the caravan.

At last, Chapuis found another turquoise, and we lost interest in everything except the clearing of that chamber before we were interrupted. We were living on our nerves, and worked on into the night, using torches and candles in the rock room.

On the following day we found a gold amulet and other ornaments. That was enough to fire anybody, for what remained was unknown: it might be anything or nothing.

The sand was all swept away. We could stand upright in the chamber. The last bit of sieving was rich in rewards. Hardly a riddle but showed some little find: cornelian, garnet, amethyst, and turquoise beads were numerous. They seemed to have been thrown in after the burial. The gold was well worked, and to me bore a resemblance to the workmanship of jewelry we had found in the tombs of Utica. There was a distinct link with the metals of ancient Carthage, handed down perhaps from generation to generation. Certainly some beads were coeval.

In all his experience of Saharan exploration, Chapuis had never discovered gold; but now he stood in the sun with his hands full of it, as we passed the objects up, and his sun-scorched, sand-blasted, grizzled face lit up with a light that was not far short of fanaticism. And suddenly there was a shadow between him and the sun. He stood, immobile, looking up to the top of the mound, face to face with Tuaregs.

There they were, gigantic, their spears in their hands, guns across their shoulders: silent, watchful. How long they had been there, or how they had approached, it was impossible to conjecture.

Chapuis, eased from his excitement, became again the cunning Saharan, and whispered that the situation was likely to be delicate. They had seen the glint of gold. Hurriedly he gave us our instructions. What we had discovered was not gold; but brass. The mound was not a Tuareg relic, since they live in tents. He worked his wily brain to the limit, to find a plausible excuse.

"De Prorok," he whispered, "this is the tomb of your ancestors! How could Tuaregs build a great stone monument? We're following that line..."

Down went the sieves, and we stood, unconcerned to all appearances; but inwardly very troubled. We could at least measure the glance of those glittering eyes, accentuated by kohl, as the grim figures approached, speaking rapidly among themselves.

Chapuis went forward to greet them. They might have been his long-lost brothers; but they returned his salutations with stony faces. We, apparently, were for it. Chapuis continued to speak in Tamashekh, extending interminable greetings.

There they stood, with shields, swords and lances, guns and, worst of all, their terrible daggers sheathed along their forearms.

Tyrrell and the others looked on, not knowing what to do or say, sorry that the guns were down at the camp. Denny patrolled the upper reaches of the mound, pretending to be busy. Chapuis still continued in his efforts to make the Tuaregs talk, explaining at length. He got no response. He tried to drive it into their minds that the excavations had nothing to do with their Queen, or with them. All he could get from them was that they had seen the glint of gold.

With a flash of genius, he pulled out his ancestral gold watch: a watch as big as a turnip, that one of his forbears had carried at Marengo, and said that that was what they had seen, and which they had nothing at all to resemble.

That, he said, was what we had discovered: and the Tuaregs had never known watches. It looked gigantic on the palm of his hand. So, ultimately, he got the nobles away from the tomb and down to the camp. They seemed to be convinced that the tomb had nothing to do with their history; but just the same, the tomb was known as the tomb of Tin Hinan, and if we touched the body, there would be trouble.

We followed, and made a sort of peace by parting with the last few things we had that could be converted into presents.

I had a precious hunting-knife. It found a different owner. Denny had a plated corkscrew. That nearly went; but he disappeared with it. Martini had a stroke of genius and produced an empty Chianti bottle, with its straw covering and loops. That went to the girdle of another noble.

Still the moment was not comfortable; things were not propitious. If the Tuaregs carried back word to the Amenokhal, we were finished. The thing was to keep them with us until the caravan arrived and we could give them a feast.

Martini tried his best, showing them the miracle of a motor at work. Bradley Tyrrell made chairs for them out of bits of wood: anything to keep them interested; but there was nothing doing. They departed as abruptly as they came, regained their *mehari*, and set off in the direction of Tamenrasset, leaving us wondering.

Our salvation now lay in speed. Chapuis insisted that we take our guns to the mound, and that we relieve each other as sentinels. The tom-toms had ceased their calling; evidently the Tuaregs had reached the village, and were raising some disturbance with the slaves. There was a piercing scream and then silence.

Chapuis was almost feverish. This was sacrilege, and if they had not been convinced by the story he had told we were not in a particularly good state. Besides; if there were gold in the tomb, sacrilege or no sacrilege, they would have preferred to dig it out themselves.

We went back to work. The burial-chamber was full of inscriptions. We made a big discovery. Object after object appeared: bracelets, anklets, and the couch on which the Queen had been laid. The skeleton was lying on its side, knees folded, and at the head was a statuette, easily recognizable as being of the Aurignacian period: a squat, crude image of a steatopygic goddess which we promptly named "The Libyan Venus." When Reygasse came to publish the results of our discoveries on his own account he called it "The Hottentot Venus"; but that meant nothing to us, then.

Our big cameras and the movie-camera were with Reygasse and Barth at Tamenrasset. I had to be content with my own small Kodak, but we brushed away the sand from the skeleton.

The shrouds went up in dust; but not before we had distinguished a sort of veil over the head.

There was a tiara, or diadem, whose cord had gone, and the pieces were among the ribs of the dead Queen. What looked like a head-dress of three feathers turned to dust as the air struck it.

Slowly, bit by bit, with Tyrrell holding a petrol tin outside, to catch and reflect the rays of the sun into the chamber, we uncovered the arms with their massive bracelets: eight of silver on the left and nine of heavy gold on the right. In the dust around the neck were cornelian, garnet, amazonite, turquoise, glass and plaster beads, with some of chalcedony and others of gold and silver, distinctly similar to beads I had found at Carthage.

The bed had collapsed, after seventeen centuries; but it had originally been of wood, worked in simple patterns, and near the head was one beaker of wood and another of glass, the wood bearing traces of design and containing coins which were later identified as belonging to the period of Constantine the Great.

As the treasures increased, excitement and haste grew. We also found pieces of iron; relics of the Amazonian arms the Queen must have carried. It was so important that even Chapuis lost control for a moment, crying, "Let's hope the caravan beats the Tuaregs, and we can get away before they realize what's happened."

Then he insisted on our putting ourselves into a state of siege, with our arms placed handily at the entrance to the tomb.

We had cleared the chamber. Reaction set in when there was nothing else to find, and we more or less collapsed. We were through our stores, there was not a grain of food left, only a little coffee, and we sat around, trying to sleep.

Somebody or other, from time to time, climbed up to see if there were any sign of the caravan, and ultimately Chapuis did see it.

Pond and Barth were coming ahead with a small load. Reygasse was staying at Tamenrasset, finishing the collection of souvenirs, and keeping the cars. He did not arrive until the following day.

We were too tired even to raise a shout. All we could do was to lift some of the objects and wave them in the air.

Pond wanted to know what was wrong. He had come through Abalessa, and the natives were excited. When we showed him what we had collected, his face was a study.

"All this," he said. "And Reygasse not here! He's still saying good-bye to his friends."

We were not interested in Reygasse and his adieux. What we wanted was food and drink, and we raided the supplies. I shall never forget the terrific effect of a small whisky. It was like drinking hot Vesuvian lava. But there were sardines, and wartime bully beef. It was the food of the gods to us. And there was bread made by the Foreign Legion. We would have eaten the "General's" boots, polish and all, had there been nothing else, for we were absolutely starving.

Pond, quick to his job, promptly got out his calipers and measured the Queen's skull, and pronounced his verdict. Tin Hinan was really a woman.

Then we put things back as they were.

The next day, Reygasse arrived. We made a procession in his honour, with specimens, and he was just a little white with emotion. It was not possible! Certainly it was not possible!

But suddenly he was excited. He was like a little volcano in unexpected eruption. He strode about in supreme isolation.

"We have made history, you and I, de Prorok!" he cried. "We have made history! We have changed all the conceptions of the Hoggar!

"You must realize," he continued, his voice a little impeded by his anxious heart. "This is a vast treasure. The Tomb of Tin Hinan! We have found it! Vive la France!"

For his benefit, and so that he could be in the picture – a little for documentation as well – we re-enacted the scene, and filmed it. Tin Hinan was packed in *bidons,* and we took her away. The *toboles* were beating in the village with an ever-increasing threat. Reygasse said that he had passed the Tuaregs on their way to Tamenrasset. They were probably on their way to protest to the Amenokhal. The village of Abalessa was "up," as we passed through, on our race to the fort. We had visions of the confederation roused to bar our way; but we were not molested.

The climax had been reached. We had a tough time driving home again from Tamenrasset. We went through a sandstorm that at other times would have merited a long account. Our supplies went wrong. We suffered many things.

At In Salah the doctor verified Pond's first pronouncement that this was a woman's skeleton we carried. We picked up the objects we had buried on the way out. Pond and Reygasse, perhaps, got their respective prehistoric collections.

Ultimately, the Queen went with me to Paris, and I drove around the city with her in a very modern taxicab, seeking the responsible authorities to whom I should make my report. But a ministry had fallen, and the new government knew not Tin Hinan. So, for a time, the queen-ancestress of all the Tuaregs reposed quietly in a cool cellar in the heart of Paris. And Reygasse, savant, explorer, discoverer, continues to make scientific reports about her.

PART II

JUPITER AMMON AND TRIPOLITANIA

PERSONNEL OF THE TRIPOLITAN EXPEDITION,
UNDER THE AUSPICES OF THE ITALIAN GOVERNMENT

COUNT BYRON DE PROROK Director

PROFESSOR R. GUIDI; Director Tripolitan Antiquities

P. LEPROU; Société de Géographie (Paris)

A. SMEDRUD; University of Oslo

LANGSTON MOFFET; Associated Press

MARQUIS H. D'AYALA; Cuba

SIG. E. RICOTTI   SIO. SPORTARI

DR. FIRELLI   INO. R, ROSSELLI

CAPT. JOHNSTON-LAVIS

ESCANDE and assistant chauffeurs

Chapter 1

My friend Gsell, it seemed, had a real understanding. There were places where, for a little time at least, one could get ahead of the *Service des Antiquites*. We had made a fairly successful raid to the Hoggar and Tin Hinan; a little too successful, perhaps, since later expeditions, and complete excavation under the direction of Reygasse, took a long time and succeeded in tracing the ground plan of the monument, as well as discovering one iron bracelet.

Chance, intuition if you like, had served me very well in directing me to the one, and only, room which contained any treasure at all. They could have the rest.

My mind was turned on other places of mystery and promise in the desert. It was my hope, before my exploring days ended, to cover as much as was interesting of the Sahara and the Libyan deserts, and after that there remained Tripoli and the Fezzan, and, if we could manage it, the Sudan and Ethiopia.

The most outstanding name, after Tin Hinan, was Jupiter Ammon, and its associations with Alexander the Great, whose trail I hoped to follow across the desert.

Therefore I organized an expedition, this time small, to the Oasis of Siwa, intending to use that oasis as a base, and scour the chain of oases along its length, coming out again in the Fayum.

The cars were Fords, with balloon tyres; the most serviceable and practical, as well as the most economical, of all desert transport. I found them better than my six-wheeler Renaults, and better than the caterpillar Citroens.

We were only four whites, with Ali Ford as chief mechanic and character of the expedition, Senussi the thief, and Hassan the fool, a full-blooded Sudanese Negro.

After covering some three hundred kilometers from Alexandria, we reached Marsa Matruh, the ancient port of Ammonia, which was doubly significant, since it was the harbour to which all the pilgrims came; from Arabia, Greece, Phoenicia, and the Mediterranean basin, to cross the pitiless desert and consult the famous oracle. It was also the site of the summer palace of Cleopatra.

Our three hundred kilometer trail had been marked every few miles by watch-towers which had served their purpose from time immemorial, indicating that fertile strip between sea and the highlands of the desert, to which the Bedouin had come with their flocks and herds. It was a trail of no mean beauty itself; but what a host had traveled that way since the trail was first made! The trail of the dead and anxious great!

Crossing the desert plateau, we came suddenly on the port of the lovely queen, a haven set in loveliness that is the equal of hers, even when described by the most romantic.

Palms nodded their royal plumes in the quiet air, lagoons were the bluest of all blues, fringed by reefs through which the slow sea broke to the ancient harbour. The beaches were of a strange, silver sand; so white that it seemed like chalk. The water was transparent; we could distinguish ruins that had fallen to the bed of the sea, and the small entrance of the port, with calm anchorage for the galleys of pilgrims on their way to the oracle.

Above was the oasis, and the summer palace of Cleopatra, where she retreated, the world, perhaps, well lost, during the battle of Actium, unnerved by the excess of slaughter; and whither she was followed by Marc Antony, to spend their last hours in this miraculous haven.

Her barge sailed the waters on which we tried out the collapsible boats we were taking with us to explore the lakes at Siwa, and with them we traced the sea-walls of buildings now sub-merged.

The palace site is partly covered with silver sand dunes and a forest of giant palms, but along the sea-front there are traces of marble steps, and the lined pool, as well as a number of corridors and subterranean chambers, which we made an effort to explore.

The natives of the village are mostly Greek sponge divers, and, as soon as they learned that we were interested in antiques, they came to our bungalow with objects found in the sea, including statuettes, lachrymatories, and coins of all epochs.

We began exploring, engaging a number of workmen to remove the sand that had filtered down to the ancient halls where the Ptolemies had held revel in the past. Very little of interest was immediately discoverable, and we had not come prepared to make a thorough investigation; but we did secure some pale emeralds and fragments of statuettes, as well as locating mosaic floors. Other beads of turquoise, cornelian, garnet, and coral were there; but it was the emeralds that interested us most, since legend says that they came from the interior.

It is a site that should be explored and thoroughly excavated. That such work would be worth while was proved by our *sond-ages,* as well as by the work of illicit diggers.

We stayed there for a glorious week, preparing the trip across the desert to Jupiter Ammon, and, immediately on leaving the coast, came face to face with the abomination of desolation. There is no more miserable tract of country than this stretch lying between Marsa Matruh and Siwa. There is neither tree nor rise for a hundred miles; only the old trail of the date caravans, using the ancient wells of the Ammonians as points of direction.

We camped, occasionally, by these wells, and found that, generally, the guardroom has doorways of giant monoliths, the well within being cut through the floor of the desert to water below. Frequently the stones are covered with Greek and Roman inscriptions.

After the second day of desert travel, we came to Djebel Iskander, or Hill of Alexander, where, legend says, he was wandering, lost on his way to the oracle, when the ravens came out to lead him to his destination. It is singular that after so many centuries the story should remain, be perpetuated in the name of a hill.

The desert was as flat as a lawn; brown, parched, dull, and monotonously smooth, without even a ripple in the sand. It appeared to stretch on to infinity, but ended abruptly in an alarming drop. We came to the edge of the plateau just as the sun was setting, and there, lying in the golden light below us, was the great oasis that gave the word to our languages; first used by Herodotus in his description of Jupiter Ammon.

Terraces, with as rich and varied colouring as the Grand Canyon, led down to the fertile region, caught and illumined by the reddening sun; beyond stretched a series of silvery lakes, with islands and millions of palm trees: a sight so unexpected and so surprising in the desolation that we stood and gazed long, before we descended. It was as though a lost world had suddenly been restored.

Those lakes and oases stretched for a hundred miles, right through to the Tripolitan border; perhaps the last remnant of a branch of the Nile that in antiquity had watered the region.

Slowly we wound our way down the terraces, noting as we went that they were filled with rock-tombs. All the dead of Ammonia might lie there, in that amphitheatre of rocks.

The tombs appeared to be in pairs, and looked like a thousand sightless eyes staring vacantly over their lost paradise, and as we descended the glory increased. The sun was caught by the translucent lakes and thrown, in vivid colours, against rocks and palms.

Before us stood the fortifications of Siwa; unreal, phantasmagoric. Battlements, towers, and minarets, great walls pierced by a hundred windows, houses piled one on top of another glistening white as silver; for the walls were built of mud and salt. The newer buildings were of snow-field intensity, reflecting the glare of the sun like a polished shield. In the slanting light, it seemed like the city of Haroun er Raschid and the brilliant caliphs of Baghdad, instead of the world's most decadent city; the Sodom of the twentieth century.

We camped well away from the city, a little apprehensive, still, of the fanatical Senussi, on the Djebel Muta; the hill of the dead. Here, a rough bungalow had been built by those British officers who took Siwa during the war, to make it the headquarters of the Libyan patrol. It was an extraordinary thing, camping on the burial-ground of some thousands of the ancient citizens of Jupiter Ammon, and, strolling about in the moonlight, it is no exaggeration to say that we trod on at least half a dozen skulls, grinning in the half-light. Those officers who chose the site had a dry sense of humour!

Almost before we were asleep, we heard a tumult in the town. The natives resented us, as they resented all new-comers then, because the advent of the whites had usually meant some display of force, and they were still afraid of the *Nazrani*.

Fanaticism was still with them, as we discovered later, when we walked through the streets, to the accompaniment of jeers and curses, and stones which, coming from nowhere, landed among us.

We began with the exploration of the hill of the dead, where there were a hundred thousand mummies in long passages and causeways. We were, if the German professor who discussed the origin of syphilis is to be believed, at the very birthplace of that malady. Judging from the Siwans of to-day, his conclusions should have a certain weight.

The outer tombs had been plundered; there were piles of discarded mummy-cloth, broken pottery, beads, and skulls lying in the open; but the inner tombs were intact, as well as some magnificent rock-chambers with painted scenes of past history. We had hopes even of finding papyrus, until Ali Ford disillusioned us. If there is papyrus to be found, it will need considerable excavation, for every scrap that could be discovered easily has been taken to the town, to be burned as incense.

By degrees we approached the town, and made the acquaintance of the chiefs, out of politeness, and thought we had succeeded in calming their fears; but on the fourth day we were disturbed, in more senses than one, by the beating of drums and the wailing of flutes in the town.

Ali Ford, who spoke English – with an Oxford accent be it known, from contact with officers during the war – came hurriedly to tell us that there was trouble. The chiefs were not at all satisfied with us and were intending to make a visit to the camp. The result might be anything but pleasant.

The truth was that the moon was in eclipse, and the chiefs had heard mutterings that the *Nazrani* had put the moon out. It had certainly disappeared from the sky.

Shortly afterwards, the procession began to wind itself from the city, and we could see the red and green flags of the people. In case of eventualities, we got out our guns, although Hillier said that first we had better try a bit of palaver and, wise man that he was, he prepared a drink that became known among us as a Siwan cocktail: petrol and gin in a great bowl.

As soon as the drink was ready, Ali Ford and Hillier went out to exchange greetings, and to explain to the chiefs that we were not sorcerers, that we had nothing whatever to do with the moon, and that in due course it would come back to shine on the splendour of Siwa. Nor should we take the sun out of the sky, as they felt was likely.

The palaver was successful. The chiefs became friendly, Ali having intimated that we had a ceremonial libation prepared. For the chiefs and people there was gin and petrol; for us, gin and water. We did not mention the difference!

The effect was almost instantaneous. Three glasses sent the chiefs into splendid hilarity. Drums and music were summoned, the people swarmed round, and we had the first exhibition of Siwan morals.

True to promise, the moon returned. The dancers lined up, men and boys. Every dancer had his boy friend. The enthusiasm could not have been approached, even in Sodom, for Siwan morals are unique.

We learned from Ali that the chiefs had harems of boys. The women were frantic by the neglect shown to them. Homosexuality was not only rampant, it was raging, and the usurping boys went in danger of their lives from the women.

We had an instance of that enmity one day when we saw a group of women stoning a boy whom they had caught unawares; but the greatest revelation was the festival of Sidi Suleyman, which was celebrated during our stay in the oasis.

Before the feast, our household went absolutely unattended. We had to fend for ourselves. The whole city was busy with preparations, and when the great day arrived we were afforded a sight which can never have been equaled in the great days of licence of decadent Rome.

Naturally, we turned to Ali Ford for guidance, and he was both nervous and apprehensive. For *Nazrani* to overlook the festival was impossible. What was worse, it was dangerous. But he got us there, just the same.

Every able-bodied man in the oasis was scrambling up the palms to collect lubki, or palm wine, which was sucked from the heart of the tree through a small tube. There they were, in the leaves of the great, royal palms, sucking away, and tipping the sap into their receptacles, emitting a cry of triumph when the palm was drained.

In the city square were piles of golden Sultana dates, believed to be possessed of aphrodisiacal qualities, and to which men and women helped themselves as and when they would, to make themselves virile and voluptuous for the coming orgy. The Siwans from outlying oases came in on mules and camels, bringing in goats and sheep for the great slaughter.

Through Ali, we discovered an abandoned house, which could be approached from the rear, through the palms, and from whose roof there was a good view of the square. When the day arrived, I confess that we were as excited as the Siwans themselves, as, towards sunset, we crept to our observation post.

The *koubba* of the saint stood on the right of the square, which had been swept clean for the occasion. In the centre stood material for a gigantic bonfire. Sheep and goats bleated and cried from every corner. From the roofs and windows of the houses, carpets and streamers were draped. Green and red flags waved from the tomb of the saint.

The square, open on one side, gave on to a vast expanse of palms, which cast lengthening shadows. The battlements, gaunt and gleaming in all shades from the brilliant white of salt to the dull tinge of older buildings, flecked with orange, red, and purple by the changing light, served as background. Around the square, little doors, dark and mysterious, seemed like the improvised entrances and exits for a thousand actors.

Yet the place was deserted. For all its decoration, it was a square of the dead; but in the houses, and in the distant oases, there began the slow, rhythmic beat of tom-toms, soon reinforced by the shrill "le le" of the women, whose excitement was no less than that of the men.

Negroes and slaves began to emerge from the shadows in barbaric costumes. There was movement in the darkening palm groves: young men busily collecting the last of the lubki into a great container, for the feast was to last three days, and much drink would be needed. Happily for them, palm wine ferments quickly.

Sunset was marked by the crash of an ancient Turkish gun in the square. The feast was officially begun, and at the signal, a staggering uproar arose. All the tin cans, drums, trumpets, and flutes of the city, with cymbals – real and improvised – were joined in a steadily increasing volume of sound. It seemed as though it had begun at its maximum; but not at all. As the populace streamed to the square like a horde of ants from every sombre doorway, the sound, already a tornado, swelled to the deafening roar of a world's end.

The dignitaries, and women, came from the three doorways of the citadel and spread around the square, gaily appareled, and began to supervise and prepare the food and drinks.

Musicians followed with drums and flutes. As if by magic, thousands of lanterns were lit, red and green, hanging from the houses on slender rods. From the outskirts a ghostly procession filed towards the town, young men carrying torches in their hands, who wound among the trees like fiery serpents with many tails, converging into one sinuous body, to the accompaniment of a syncopated drumming, as they brought to the square great calabashes of lubki.

The place was full of shadows standing round a deeper shadow, the pyre. A torch was applied, and we saw the flames licking their way round and upwards, until the great pyramid was alight, throwing grotesque and magnified shapes on the walls. Hundreds of young men with cymbals danced round the flame, pirouetting like dervishes, their exaggerated shadows climbing the walls, their robes in the wind, arms in the air. Everything was intensified by the flickering light until it became a scene reminiscent and redolent of Hell.

The drums increased their tempo. Drink was poured down eager throats and over sweating forms. There was the odour of acrid brown bodies, and clouds of incense.

We were in our shelter, looking down, wondering if these things could really be. All the devils of Siwa were in the main square. A general slaughter of sheep and goats followed, before the bonfire. We were spared none of the details; nor did we wish to lose any particle of the event. The screams of the dying and sometimes tortured animals were added to the tumult, and the sharp smell of blood was wafted up to us; a new ingredient in the maniacal horror of the night.

The feast had begun in earnest. There was the noise of gorging multitudes, of the swilling of wine, the fanatical banging of drums and crashing of cymbals, and the sharp, piercing screams of men and women, with a dull undertone of movement and excitement which never varied.

Still good-natured, the people were rapidly reaching hysteria. Animals were dragged to pieces, and eaten half-raw. The taste of blood probably added something to the exaltation of the Siwans, urged on by the insistent beat of drums and the wail of flutes. Little by little, the dancers discarded their clothing, soaked in blood and lubki. Their sinewy bodies glistened in the light. The women began again their incantations, keeping time by clapping their hands, and the general dance around the tomb of the saint was commenced. There was probably not a sober individual in Siwa, and steadily, relentlessly, the feast expanded into an orgy that could never have been surpassed. Gorged and inflamed, brains and bodies fired, men and women, and men and men, with bodies interlaced thrust and retreated, fell to the ground, or grappled and fought in a frenzied hold. Even the children tasted all the excitement of the night, and shared with the rest the fullness of the feast. The square was no longer a place of the twentieth century. Time had receded. It was the grove of Astarte. All the gods and all the lesser gods were there, combined in one great festival of fecundation. On the hard earth of the swept square new life was being conceived at the bidding of the saint who lay dead in his *koubba*.

Gradually, the crisis passed, the noise subsided; the lovers lay still by the dying embers of the fire. One day had ended.

When the sun began to rise, the revelers crept away, to escape the heat of the day; but, at the same hour, for the next and the next day, the feast was recommenced.

Siwa knew no morality during those days when we were there; whatever may have happened to change the city's face since. There is no crime that is not native to the place. Sodomy is almost a virtue. It used to happen that when there were too many girls in the family, the unwanted ones were thrown from the top of the battlements. We saw with our own eyes what happened when jealous women caught the boy favourites of the town.

We saw, too, the spectacle of a widow seeking relief from her curse, one day as we went through the town, and Ali, hearing a familiar sound, dragged us into the nearest convenient doorway and told us to hide. Should a woman be so unfortunate as to lose her husband, she is accursed, and must perform the rites of her cleansing. When she is advancing, natives on the streets scurry like rabbits for shelter, since to be seen by her is to be cursed also.

We saw that woman, preceded by a running boy with a bell, going on her way to wash herself clean in the Fountain of the Sun. For six weeks she must continue the rite.

Superstition, of course, was rife. Anything might be the vehicle of the evil eye, so the houses were invariably protected by the skulls of animals, preferably horned, although we found the skulls of camels, horses, and dogs, and the hand of Fatima everywhere apparent.

Women who cannot bear male children are doubly cursed, which leads to a certain deception.

We knew from Herodotus that the Fountain of the Sun was held in some sacred estimation in the past, that rites both strange and secret took place there; and when we came to study the question, to see if the old romancer had foundation in fact, we could at least accept the strangeness of the practices.

The Fountain of the Sun lay about two miles away from the town of Siwa, in the heart of a magnificent grove of royal palms, and was known to almost all of the ancient historians as being hot in the evening and cool during the day.

We tried it frequently, but found no change whatever in temperature that could account for the tradition; all that happens is that the waters are of a fairly even temperature, which means that they feel agreeably cool to the body during the heat of the day, and in the chill of a Siwan night as agreeably warm. The contrast with air temperature is certainly marked, and the beauty of situation unique.

Old stones lie around the pool, covered with sweet moss; there are flowers among the pomegranate groves, jasmine blooms in abundance, and vivid golden fingers of Siwan dates shine among the palms and are reflected in the limpid waters, to which come the women of the town when all other means have failed.

The sorcerers and charms unavailing, concoctions of toads and mummies' skulls useless, the disappointed women come to the Fountain to bathe in the waters and receive the visitations of the gods, to relieve them of their barrenness. The spirits that abide in the grove follow them into the waters and yield to their pleadings. Embraced by the gods, they are freed of their curse and there is rejoicing in the houses of their husbands.

So runs the tradition; but what actually happens, as we saw from our shelter when led there by Ali, is that the young rakes of the town take advantage of the tradition and, known or unknown to the women, follow them into the water and impersonate the gods.

In the Fountain of the Sun, the play progresses through the night, and with the appearance of the sun the women seek the shores to lie with their backs exposed to the rays, completing the rite. We saw them as they entered and emerged praying, not towards Mecca, but rather in the direction of Jupiter Ammon.

For ten days we lived among the dead on the Djebel Muta, exploring the corridors, only to come on disappointment after disappointment until one morning I crashed through a weak spot in the flooring, and landed among the suffocating remains of dozens of mummies. That accident, macabre as it was for some time, since I was alone and could not climb out unaided, but had to wait for hours before I was found; changed the whole aspect of our last few days.

The result, was that we had a series of unpillaged tombs to explore, crowded with mummies in a state of perfect preservation, and here we found a bronze sacred cat, statuettes of Ammon Ra, and a quantity of fine chains of mummy-beads, which had naturally fallen apart, but had left their imprint on the mummy cloth so that we were able immediately to reconstruct them.

At the ends of the corridors were inscriptions which we copied, some dealing with the cult of Ammon; and drawings, still vivid, of the priests and their office. Papyrus was as rare as we had been told to expect; but we discovered a few pieces.

Continuing the exploration, we found a mummified skeleton, on whose hand was a perfect ring, with the eye of Osiris, and a scarab which gave us the probable date, estimated by authorities at 1750 B.C.

Apart from these discoveries, there was nothing of major importance discernible. It would need a long and detailed excavation, so we decided to move on to another site.

Chapter 2

Two miles away stood the most famous spot of the whole of the Libyan desert: the temple of the oracle at Agourmi. The site is remarkable, with vivid red rock standing out above the plain, sheer walls in a great circle, with the ruins of the temple showing here and there below the crude but picturesque village that had been built on the ancient stones.

The only way up to the citadel-temple was through a great, arched doorway and a carved path which wound up the side of the rise. This we climbed, and sat among the ruins, to enjoy the wonderful spectacle of three hundred thousand palm trees in the oases below, which would have been the scene enjoyed from the temple steps; with lakes shining on either side, between the receding groves.

Ruined temples and ancient stones raised their heads here and there on the edge of the deserted shores, and the sapphire waters caught the reflection of trees and temples and terraces on their blue, unmoved surface that was one with the blue of the African sky.

Such a spectacle must have greeted the eyes of the great men of the past. Ours was the platform where the priests of Ammon received the caravans of elephants bearing the royal pilgrims, and the gold dust and ivory which should provide the necessary offerings to the oracle.

Here Herodotus (or one of his secretaries) must have stood, taking in the scene. Here came the Pharaohs, and Croesus seeking immunity in the after-life, with the first coins known to men among his treasures.

Greatest of all, Alexander here sought evidence of his divine origin and, of course, the priests, seeing that his hands were not empty, made the oracle speak. There must have been misgivings, however, when the sinister figure of Cato appeared.

Most romantic of all, to me, must have been Hannibal, wondering why, with victory so near, he yet tasted defeat.

We sat there, ruminating, looking over the glorious scene, the stage of a gigantic phase of history, and a procession came out of the bowels of the ruins, as if to add point to our thoughts.

It was only a Siwan marriage; but it meant an opportunity for the camera-man; he hid behind the walls at the bidding of Ali Ford, who pushed the rest of us also into secure hiding, knowing that nothing could be done openly.

The priests of Ammon must have had their excesses; but we were really shocked to see the parties to the marriage: the tough old sheikh of Agourmi, and a child – she was no more – who could hardly have reached adolescence.

The bride was covered with bangles and silver bracelets, and carried round her neck the great silver plaque of the virgins of Siwa – a decoration unique in the Sahara – while round her clustered a group of virgin friends. They looked like a little Sunday-school class, eagerly anticipating the sweets that would be their portion.

The old satyr waited down below for his newest victim. After the ceremony, which we were lucky enough to film, Ali arranged for us to interview the bride, so that we could take close-ups. Then, she went on to her sacrifice, while we continued to examine the walls.

We found remains of the once-magnificent building. There were inscriptions and broken stones, the debris of altars, enormous arches fallen into ruin. Great monoliths barred our way. On either side could be distinguished the sacred emblems of Egypt and Ammon; but decay was everywhere. Perhaps some reconstruction might be possible; but the labour would be great.

Ali took us to a hole in the ground, where we were astonished to find a well that had been cut through the rock to the lake, forty yards deep.

This spot, he said, hid the iron door which led to the tomb of Alexander, or the treasure of the priests. We could not get down to it; but it is certainly worth investigating. There are so many stories. Occasionally, one of the legends will lead to something; but at Siwa, every hole, every well, is confidently pointed out as being the tomb of Alexander.

That many legends are founded on fact is proved by the repeated discoveries made by the Siwans working at the base of ruins. Amulets, rings, coins, statuettes, and scarabs are found from time to time and, unlike Egypt, where the beggars force these things on you, here we had to use diplomacy to get into the houses of the people who had dug up historic things near the temples.

One vase which I managed to obtain, after three days of preliminary negotiation, was a beautiful bronze, with a well-worked lid in the shape of an alligator's head, and inside was a magnificent necklace of cornelians and a dozen small gods: the gods of Ammon, in beaten gold. The workmanship of the gods was not of such finish as others that I have seen; but they marked a very definite link. Gold was brought into Siwa in its early history along the ancient trails.

Slowly, we collected several coins, showing that Siwa had been in constant touch with the outer world. There were Ptolemaic and Roman coins in numbers, and a few Greek coins; but the greatest stroke of good fortune was ours after we had made a friend of the sheikh of Agourmi, and he poured out on the floor a lot of odds and ends, mostly bits of pottery, broken statuettes, and rubbish. Among the waste, however, we saw coins, some of which bore the actual effigy of Alexander as Pharaoh of Egypt and God of Ammon.

We inquired discreetly where the coins came from, and were at first told that they had been found casually among the ruins; but Ali Ford wormed out of the sheikh that they had come from the Djebel Dakrour, where we finally persuaded him to lead us. There, vast tombs had been pillaged.

We climbed the rock terraces, discovering a Greek inscription, not easily decipherable because of erosion, whose lettering corresponded to that of the third century B.C.

One of the tombs had central columns, and looking between them we saw the temple of Jupiter Ammon below. It must have been located with definite purpose: a royal tomb, perhaps, commanding the sacred spot. We filmed the scene from within the tomb, to preserve, in so far as was possible, the view that must have led some powerful ruler to decide on this as his last home.

Other royal tombs were near; but they yielded little to us. The coins and inscriptions which we brought away from Siwa were the first definite relics of Alexander to be found in the oasis, and have since been published.

In the caves underneath the great citadel we found fine rock drawings, and to our amazement they included pictorial representation of the ships of the Nile in the time of the Pharaohs; a suggestion that at the date of the oracle the lakes communicated from oasis to oasis. One spot, indeed, seemed extremely suggestive of the landing-place. Those waters had been crossed, at one time or another, by the galleys of the pilgrims, guests, and priests.

Two exploratory trips were made, using the main camp as base; the first to reach the ruins of Zeitun, which we knew were on an island in one of the lakes.

For this, we used our collapsible boats, and sailed across the still waters, making a picnic camp on the island by the ruins. This was the spot where, according to yet another traditional tale, the treasures of Jupiter Ammon had been thrown into the lake.

We found no treasure, although here again were strong indications that a thorough investigation would be worth while, for we could see the old wharf, now high above the level of the lake and, in the swamps that had once been places of real beauty, other ruins were visible.

The whole area was malarial; but malaria will soon be wiped out by the efforts of the military authorities, and this, with the whole of the Siwan oases, should more than repay complete excavation. Roman ruins, tumuli, broken pottery, and beads gave the usual surface evidence of a good site.

The second trip, still following the legends, was south to the fields where, it is said, the army of Cambyses still lies mummified in the sands: the army that marched on the city from Thebes with orders to sack and destroy the temple. Ammonian chroniclers say that, three days from Siwa, a vast sandstorm suddenly wiped out the mighty host.

This time we went on camels, and succeeded in finding a series of abandoned oases, with tombs in the melancholy valley. It was a dead, unexplored, deserted world, where travel was completely blocked by giant sand dunes. This, it is almost possible to say, is the most forbidding and impassable part of the whole of the Libyan desert.

The dunes were too great for us. Ali and the Siwans could go no farther. Beyond, they said, was the land of the devil; but it may still be possible that somewhere in that terrible stretch lies the lost oasis of Zenzura, that city which legend has called the City of Brass.

On the way back, we did see an extraordinary sight connected with mummies; but not the remains of that vanished host. Instead, we came upon a Bedouin tribe who had travelled to one of these abandoned oases to collect wild dates, and had made their camp in the very skeletons of camels which had died on some caravan or other. It was an amazing thing, seeing the little brown children coming out of the ribs of the camels, ribs dried and cleaned by the sun and sand.

Siwa itself was only a point on our journey. We had intended to make a survey and to trace as much as we could of the plan, before moving on. This we had done, and now began our expedition to the west.

Traveling a little south and west, we had the idea of following the old trail of Herodotus, which went from Jupiter Ammon to Augila, and thence to the Djebel Soda and the land of the Garamantes and the Nazimons.

By now, the incidents of desert travel must have become familiar. Nothing of outstanding interest happened on the first day. The cars ran well, and although the country was somewhat unusually against us, we reached the oasis of Maraghi, there to observe the definite geological formation of the Siwan depression, which conformed with the changing civilization of man.

Reading down the terraces, we found palæolithic man on the upper plateau, camp fires and caves of Neolithic man lower, and then the remains of an Ammonian temple. More amazing was the Byzantine basilica low down on the terraces, succeeded by the present Berber settlements.

These terraced civilizations, which are discovered elsewhere, offer certain evidence of the altered state of the Sahara. Now, the whole region is practically deserted. The tombs have been cleared out by the troglodytes, distinctly Berber people, and quite savage, who live there.

Like the troglodytes of Tunisia and Tripoli, they are the lowest form of humanity; often earth-eaters; but living also on snails, lizards, snakes, and earthworms. Too lazy to build, they use old tombs whenever they can find them.

Our way thence was to Araschie, not only because we wished to follow as much as possible of the old caravan route; but also because this used to be the sacred lake of the Ammonians, which sanctity has been handed down to the Senussi. It is supposed to be the place where the sword of Muhammed and his treasure are buried. An island in the middle of the lake is the legendary hiding-place.

The lake lies somewhat off the cross-roads of the caravan routes from Carthage, and Djarabub a hundred miles west, the centre of the Senussi Confederation.

Pilgrims cross the Sahara to the sacred city of Djarabub, taking their pilgrimage seriously and earning double merit by attaining this town before going on to Mecca, when they are cer-

tain that there is a commensurate reward in the riches and plea-
sures of the hereafter awaiting them.

As the lake is commonly supposed to be haunted, it is carefully avoided by the Arabs of this era.

Our way crossed the rock plateaux of the higher desert, and
we were ploughing a slow way across that none too encouraging
surface when we suddenly looked down on to a hollow where
stood groves of abandoned palm trees in dark masses along the
shores of a still, blue lake, beyond which rose dunes really
deserving the description of mountainous. These dunes are said
to be the highest in the world, and were reflected in the lake like
snowy Alps. A group of perhaps a score of gazelles stood at the
water's edge, dipping their muzzles daintily down. Tombs stood
all around, as though, in ancient times, this had been some centre of pilgrimage in which either thousands had died, or had
been brought, according to custom, to a hallowed place.

Climbing down, we excavated several of the tombs; not at all
easily done, for they were built of stone, and giant masses had to
be removed before we could reach the funeral chamber.

In every one that we opened we found skeletons in the pos-
ture of the Libyan dead, in many cases intact, their knees up to
their chin and ankles tied. The stones piled above were there for
the purpose of keeping the dead in their places. The Libyans,
evidently, were of the opinion that when a man was down he
should stay down!

Flint instruments taken from the tombs belonged to the
Neolithic period; but in some cases there were evidences of a
civilization bordering on the Ammonian. The skulls were char-
acteristically Berber, similar to the Tuareg and Atlas types.

We were moving in dead valleys, honeycombed with the
graves of another dead world; but, after excavating the mounds,
we left the terraces and made our way to the lake shore, where
we put up our tents and made a comfortable camp.

That evening, we unloaded and prepared the collapsible
boats, and towards nightfall were lucky enough to bag two
gazelles: welcome food after tinned provisions.

The stories concerning the lake were multitude; what seemed to be well established was that Colonel Burtin, a French explorer, had been drowned while trying to get to the island, sucked under by the whirlpools.

It was difficult to believe that whirlpools existed; but there was also the tale of an English explorer who had similarly been lost while trying to swim his horse across.

Ali said that the island was protected by poisonous snakes of great size. We lived to see the whirlpools and the snakes, and still came back alive, thanks to the boats.

The next morning I went ahead with the camera-man, and Hillier came after with the Senussi. We knew the boats were stout enough, and that they answered well, and we made a straight course for the objective; but my boat, instead of keeping straight on, began to swing in a circle.

Hillier, thinking that I had not noticed the deviation, shouted to me, to know "why the hell I wasn't keeping my eye on the island," instead of wandering all over the lake; but I was doing my best, and a few seconds later Hillier was doing likewise and circling after me, with a steadily increasing drag. Looking down into the clear water over the edge of the boats, we saw, in the green depths, plants and submarine growth rising like a volcanic eruption from the bowels of the earth, twirling and twisting in some current or other.

Obviously there was a great force at work down below, perhaps due to the rock formation of the lake. We could trace the intensity of the maelstrom, which increased towards the centre. Then we understood more readily the fate of the swimmers who, not perceiving the danger from the surface, would be drawn into the current and slowly sucked down. It gave us all cause to think, and if we were not panicky we were a little more than anxious. Obviously, the lakes were fed by a subterranean source. Rowing harder, and still harder, we came clear, and made for the island, half a mile to the south. We had solved one mystery. The other guardian might be equally authentic.

On landing, I failed to see any snakes; but we did see a great *ouragen,* that deadly lizard, sunning himself on a rock. Hillier shot him, spoiling my chance of a live specimen for the zoo.

We climbed up, going warily and well-booted, to explore, discovering at once that tombs had been sunk vertically into the rock of the island. They had filled with sand, however, and needed to be cleared before we found any direct evidence of their origin.

While we were digging, we were all startled by an incredible noise that floated, softly at first, but with ever-increasing intensity, from the direction of the sand dunes. Ḥassan, who had come with Hillier in the second boat, turned tremblingly to us. "No touch the tomb," he pleaded. "Dunes talking!"

The noise developed into an absolute roar in the stillness, ending with a staccato rattle, like the angry beat of drums, and that brought us all to a standstill.

Hillier said, "What the hell's that?" and Hassan, though shivering in apprehension, pointed across to the dunes. One giant, encircled by others, stood out majestically. That was it; the famous singing dune, the real sentinel of the lake, which worked on the superstitious Siwans and other tribes of the desert, so that they would not camp within miles of it.

We shouted across to Ali, who was distinctly agitated on the far shore, waving his arms and summoning us to return, that we were not coming back yet; but he demanded that we should pack up and be gone. I have never seen natives in such terror; Hassan, for all his colour, was a sickly, ashen grey.

The sound was doubtless amplified by echo among the cliffs; but it was certainly haunting and unreal, and so well timed that the natives took it as a definite warning. We, however, decided that we would continue our exploration, and when that was done, follow on to the dune and see, if we could, what it was all about.

We found that the tombs had long been rifled; certainly not by modern hands. As certainly there are others to be discovered. The top stones are so well cut, and fit so closely, that it would take a considerable time to cover the rock surface and tap out the whereabouts of the remaining tombs.

We discovered no sword of Muhammed, but there were plenty of broken pottery, flints, and arrow heads, which seemed to indicate that in earlier times the island had been a place of refuge.

The next day, despite Hassan's ultimatum that we should "all die," we moved over to the singing dune, which meant that Hillier and the rest of the whites had to tramp the most of the way, for the Arabs came to an abrupt halt at what they deemed a safe distance. We had to camp alone.

We had all heard, and read, of the singing dunes; but this was the first identifiable dune that I had seen, so we camped there and waited for the phenomenon to begin.

Sure enough, about an hour after sunset, while we were calmly munching our bully beef, a low sound, which might have been imagination, began to be felt rather than heard.

We turned to each other. Yes! we had all heard the same thing, and by now it was distinctly moaning. Being too tough a band to believe in the supernatural, we advanced to the base of the dune and got our ears down, to work it out.

We concluded that the cause of the moaning was due to the fact that this great mountain, being in the midst of a circle of other dunes, terraces, and precipices, was caught in a current of air. In the evening, as the hot air rises and the cold air comes down, it sweeps round the base of the dune in a minor cyclone, causing the sand to move. We could actually see the current in action, removing tons of sand, which was replaced by a slow-starting avalanche. The millions of moving particles set up friction, and the dune "talked."

The rattling sound was due to the cracking of the sand. The Siwans unanimously ascribed the noise to the voice of the devil. We tried to explain to them; but there was nothing doing. We rubbed our hands together till they rasped and whistled, and all the reply we could evoke was *"Ya es salaam!"* which is to say "Fancy that!"

Thereafter, we tried something which we had been forbidden to do, to proceed to Djarabub. The Officer Commanding the Western Desert had been definite in his antagonism to this project, since Italian forces were operating against the native tribes; and ordered us under no circumstances to pass into Tripolitan territory. But the inclination was too strong. We decided to push on, and see what happened. Fighting might be over, or we might find the Italian forces amenable to our adventure. So we pressed on through a territory commonly regarded by the Arabs as the stronghold of the devils of the desert.

Ali, who had served with the British during the war, said that he knew where there were ruins, and his rough indication coincided well enough with the account of Herodotus. It might easily be on the old trail to Carthage.

We wound through a section of desert that was as beautiful as it was difficult; canyons were on either side of us, and the pass through which we were driving narrowed as it neared a ridge, and then began a sheer descent.

This, said Ali, was about the place.

Hillier said he would like to see where the things were, and that if Ali had been leading us on a false scent he would wring his neck. Ali only smiled. He was sure – and there they were a little later, under the rock-ledges. Ali's word of honour as a Siwan had not been broken.

We came to a place where there were definite signs of an ancient outpost guarding the trail, and where hundreds of amphoras, precisely similar to the multitudes we had found at Carthage, had been stored, full of wine and provisions, in the days of the Phoenicians or Romans. Here they had halted, between Carthage and Ghadames, on the way to Thebes.

Roman legions had held the post, and we collected a few of the amphoras, leaving the rest, since we had insufficient transport.

From that point we followed the ancient route, lunging terribly among the great boulders, which we had to go over, since there was neither way round nor could we move the obstacles.

Apart from the roadway, everything seemed to be going well. We had seen no refugees. There had been no sound of fighting. Possibly the action had been decided and the Italian army had moved its scene of operations. We hoped so, and that it would be within the bounds of possibility to reach Ghat.

But, while we were eating lunch among the great rocks, Hassan let out an unearthly howl. We had heard nothing to occasion fright, but he turned that peculiar grey that spoke of a fright incomprehensible to non-superstitious people. Even Ali was shocked into fear; his spring-like, tough hair lifted his *chechia,* and, a moment later, we too shared the alarm. There was a roar that boomed like the fall of a city, echoing and reverberating among the rocks.

We had run into an Italian desert patrol, and their cars came towards us with an alarming resolution. We could see the gunners standing-to at their machine-guns.

We got to the top of the boulders and waved our hats, taking care to keep our hands well in the air, having no desire to be shot first and explain later.

The attack on Kufara had begun, we learned, and this patrol was hunting refugees. They had taken us for fugitives and would have attacked, had we not made ourselves known.

Our moment of panic faded; but it meant the end of one trip and the beginning of another. After we had explained our mission, and there had been a little private exchange between Hillier and the commanding officer, we talked.

Hillier was a little distant, and showed it, when the young commandant asked what we were doing on Italian territory without permission. "It may be Italian to-day," said Hillier sarcastically, "but last night it was Egyptian, to the best of my knowledge!"

Still, nothing worse followed. We learned that the Italians had captured Djarabub, and that the Arabs were in flight, as we joined forces and shared our meal, which the Italians enlivened with a little chianti.

We were sent back, however, since it was obviously impossible to continue; but, as a consolation, the young officer gave me an introduction to del Bono, the Italian Minister for the Colonies, who, he said, would be greatly interested in the expedition through Italian territory as soon as it was practicable. We might even be permitted to follow the advance of the Italian army, as Signor Mussolini was intensely interested in archaeological research.

So we obeyed instructions, retracing our steps and picking up the various collections of objects that we had stored, following the depressions of the Libyan desert from Siwa to Cairo, where, in antiquity, there had been a much more populous and expansive civilization.

It was simply a matter of labour, of pushing cars through sand and across rock, and stopping, in more favoured places, to collect, literally, thousands of prehistoric remains, including a great number of Fayum flints of the half-moon, fishtail, and Eiffel-tower types; which also, incidentally, showed that we were on the trail that had been used by men of all the ages, traveling from the Atlantic to the heart of the desert.

Chapter 3

As a result of that chance encounter in the desert, the following year I communicated with Signor del Bono, who put me into touch with Commandatore Miccachi.

After months of negotiation, which involved a dozen trips to Rome, we finally received the authority of Signor Mussolini, supported by the Archaeological Department and the Governor of Tripoli, to make our expedition.

The only stipulations were that the news of discoveries should first be communicated to the Italian press, and the films be taken by an Italian operator.

So, after slight preliminaries, we sailed for Algiers, where I was to pick up the cars I had bought from the late Prince Sixte de Bourbon.

These cars were the last word in equipment: the seats so comfortable that we might have been going for a joy-ride. There was a Pullman chair for each passenger, and each chair had a thermos flask in a specially contrived pocket. In the roof were straps for our guns, so arranged that we simply pulled the guns down when we wanted to use them and, after use, let them automatically return to their places.

Compartments for ammunition, water, oil, petrol, and for objects found were arranged so that everything was packed in the least possible time and the greatest safety. The searchlights were detachable, and could be carried on cords to the centre-poles of our tents when we camped. Each car also had a filter, and there was a heat-proof container for our films.

Only a minimum amount of refitting was necessary, although the cars were just back from Lake Chad, and that was soon done.

Then we followed the coast of Algeria and Tunisia to Tripoli without halting, much as we should have liked to stay, until we reached the Matmatas and Gigthis, which it was impossible to neglect.

We camped in the temple of Apollo, our headlights lifting the majestic ruins to a marvellous softness of gold and ivory, and the next morning, for sentiment's sake, I went to find the buoy that marked the site of submarine excavations I had made some years previously. It was still there, waiting for that day when, with luck, I shall continue one of the most fascinating chapters of my experience.

After that we made straight for Tripoli, and, apart from a bullet through the roof of my car, fired by an over-zealous Arab, reached our hotel without incident.

It was made clear immediately that when the Italians undertook a job they carried it through, not only with exactitude but with a genial charm: which will, of course, ultimately carry them to their great objective in North Africa. I think I have never known enthusiasm and kindness so great as was shown on that occasion. It seemed as though entertainment would never cease, and the day of our departure was a festival throughout the town. The people of Tripoli brought us presents to take to the officers and soldiers in the desert; letters, and gifts for Christmas, although we should deliver them long before that festival.

The Grand Hotel had all its flags flying, and the cars were drawn up and decorated, surrounded by the camel corps, officers, and photographers, besides half the population of the town.

With exhausts cut out, we roared up to the white steps of the Governor's Palace for the formal leave-taking, and so we were off, making our way to Leptis Magna, where we camped among the ruins of the most wonderful Roman city of North Africa.

There are marvellous sites in Tunisia and Algeria, eloquent of the majesty that once was Rome; but nothing on this earth can approach Leptis Magna for perfection and splendour.

Much of the city has been saved from destruction because the Vandals, finding it already abandoned, spent no fury of vengeance and spite on its stones. The drifting sand saved it from later invasions, and now, when the sand is being cleared, and careful administration is watching over the restoration, the ruins come out in no great damage.

We camped on mosaic floors near the forum, still beautiful and intact, and wandered for hours among golden columns glittering in the moonlight, their colour intensified by contrast with the silvery dunes. Vast temples, harbours, theatres, and palaces looked on to emerald waters on one side and the soft lace of a palm grove on the other: the giant skeleton of a once mighty city, birthplace of Septimius Severus. A strange character, that noble Roman: born in Leptis Magna of Punic origin; Emperor of Rome; died at York.

We saw the evidence of the careful labour that was restoring the city. The maritime ports and the naval basin still had their mooring-rings on the quayside. Shops in a delightful semicircle spoke of trade that had once been prosperous. Temples to marine gods spoke of the devotions of sailors who, perhaps, did not care too much about blue-water sailing.

From Leptis Magna, we plunged into the desert with Ghirza as our first objective, hoping to be the first archaeological expedition to reach that mysterious ruined city. It was only about three hundred miles away; not far, as distance goes; but across appalling desert, without vestige of trail. No cars, so far as we could discover, had yet reached it, and our task was considered to be impossible by the authorities.

Certainly, our difficulties were not lessened by the incompetence of our guides, who had a private quarrel of their own. It happened that they belonged to two tribes, with a dispute almost amounting to a blood feud unsettled between them.

Of the parentage of each, according to the other, there was at once considerable doubt and no question, and the quarrel almost ended in murder when one, outraged by the other's insolence, retaliated by saying that he was at least a more attractive man, and that his enemy's wife thought so too, not withholding her favours.

To settle that particular matter, we established each on the roof of a different car, and they rode so, waving contrary hands as to direction, with the result that when we were two days out we were completely lost.

Hussein ben Aksobar pointed south. Sidi Muhammed Askala insisted on traveling south-east, calling his colleague the seven-fold son of a dog.

There was nothing for it. We left the guides to their squabble, and by scouting around found the traces of an old Roman trail leading south, which we decided to follow.

For several days we crashed through rocky country, or ploughed yielding sands, with occasional good, level surfaces; going more or less blind when we branched off to follow the dried beds of streams which gave us easier going.

Bitter work for us; it was a fine picture. The camera-man enjoyed every minute of the trail, and our profane advance.

Salvation came through the discovery of a Roman military sign-post by Captain Lavis. Professor Guidi deciphered the inscription, although it was much worn by time and weather, which indicated a chain of forts lying ahead.

By sunset we had demonstrated the truth of the sign-post and camped in one of the little forts, from which we gathered that there was a town of some size in the near vicinity.

That drive was worse than anything we had experienced before. The path to the Hoggar was nothing in comparison to the hardship and uncertainty of the trail that we followed after sunrise the next morning. To the French Hoggar, we had at least camel tracks as guides. Here we had nothing. It was an absolute blank, and we had to take whatever came: canyons, ravines, mountains of rock and sand, as we travelled by compass and guesses, with occasional easy patches among the river beds.

Even in those dried courses there was a growth of bush and brush so thick that we had to descend and chop our way through, cutting a swathe just broad enough to permit the cars to pass in single file, and when we left the bed we found ourselves in loose, soft sand, in which the wheels of the cars spun with a familiar and disappointing whistle, churning a small sandstorm before they began to settle deeper and deeper. Our entire force was necessary to dig them out. We were compelled to unload and start again.

Still we continued to follow the chain of ruined fortresses which seemed to be stationed on the heights at about every twenty miles, overlooking the river, and suddenly, almost mysteriously we saw what appeared to be the smoke-stacks of a modern city on the far horizon.

Both guides claimed the discovery at the same moment, shouting and gesticulating from their seats on the roof.

"Ghirza," they screamed, although we had been heading for it for hours.

Then we got a taste of the real treachery of the desert, for we ploughed on and on, with the ruins as far off as ever. The surface was now almost impracticable, and we were compelled to fashion a road to the plateau above, when the great monuments came slowly into fuller design.

There were mausoleums such as we had never before encountered in desert travel, and to say that we were thrilled is to understate our enthusiasm as we blasted our way across: a way that had been dismissed as impossible by the authorities at Tripoli.

Yet it was still a question as to whether we should be able to fight it out. Night fell, and still we wound painfully on, with car number three crashing into a jagged boulder, which ripped off the mudguards and exploded the flint-filled tyres.

We effected repairs, and went on again. Rosselli's car fell into a sandpit, and had to be dug out. In the deceptive light of the moon we saw dark masses looming ahead, and half an hour later our headlights lit up the ancient city.

It was a scene of rare, romantic beauty, and we yelled ourselves hoarse with joy. At every turn there was a new ruin, and at midnight we camped near the moonlit columns of a gorgeous temple, where the silence was really tangible. We were too tired to put up our tents, or even to make beds. I crept into my sleeping-bag, to hear the sonorous, expressive voice of a hard-bitten English captain saying, "What a hell of a place to build a town!"

His was just another, unconscious, testimony to the change that has come over the Sahara. On either side of the city were the sun-scorched plains of utter desolation. There was neither beauty nor hope within a hundred miles; only this silent, deserted city.

In the morning, we explored it thoroughly, discovering that it must have been prosperous about the third or fourth century. There were certain Garamantian and phallic signs; but the ruins were definitely Roman in the mass.

When we crept out of our sleeping-bags in the dawn, it seemed incredible: the ruins had been left untouched for centuries. It was one of the capitals of a lost and great civilization.

Italian desert patrols had been there; but that, so far as we knew, was the only occasion on which it had been visited by Europeans. It had never been photographed, never surveyed prior to our arrival.

Sunrise was already painting the mausoleum of a forgotten king with tints fit for his state as we sounded the alarm to rouse the rest of the camp, that they too might enjoy the spectacle of sunrise in an abandoned city, Yet, I am afraid, the appreciation was mixed, and ranged from the finest profanity to the poetry in smooth-flowing Italian that came from one of the professors. Truly, it was beyond the hope of men to see anything so supremely beautiful. The early purple shadows faded to blue. The cream and silver of the stones rouged and mellowed. The sun climbed higher into the heavens and a wave of rosy light flooded the city, followed by pulsating gold, offset by the faintest of mauve shadows for a while. Then all was clear, sharp and shadowless. The sun poured its unrefracted light full on to the stones, robbing them of all life. What had throbbed in the dawn now stood dead and dried. Sometimes, it is possible to hate the sun.

The cook was bundled about his job, preparing breakfast, and shortly afterwards we were able to proceed with the real examination of the ruins. We climbed among the temples and palaces, and made a rough plan of the position of the monuments.

Professor Guidi was hoisted on to our shoulders so that he could transcribe the inscriptions and examine the strange architectural features not hitherto encountered in any Roman city. There were details Roman, and things not Roman; Greek, and not Greek; Phoenician, and not Phoenician. There was something new. It might even be the lost capital of the Garamantes. Or, it might not.

For days we pored over the ruins, considered the mysterious square columns of temples, and the designs that were almost cabalistic.

Some buildings made of dried mud appeared to have been intended for barracks. They gave us much to do.

Our immediate need, after the first survey, was to locate the tombs of the common people. The royal tombs had been rifled, long ago, we soon discovered. The robbers had made a quick haul, and gone. Doubtless a full excavation will bring to light objects and evidences which we had neither time nor equipment to find. We were successful only in recovering some beads and debris, which was of course carefully sieved for pottery and small objects.

We knew that the common people's tombs must be somewhere not far distant, for the town must have contained between fifteen and twenty thousand people at the time of its desertion. Following the bed of an old river for several miles, we located rock-tombs that had been carved from the masses, and which resembled the tombs of Siwa and of the Ammonian civilization, and were not unlike those of Carthage and Utica.

We cut our way into one; but it afforded nothing beyond the traces of the skeleton, jars of food, some rough pottery, and cornelian beads. The skeleton was drawn up, knees to chin, in the expected fashion, and must have been that of an elderly man, since most of the teeth were gone.

Further search revealed a number of worked flints and several bronze instruments, which made us wonder was this the tomb of a general practitioner of twenty centuries ago. Pots and jars showed traces of dried substances which might have been his simples. The contents were carefully packed for scientific investigation, and the instruments and skull were taken for measurement, to see whether he were Garamantian or Roman.

We made a plan of the city, Professor Guidi arranging with the Italian Government for the complete exploration of the site by a thoroughly equipped expedition to be sent the following year.

From the drawings we traced, Ghirza must have been a pretty wicked city. The phallic cult was well portrayed, and many scenes told us that we were exploring a desert Pompeii.

The Arabs had legends, as usual, of its accursed state. Once, it appeared, Muhammed's grandfather had been there, when lost in the desert, and found the city full of marble statues.

We wondered what had become of them; for there is generally some foundation in fact of many of the Arab tales.

Possibly a wandering tribe had destroyed them. Perhaps they were buried somewhere in the sands. Muhammed had no news on that point; but he knew that Ghirza had been a city full of wicked, dark, dancing girls and satyrs. Allah had seen fit to destroy it as a punishment. There had been a great earthquake, in which all the houses had collapsed, and God had converted the inhabitants into stone. So he accounted for the presence of the statues.

We ourselves found, as evidence of their existence, fragments of marble: hands; arms; pieces of the torso.

From Ghirza, our next job was to pull clear and get to Bu Djem.

We had the same struggle with difficult country, perhaps more intensified, which once more drove us to the river-beds, in a direction vaguely south-east. Our guides had only the haziest general idea of the position of the military outpost, and, since they were both still enraged and quarrelling, we isolated them again on separate cars, from which elevation they searched the horizon for mythical indications.

I was positive they had never been in the country before, but we followed the map as well as we could, and our annoyance with them was lessened by the discovery of prehistoric flints of the greatest importance.

On the side of the river-bed we discovered a number of sites of Chellean and Mousterian flints, and Professor Guidi and the others, who had little experience of flints, were delighted to find these traces of palæolithic man in Italian territory. It was the first location of this period in the country, and we piled our specimens into cases for the various museums. Continuing, we found the traces of hundreds of years of tribal fires on the river, which led to the conclusion that, centuries ago, it had been an area capable of supporting a large population.

Unfortunately, we began to run short of water; but when we were at our lowest ebb our glasses picked up the welcome figures of the Italian Camel Corps, in their picturesque white uniforms, who had been sent out on the search for us.

There is no uniform, I think, quite so picturesque – and so forbidding – as that of the Italian Meharist. Perhaps it is protective: certainly it fades into the sand readily enough on occasion. The steeds themselves are white. The uniforms, lances, and turbans, even the half-veils that are worn as protection against sand and dust, are white and, unless the rider wishes to show himself, it is hard to distinguish him at more than a few yards' distance.

Led into Bu Diem, we were received with the customary Italian enthusiasm. The garrison had all its flags out, and the troops were lined up on either side, while the Commandant and his lieutenants came forward to greet us.

In addition to archaeological information, we brought them welcome and essential news of the trails, for which they were thankful enough.

Professor Guidi had the news of our discoveries telegraphed to Tripoli and Rome, and the camera-man arranged for a full-dress film of the life of the Camel Corps among the dunes.

A marvellous picture it made, with the silent shadows filing by, their lank mounts covering the sand tirelessly in great strides, or stealing through the darkness into the full glare of our flares and headlights, topping the hills and giving us the unspeakably beautiful silhouette of a full company against the black pall of the night.

Bu Djem was only a halt for water and petrol; but we made one excellent find: a stone bearing an inscription to Valerian which we discovered in the sand dunes to the south of the fort; relic of the little post of the Roman Legionaries. Italy still treads in the path of the Caesars.

Our route was to Oueddan, to visit and explore, if possible, the place where treasure had been discovered in the oasis of Djofara a year previously.

At Hon we had the amazing spectacle of the Italian expeditionary force setting off for its attack on the last stronghold of the Senussi: Kufara. One of the planes made it possible for our operator to take a film of the four hundred motor trucks fighting their way through the sand.

Not a tenth of the labour and organization of desert warfare has been told to the world. It is an undertaking beyond ordinary comprehension.

From Hon, after the departure of the army, we had a stretch of about a hundred kilometers before reaching Djofara, and when we arrived in the settlement we wasted no time, but began our quest immediately.

The opinion of the town was divided as to the location of the treasure. Half said that it had been found on the great plateau overlooking the oasis, near a Turkish fort taken over by the Italians.

The other half contended that the treasure had been found in one of the Arab houses in the village that nestled at the base of the rock.

Professor Guidi and an assistant began digging on the Gara at first; but after two days of hard labour, all there was to show for the effort was a small bit of gold-leaf in the hole that the Arabs had indicated. It must have been no more than a temporary hiding-place.

There, however, we did see something perhaps even more impressive than the discovery of ancient treasure. The Italians, taking to heart a bit of Senussi craft and courage, were painting great letters on the walls of the fort.

"Remember Sebha!" was the inscription that some spelled out, as others mounted and manned their guns.

The reason was that, some weeks previously, at the fortress of Sebha, the Italians had been surprised during mess, after capturing the place and establishing their machine-guns on the parapet of the fort.

Unobserved, a body of Senussi had approached, rushed the post, and turned the guns on the garrison, with the consequence that the victors were wiped out. The lesson would not need to be repeated.

Our scent having failed, we then spent a long time digging into various houses, trying to find where the treasure of Oueddan had been discovered: a really considerable treasure, consisting of ten golden idols, rings, buckles, fine spirals, and amulets of excellent workmanship.

Finally we found one workman, an Arab, who claimed to have made the original discovery and would reveal the site for liberal pay and the promise that I would deal with him myself, independently of the Italian "oppressors."

I was taken to the north of the fortress, to the Oued er Ramada, where it was said that rock-tombs existed. The others were left busily at work on other locations.

Crossing an entirely barren region, north of the old caravan trail from Jupiter Ammon to the valley of the Nile, we came to the lower slopes of the vast rock-terraces of the Djebel Oueddan, where at least we had a magnificent view of the fortress on the rock, surrounded by its depression of charred and arid desert.

A vast, unexplored region lay before me, intersected by dead river-beds emerging from the mysterious plateau. There was not a sign of life, beyond the tracks of jackals or hyænas in the sand. My dour Arab guide did not utter a word for hours, save that now and again he pointed forward, muttering *"Henak! Henak!"*

After a long, hot climb we reached the upper terraces and found rock-tombs in the face of the mountain. On every side were traces of recent excavation: shreds of mummy cloth, bits of pottery and bones where the illicit diggers had hurried their work ahead of the arrival of the Italians.

I noticed that a series of tombs led across the plateau in the direction of Augila and Jupiter Ammon. The ancient trail must have passed at the base of this rock.

My guide explained that the idols had been found in a tomb whose broken entrance he indicated. After discovery, they had been hurried away, and buried elsewhere. An Italian soldier, digging haphazard, had come upon the secret, to their dismay.

I collected beads and bits of pottery, and photographed the site because of its archaeological importance. Ultimately a properly staffed and equipped excavation will need to be made, for there is no doubt in my mind that the Arab told the truth. There are other discoveries to be made.

The pottery and beads were similar to those found in Siwa, and a perfect, mummified skull showed typical Libyan characteristics.

The Siwan statuettes were rougher than those found at Oueddan and I was reminded again of the fact that there is no gold to be mined in the neighbourhood of Siwa. The metal must have come from Ophir, from Ethiopia. I decided that when occasion served I would press these old routes back to the boundaries of the ancient Libyan kingdom.

Our next point was to have been Kufara; but we were prevented by the authorities, who informed us that on no account could we penetrate, as fighting was still proceeding. Not only that, the resistance had been greater than was anticipated, and bombing planes were employed.

Italian casualties, it was said, amounted to five thousand men; but whether that was rumour or fact I could not discover. Certain it was that the Senussi were formidable enemies; certain, too, that war was pushed forward without respite as the villages were wiped out from the skies in a steady advance.

We saw the Italians off on their way, and ourselves travelled west, to cross the strange region of the Djebel es Soda, described by Herodotus as "the great black mountain"; not a bad description at that, since it was an area of extinct volcanoes, where our cars had an appalling time, due to the laceration of the tyres by flints.

An extremely rough trail had been made, for some of the way, by the Italian forces, and we crossed to Murzuk, where a good camp had been arranged for us by the Italian authorities.

Murzuk proved to be one of the most miserable of places. The inhabitants, due to Turkish cruelty and misrule, and in no small part to the present war and the termination of the slave trade, were in a tragic condition. Some were actually starving to death. The town was in a state of famine when we arrived, and relief was still afar off, as no supplies had been brought through.

Some day, perhaps, the full tale of privation following desert warfare will be told. Conquest had been accomplished. The fighting forces had been defeated; but the poor civilians – the children and the women, the old and the infirm – were suffering as civilians habitually suffer in warfare.

Swarms of children, little better than skeletons, crowded round our tents, their little hands outstretched in a gesture more eloquent than their hoarse cries for food. They ate anything we offered to them, and we had not enough to touch even the fringe of their needs.

Still, we had a fair supply of macaroni and other paste, and we fed what we could, though our best was only an aggravation of their case. Ultimately we had to harden ourselves against their importunity, and hope that relief would soon break through from the north, with food for the starving population.

Nor were the soldiery in much better case. The greater the distance from the coast; the longer, it seemed, they had to wait for rationing.

Malaria was raging, and although the military were doing all that was humanly possible, not a great headway was being made against that plague; or against a sadder, more revealing epidemic that was prevalent. Little children were being strangled by their parents, due to the misery of starvation.

We went to the house where Ritchie had died, probably murdered at the instigation of the Turkish governor; and the house where Mlle. Tinne had stayed, on the expedition she led to Ghat and Ghadames. She made a few kilometers more before she, too, was ambushed outside Murzuk, murdered and robbed. For years after her death, her belongings were being sold or bartered in different parts of the Sahara.

We tried to locate Ritchie's grave, from indications in old journals that we carried with us on the journey; but nothing remained, capable of identification. Even the Italian officers had no information.

So we visited the dungeons of the towering old fortress, in which the Turks held their harems and their slaves and prisoners; dungeons just as terrible as those of medieval Europe, below ground-level: which means that they were veritable swamps in which the unfortunate prisoners were chained.

Chapter 4

From Murzuk we drove through to the Fezzan and the chain of oases known to the Carthaginians, Greeks, and Romans; but little known to-day.

Oued el Adjal we entered by a rocky canyon that opened unexpectedly on to the oases, which extended for nearly two hundred kilometers. The Oued was bounded on the north by the most formidable ocean of sand I have seen anywhere in the Sahara: the Hamada el Hamra, or Red Desert, which was nothing less than a blazing wilderness.

Continuing along the river-bed, trying to discover our direction, we found magnificent rock-drawings on the heights, the work of real artists of prehistoric times.

Among the groups were lions, ostriches, and antelopes, crocodiles, and, most astonishing of all, *Bubalus anticus,* showing that the drawings were of great age. We appeared to be in the very heart of the ancient land of the Garamantes.

We knew, from the old chronicles, and from the accounts of Balbus, in the year 19 B.C., that their method of penetration was by the horned-buffalo chariot: an account supplemented by the records of Suellus Flaccus in the first century A.D.

We camped on the spot, and began to take our photographs and drawings of the ancient chariots and their humped animals.

To save time, we had the Arab guides haul food up the cliffs to us, and our camera-man made the first moving picture of the work of the primitives of the Central Sahara.

Our problem was to discover why the prehistoric people had worked so lavishly on these drawings, and had chosen such a strange place as the summit of a precipitous mountain. Certainly their experience of the country was different from ours, for the drawings showed also rhinoceros and hippopotamus, which were long-vanished from this region. Had it been a jungle when the drawings were made?

Climbing the precipices we found a natural arch, and through the arch, as far as the eye could reach, there ranged mile after mile of sand dunes, across which we were able to make a perfect moving picture of that commonest, yet most remarkable, event of the desert: the setting sun.

The varying lights played among the dunes. Gold gave way to red, and red to purple before the shadows deepened, and thereafter we saw the purple fade through violet to blue, and at last to that strange and incredible steely grey that awaits the moon before becoming positively Arctic in the night. We might well have been on a snowfield when the moon shone.

Our enthusiasm over the discoveries was great. We had found traces of a definite civilization, and whether our Tuareg guides understood us or not, we did not much mind.

It was cold, sleeping on the heights; but in the morning, hot coffee loosened our joints, and we went to work again until the heat was too great, not having covered even a fraction of our task.

The second day brought a greater discovery. Traveling along the river-bed, and scouting every gully as we went, we came upon a vast burial-ground that antedated anything we had expected to find. Camp was promptly made, and with pick and shovel we began a preliminary excavation of some of the tombs which nestled under the precipices.

It was a real valley of the dead; in all, we estimated the number of the tombs to be in the neighbourhood of forty-five thousand.

The guides promptly labeled them the tombs of the evil spirits, as they looked on them, clustered in dead villages under the walls of the cliff.

It was the valley burial-ground of the Garamantes, we later discovered. The tombs themselves varied in height from ten to twenty feet, with circular bases made of great slabs of stone, rising in diminishing circumference until the dome was completed: very similar in form to the tombs of the French Hoggar and the Southern Atlas.

We worked all day, clearing away the giant boulders; worked until dinner, and then through the night, to reach the excavated tomb below the dome, in which the offerings were usually to be found.

Oudney, Barth, Richardson, and Duveyrier had passed along the main valley; but, neglecting to explore the canyons on either side (although they mention having seen one or two isolated tombs), had passed by without noting the vast extent of this lost burial-ground.

Dawn saw us once more at the stones, and this time the camera recorded the whole operation, for there are few sensations to equal the opening of an ancient tomb. The excitement and anxiety alike are painful. Nobody knows what is likely to appear. The slab is raised, and the dead begins to tell his tale. Every one has a tale to tell.

Will it be the golden opulence of Tutankhamen, or the sad little story of the dancing girl whose tomb we opened at Utica, with its evidence of a world of slumbering passions? Will it be the tale of a vanished Queen, like Tin Hinan in the Hoggar, whose Amazonian equipment opened a new page of African history; or will it be banker, soldier, fisherman, or priest, such as we found, day after day, at Carthage? Whoever, whatever they were, they all bring back a forgotten world.

The stone was off! We were so nervous that we could hardly wait to document the find.

It was a typical Libyan burial. The dead man lay with his knees up. There were three rough pots around his head. A necklace of huge cornelians had fallen into the sand. By his side were weapons and little gods: spear heads, lance heads in silex and bronze. Round his ear was a finely-worked silex which fitted closely: an ornament, no doubt.

Of the small, stone gods, one distinctly resembled the steato-pygic figure we had found in the Tomb of Tin Hinan and had profanely called the Libyan Venus. Very little remained of his wooden shield, save the battered bronze edging.

He was lying on some sort of a skin, from which the hair had vanished; only the desiccated leather remained. On either side of the dead man were pots, and some basketry which had held grain. The pottery and beads proclaimed their origin, being sim-ilar in design and incised decoration to those of the Hoggar and of Carthage. We knew he was a warrior, from his weapons.

Everything was thoroughly documented and photographed. The skull was carefully waxed for preservation, and then we began to remove the objects and take the usual measurements.

The skull was dolichocephalic, similar to the skulls of the Tuaregs, and the tomb probably dated between the first and third centuries B.C., corresponding to the height of the Saharan King-dom of the Garamantes.

These were the people Hannibal used in the second century B.C., in his mercenary armies. Alexander was confronted by them in his march to the Oasis of Jupiter Ammon. Twelve centu-ries earlier, the Pharaohs were fighting the Libyans, whose terri-tory stretched, at one time, from the Atlantic to the Nile, and from the Mediterranean to the land of the ancient Ethiopians: a race that has almost disappeared because the elements have dried up their continent.

We closed each tomb as we finished its examination; but the remaining tombs which we excavated were not in very good condition.

Then, from the valley of the dead, we continued due west, making for Garama, the ancient capital of the Garamantes, which still preserves its name in the modern Arabic "Djerma."

Here, a few inhabitants came from their crude straw huts to see our roaring caravan approach. They left their wells, which were operated by weary donkeys who walked their little paths and dragged on a rope, hauling a little water to the surface.

The Fezzanians of to-day – what is left of them – are a mixture of Negro, Arab, Turk, and Tuareg; mostly miserable ex-
slaves of the epoch when the land was subject to the Turks: victims of cruel misgovernment.

To-day, thanks to the change in their fortune, there are no
longer thin and weary lines of slaves moving north, dragging
their chains until some slave-master frees them from the awful
burden. It is a kindlier and more constructive rule under Mussolini, strict as it may be.

The contrast of the ancient capital with the little hovels that
mark it – hovels simply made of bamboo canes and leaves – is a
mute testimony to departed glory. Only a few fields of grain,
sufficient to provide for the couscous of the people; palm trees,
almost derelict; and a few meagre animals are there for the sus-
tenance of the natives to-day; but along the Oued Ahal, lay the
ruins of a mighty city.

The ruins were in desperate condition, which we spent the
day in visiting, and where we succeeded in finding evidence of
Libyan and Roman foundations. We calculated that fifteen thousand people must have existed in this region prior to the Turkish
conquest; but that slavery and barbarism had wiped out the population.

One old Fezzanian, seated in the shade of his tumbledown
hut, epitomized the change. There he sat, his almost expression-
less face showing little sign of intelligence as he searched his
body for lice; caught, and ate them.

We were trying to reach the Roman mausoleum, which
marks the farthest-south outpost of Roman civilization known,
to this time, and the going was hard for the cars. We had to force
them over territory that would have given a tank something to
do.

The mausoleum, which is that of a young Roman girl, stood
lonely and desolate under the precipice that towered behind, and
when we reached the spot we made our camp, intending, as was
our general habit, to explore in all directions, to see if trace
could be found of other ruins with a tale to tell.

History seems to indicate that this was the approximate site of the carbuncle mines, and we climbed the terraces, making in the direction of Oued Tilizzarhen, across the rock plateau.

We came upon the bed of a stream that had worn its way down through the cliffs to the main valley, where again we saw thousands of tombs and, what was more astonishing still, vast walls in the distance on the opposite hill.

We had read almost all, if not all, the books that had been written on previous exploration in this neighbourhood; but this was something new.

We rubbed our eyes, wondering if it were mirage or some curious rock formation. It was evident that we were coming on something big and unknown (unknown, so far as we could discover), and we tore ahead down one side of the ravine and up the other, on to sheer heights, the rock towering above us as we approached, crowned with gigantic stones laid one on top of another in the form of cyclopean walls.

This promised to be a long job, so we sent back for the cars to be brought to the base of the cliffs, and, excitement running high, set to work, seeking entry.

Only a few places promised well, for the city must have been impregnable before ruin broached the walls. In one place we photographed walls twenty feet high, made of massive blocks that must have needed an army of men to handle.

When we made our entry into the stronghold we found a vast, prehistoric city, whose level spaces were almost carpeted with flint instruments of different epochs. These we gathered together in heaps for transportation, and recognized immediately three distinct periods from the massive, roughly-worked stone hatchets of palæolithic man through the African intermediate (Capsian) period to Neolithic times.

The town had evidently been marked off by rough walls, like stone hurdles: probably to afford protection. Great holes had also been worked into the floor of the rock; probably to serve as cisterns in time of trouble.

Apart from the Mousterian and Capsian hatchets, we found numbers of magnificent daggers, all made in flint, which had been chipped to triangular section and the handle worked down.

Exploring the site, and taking the measurements of the gigantic walls, we discovered splendid rock-drawings that the inhabitants had probably engraved during some siege or other: they were carefully and beautifully executed.

Water, evidently, had been accessible in those days. It could not have been the desolate, blank plateau that we looked out over. The river must have been a fresh stream. There must have been pastures. We saw thousands of bones lying at the base of the precipice.

The inhabitants must have been of the race whose tombs we saw in the valley. It was one of the greatest prehistoric centres of the world; never, so far as I knew, had there been recorded a walled city like this belonging to men of the old Stone Age.

We had made a discovery of major importance, which was recognized by the Italian Government, who, following our detailed report, caused it to be fully explored and investigated. Naturally, we pressed as far as possible into the surrounding area, to find more rock-drawings, and to demonstrate fairly conclusively that there must have been colonies of prehistoric man every few miles.

Our collections we took back to Djerma, to be picked up on our way back from Ghat. Then we continued to Ubari, where we were frantically welcomed by the garrison to whom we were carrying Christmas mail, and presents, from Tripoli, although it was then only November.

The garrison was almost exhausted, and in a sorry plight. Fighting was not over, and the Meharists were almost daily engaged in a search for stragglers of the rebel tribes.

At Serdeles, our dump, we camped under the tree that is famous in the annals of the Sahara: a tree described by Barth, Duveyrier, and Richardson. Here we filled up, preparatory to the last stage to Ghat.

We were now in the mountains of the Azdjer Tuaregs, and along our trail were the fresh evidences of the bitterness with which war had been waged: the bare mounds of the Arab dead, and the cross-marked graves of the Italians. Fighting was barely finished before we reached the territory.

Our present guides were as efficient as any could be; but, even so, before we reached Ghat we were lost from time to time in the labyrinth of mountain passes. The guides knew well enough how to take a camel through; but finding a passable route for the cars was a different matter. We tried, came to an impasse, turned round, and tried again.

Finally, we were driven north, to take a pass at the extreme end of the chain, coming out above the Oued Tanezzouft on to a great plateau from which we had a most spectacular view of the peaks of the mountains, whose slender shafts stood straight up to the sky. They were the volcanic peaks of the Tripolitan Hoggar, and when the rubble-strewn surface cleared, our going was as smooth and easy as on paved roads. We accelerated to racing speed, charging for Mount Idinin, whose bulk stood high and separate, like a purple mass veiled in golden net.

As we approached, the mountain appeared to rise steadily in grandeur, seemingly crowned with the spires and towers of a score of cathedrals.

We camped at the base of this *Ksar Djenoun*, or Devils' Stronghold, and were almost inclined to agree with the natives in their abhorrence and fear of the mountain. Barth was lost here for three days, and to save his life bit his veins and drank his own blood.

Superstition is still rife. Our guides refused to approach the mountain at any price. We, haunted by the memory of Barth, stuck as close together as was possible, when we scaled the terraces.

Hoping for the chance of climbing the mountain, we had brought complete Alpine equipment with us, so that we succeeded where others had failed.

The first night we camped on a high ledge, with a stupendous view of the whole *massif;* thousands of peaks were to be seen from our resting-place, and, as we had a portable moving-picture camera with us, we were able to film practically the whole ascent of the northerly peak we climbed.

On the mountain, we experienced the same phenomenon that we had noticed in the Gorges of Arak, on our way to the French Hoggar. The rocks exploded here and there from the sudden changes of temperature. Small avalanches began, and increased in volume and noise as they ultimately crashed down the mountain-side like the crack of doom.

Legends connected with the mountain are many, mostly including the mysterious white Queen who lived there with an army of Amazons. Benoit used the story in his *Atlantide,* and there is no doubt that the mountain was at some time inhabited, for we saw numbers of rough tombs in hollows between the precipices, and some ruins, which had been either outpost or fortress.

At the base of the great rocks were flint implements in the sand, belonging to the ancient inhabitants of Mount Idinin.

Once, also, we made out a path carved in the rock; but this we could not reach.

Down at the foot of the mountain, also, we found rock-drawings and Tifinar inscriptions. These were the first signs we had had of Libyan script, indicating that probably the mountain had at one time been a place of pilgrimage. The pilgrims had left their signatures.

It is a fine field for future research; but we had neither time nor means to continue. We were lucky, as it was, to reach our cars again, for the descent was more perilous than the climb.

Thence we went straight on to Ghat: the ancient Rapsus of the Romans.

Ghat, which was only beginning to quieten down after the Italian occupation, is a white-walled city lying under the shadow of a great rock, from which the garrison had marked our approach.

When we arrived, they hoisted the flags and gave us a salute of guns, while we circled the walls looking for the one and only entrance.

It was a moment of considerable satisfaction. We had reached the outward objective. The journey had not been without some real value. We had still the mysterious city to explore: that city of which we had heard so many stories, and which few had really studied.

We were escorted to our base through a maze of narrow streets, which hardly gave room for two pedestrians, where the inhabitants could reach almost from house to house; where murder could, and did, happen, by a hand stretched from a window in the dark, to stab the enemy as he passed.

Our refuge was the abandoned house of one of the notabilities of the old city. Our cars, under guard, were lined against the fortress walls.

During the first two or three days, we were mostly lost, unable to recognize any of the alleys. Our straying was so frequent that we finally dismounted one of the klaxons from the cars and stationed a servant on the roof with the horn in his hand. At specified hours, mostly meal-times, he would sound it so that we should at least have something to guide us.

The old metropolis of the slave-dealers belonged to any but our own time. In its very walls, white slaves, trophies of some Mediterranean corsair, had found their burial.

Being Christian, they were unfit for the hallowed ground of Muhammedan cemeteries when death took them from the service of the desert sultans.

The slave-market was the setting for tragedy, only lately fallen from commercial importance. While the Italians were at the walls, we learned, the last public sale of slaves had taken place: at bargain prices.

The market-place is in the very heart of the town; a great, open square with white columns on all sides, well plastered, and with rings for the fetters of the slaves. Until the time of their exhibition, there they were held manacled; but when a prospective buyer appeared, they were raised to the top of the column, for better inspection, stripped of every rag of covering.

We found an ex-slave with his tale to tell, and from him and his companions we were able to piece together the vivid spectacle of the merchants arriving in strength from the north, while the slave-trains came up from the Sudan, with hundreds of terrified human beings chained together. These were the real black diamonds of the traders of Ghadames and Tripoli and the Barbary coast, seeking gems for some exclusive harem, or labourers for a princely domain.

In that market-place many a battle-royal was staged for first choice, and the owners of Ghat grew rich by competition among their visitors.

The women, who were destined, perhaps, for Turkey, were paraded and examined to discover that their virginity was genuine, and that was a great occasion, since every old satyr of the town could take part on the pretext of making a bid.

It must have been the cruelest city of all time. We were told that that human meat-market, after the first great display, was maniacal at night because, though the merchants were careful of the most beautiful slaves, to command a high price from their clients, they made it the occasion of grabbing what they could for themselves. The old slave told us that the screams and wailings of terror-stricken girls filled the square, as by scores they were violated on the roofs of the houses of Ghat.

For the slave auction, the town was crowded, and our guide took us to the roofs, where the parapets had been worn smooth by the sadistic spectators who had collected for the great performance in the square, when the girls danced and postured, showed off their physical perfection and allure, obedient to the careful training of their owners, who well understood the cupidity and passions of their clients.

In many of the houses we found the chains still attached to the walls of great rooms where slaves who had found new owners were locked up until the caravans began to form for the north: those caravans of sorrow and heartbreak.

But Ghat had another memory for us. It was here that the great German explorer Erwin von Bary was murdered and buried. We had some slight indication of the position of the tomb, knowing that he had been buried without the city, and due south.

There we found a neglected tomb, and a mound half-covered by sand. This we cleared away, and reconstructed the grave, making a little cross, which we mounted and inscribed with his name, gathering what palms we could from the oasis, before holding a simple ceremony in memory of the greatest of African explorers.

We were tolerably certain that this was the authentic spot. Had it been a Muhammedan grave, it would have been in the cemetery to the north. This was the opposite side of the city, and lay as we expected to find it, under the shadow of the old Turkish fort.

The next day was Armistice Day, and we celebrated it by opening the case of champagne we had carried across the desert to share with the Italian garrison.

It was also the day appointed for our meeting with the Sultan of the Azdjer Tuaregs; not altogether a happy day, since the garrison was in too sore straits to invite us to share their mess. We were the hosts.

It was pitiful to see the extremes to which the forces had been reduced by the difficulties of the campaign and the impediments in the way of regular provisioning. Desert warfare over so large an area is no light matter. The garrison had only the minimum of food, and even ammunition was short. They were almost isolated. The doctor was nearly off his head with overwork and lack of supplies. He commandeered most of our medical equipment, which we were glad enough to let go, as we were soon returning to civilization.

The meeting with the Sultan was arranged by the Italian officers, since the confederation of the tribes was assembled outside the city, for the purpose of pledging their allegiance to the new governors of the country.

The Italians came from the fort, with their flags flying. We approached from another direction, also flying flags. The Tuaregs came from their encampment to the open plain, where they stood awaiting our arrival.

The Amenokhal of the Azdjer was a gigantic, magnificent fellow and, surrounded by his nobles, appeared to me to be much more dignified than the Amenokhal of the Hoggar tribes whom we had encountered in the neighbourhood of Tamenrasset. He was still unspoiled by idleness, favours, and gifts, and, as he stood there, looking down on us all from his great stature, he seemed to be in the line of the great ones of the earth, with his gold stick of office in his hand.

We could get nothing out of him. He refused to speak the pleasantries he did not feel. Our gifts he ignored. We were just as unwelcome as the Italian conquerors. All we succeeded in doing was to obtain some photographs, and then the Sultan and his nobles disappeared on their fine animals, scowling as they went, with vengeance still burning in their hearts: phantoms of the past. They went from sight towards the mountains to which they had resorted, seeking refuge on the borders of French and Italian territory.

We continued our photography of Ghat for a while, and then, hearing from one or two of the Tuaregs who still remained in the town that there were tombs in the sand dunes south-west, I went off with two companions in one of the cars, taking a Tuareg as guide.

After traveling for about five miles we were unable to go farther with the car, so we left it in the care of the mechanic. The rest of us, taking our haversacks, went on foot to the dunes, where the guide promptly located the tombs.

What he did not value so highly, but what we were delighted to see, were rock-drawings. The site was a chaos of tumbled rocks, the home of hyænas and jackals, and we set to work in the caves, transcribing the inscriptions, copying the drawings, and investigating the tombs.

We had left Ghat at dawn, reaching our site about eleven o'clock, and, although we were on the fired side, we kept at work. The tombs were not of any great importance, but the rock-drawings were good, and we were busily engaged on them when a shout from the guide called us to the open. We saw that a cloud had appeared, with lightning suddenness, cutting off the sun. The guide insisted that we should pack up and return at once; but we, in ignorance of the real situation, insisted on staying, as we had not finished.

He, however, dragged us out again, and by sheer force compelled us to follow. The cloud had become a yellow wall. A sandstorm was driving on.

"Run! Run!" he cried, urging us away.

He knew, far better than we did, what such a storm meant. It was out of season, but that was nothing. We had believed ourselves free of the menace, choosing the best time for travel. Just the same, he made us understand that the storm could last for days, and that we had come unprepared. We had our sunglasses, but not our sand-glasses; so, yielding to his entreaties we packed up and ran, trying to make our way back to the car.

As we ran, the hot wind caught us and helped us on. The sand had not yet arrived, and, although we could see the swirling veil coming up on the wind, it looked as though we might out-distance it, could we once reach the car and get under way.

The heat was terrific, and still increased. The sand began to dive at us, like fine shot, stinging our ears; before we reached the car we were in a cloud of whirling grains that buffeted us with a force not easily believable. All we could do was to run straight on, following the Tuareg, who easily out-distanced us, despite the fact that we were in good training. His purple robes were our beacon as we crossed the dunes and boulders.

We missed the car. Later, we discovered that the chauffeur had been surprised, and had failed to start the engine. He himself travelled back on foot.

We were caught about by the sand. Every breath was a furnace blast: gritty and searing. The sand flew by in eddies. We seemed to be running through dry, breaking waves. We were crying for breath by the time we were within a mile of the city.

That last mile was worse than any, for the sun was blotted out. We were struggling in a tangible twilight, disoriented, and somewhat desperate, until one of us stumbled over a tomb.

We had reached the Muhammedan cemetery and, crawling on hands and knees from tomb to tomb, we fought our way to the walls, round which we groped with our fingers, seeking the entrance.

Whether we should have found it without aid, it is not easy to say; but the Italian officers, knowing we had gone afield and sensing our difficulty, had mounted a squad at the gate with klaxons and tin cans, to make as much noise as was possible, in order to guide us home.

One by one, standing close in to the wall, we arrived, and were hurried to our headquarters.

Even within the walls of the city it was not much better. There was sand everywhere. We closed doors; but still the sand came through, filtering under covers.

Yet, such is the professional instinct, our operator, sorry as he may have been for our plight, had gone to work. Mounting his camera on the highest roof in the city, he had taken a complete picture of the approach of the storm and its effect. It was a most excellent shot, with the sand driving before a wind which bent the palm trees almost double, and poured a thick cloud down the narrow streets.

The storm lasted the whole of the day, and through the night, without sign of cessation. The next day showed some slight abatement, and at nightfall it dropped off as suddenly as it had risen.

Our cars were practically covered, and, what was more annoying to the mechanics, disabled, for the engines had been taken down in preparation for the next run. Grease-covered parts lay buried in the sand, which necessitated a thorough and unpleasant overhaul before they could be reassembled.

Our guide was soundly berated by the Italians, who accused him of incompetence; but it was our fault. He had warned us honestly enough and we, thinking we knew better, had brought most of the trouble on our own heads. We explained to the authorities, and the guide was not troubled by official action.

Chapter 5

Leaving Ghat, we attempted to find the roads of the lost Garamantes, the *Iter Praeter Caput Saxi,* returning along our trail towards Murzuk, to pick up the specimens already collected; and from Murzuk to Sebha, where the Italians were building a major military post in the desert, as well as a base for aviation.

Here we slept in the first Saharan hangar, and learned what Italian thoroughness meant. Great motor-lorries were parked in the neighbourhood, and camel-guns and machine-guns were mounted everywhere.

At Sebha, also, we were entertained to a real banquet, when the usual speeches were delivered in flowing oratory. This was a frontier fort, and many an eye was turned towards Tunisia; that province lost to Italy by so little a margin. All the officers were of the finest type of firebrand, and many of them had a feeling for France that can best be described as warm. Perhaps it was something of a disappointment to these intensely patriotic young men that Italy should have to be content with desert, despite the fact that they are making that desert blossom like the rose in places; when across the border is a land flowing with milk and honey, and possessing enormous mineral deposits and agricultural possibilities.

The spirits of the Italian Colonial army ran high. We were received by the Askari, fine warriors from Somaliland, and indispensable in warfare such as Italy was then waging. They gave us one of their characteristic fantasias, with war dances, and tom-toms talking.

Whirling round us, in pow-wow or impi none could say, they crept closer and closer to me in narrowing circles. Suddenly, they had me in their hands, powerless, without changing the beat of the dance by the fraction of a second, and, at a prearranged signal, I was thrown into the air.

It was their way of showing honour to a visitor, and doubtless they enjoyed it. So, also, did our camera-man who had been warned and, true to his craft, had his machine ready to take a shot of me as I was thrown, by no means gently, into the air. And kept there; for my feet were not allowed to touch the ground until the dance ended.

The joke was on me, and my body later was blue from their kindly attention; but I tried to smile. The smile was successful when the same courtesy was extended to the Italian colonel; but I swear they handled him more gently! In my disposition were no stripes – of either kind!

From Sebha, our road led to Brach, one of the most beautiful of Tripolitan oases, not much less in grandeur than that of Jupiter Ammon. A forest of palms encloses river and lakes of topaz water. Walled fountains in the fashion of the Fountain of the Sun at Siwa bear evidences of Roman handiwork, and constructions dating to the Garamantes assured us that we still travelled the ancient routes.

Brach must certainly have been on the cross-roads of Saharan trails, and here we began to explore those trails that led to Ghadames and Carthage to the north-west, to Tripoli to the north, to Ghat and the Sudan, south-west, and to Ophir and Ethiopia, due south. Seeking for evidence, we came upon two Roman coins of 50 B.C. which might, perhaps, have been left by the expedition of the pro-Consul Cornelius Balbus minor, known to have travelled the area in the year 19 B.C.

Incidentally, also, we found that there was a small and hardy company of ladies (not honestly to be called "pretty") who, in the pursuit of a profession older even than the trails we were seeking, had forced their way across the desert, as stowaways in some transport, concealed in sacks. This was devotion to duty seldom excelled in any history.

After a delightful sojourn in this "Paris of the Sahara," we went north to the Gal Maia, where we discovered an important link in the prehistoric chain: flints of the Sbaikian epoch, which is the African counterpart of Mousterian.

The trail was decidedly ill-suited to travel, as we explored the Oued esc Chiati, although the Italians had been at work on a trail north, and ultimately hoped to link up with other workers coming south. The actual trail, however, ended here, and we had our own way to make across the Hamada el Hamra.

We had to battle with dead rivers, gullies, rocks, and sands, which made progress difficult, and as the wind was strong we had ample opportunity to witness the movement of the "traveling dunes." The tops of the dunes, lashed by the wind, cascaded down in a steady stream and slowly formed a new mound, the old one as steadily, disappearing. This was an army that knew neither defeat nor halt. The desert went forward without cease: all-conquering, all-devouring.

On the third day out from Brach, with some other members of the expedition, I went ahead, to explore a dried-up river-bed, and found the remains of several Roman mausoleums, about fifteen miles from camp. The most important of them bore strange symbols, showing the designs of the Garamantes, and what looked like traces of the phallic and Sun cults. We concluded that it was the tomb of a Libyan official in the pay of Rome. The work was definitely of the Roman era, and the pottery arratine. We had seen a similar mausoleum at Garama, and a number of amphores added to the evidence of origin; but what was most conclusive was the discovery of a lamp bearing the potter's mark: Juni. Alexi.

This was in the Oued el Had, a completely waterless course; but certainly on the trail of the Garamantes, running south.

The next day we camped in a river-bed full of bamboo canes and, on the slope leading down to the river, found Acheulian hatchets and objects that were apparently in the Levallois category. We collected one hundred and sixty arrow heads, scrapers, and flint daggers.

Escande, our chief mechanic, found a fine Campiegnian adze when we were making camp, and we later discovered that we had chanced on a fine park of prehistoric sites, with implements of quartzite, chert, petrified wood, agate, chalcedony, and jasper. We found other things, also, for, during the night we were roused by the eerie sound of a pack of jackals on the hunt. They had been attracted by the scent of gazelle which we had shot the day before, and had actually raided the camp before we awoke.

Rosselli, rudely wakened, let fly right and left at the circle of gleaming yellow eyes that surrounded the camp; but the animals appeared to take no notice, although the shots echoed through the canyon. All night, one or other of us would take a shot; but the animals stayed there till dawn.

From this point we went to El Bab, still following the old trail of the Garamantes, by *oued* and valley, which we invariably explored on foot, to right and left, finding mounds at the base of the cliffs on either side.

At El Bab stood another ruined mausoleum, with stones lying about, half-buried in the sand. To the east stood an ancient Libyan "sacred mountain," covered with Tifinar inscriptions and rock-drawings, in which buffalo figured. Sculptured in the rock was a cup-like hole, with a duct discharging over the precipice, which indicated the sacrificial nature of the platform on the summit.

The line of this unknown cult of the Libyans was complete from the Atlas to the Hoggar, from Ghat to Jupiter Ammon.

Right across North Africa we had found similar inscriptions of the crude hand carved in the rock, and two feet, standing close together.

Soon afterwards, we were reminded of a fact that we had almost lost sight of in our exploring: there was a war raging in the country.

With our guide, d'Ayala and I were following the Bir el Fatia
in search of ruins and flints when we came suddenly on a man
busily filling old petrol cans at a disused well.

To say that we were surprised to find another human being in
that wilderness is perhaps needless; but we noticed that a gun lay
near the edge of the well and that a decrepit donkey was tied to
the scrub.

Ben Ahmed, our guide, showed that he did not like the look
of things for some reason or other, and scanned the gully for
signs of companions, while we quietly approached the man at
the well.

We were within about thirty yards of him when he turned,
and sprang for his gun, taking aim at us. It seemed, for an
instant, that one of us would suffer, but the old Mannlicher
failed, and Ben Ahmed yelled that we were friends, while Hector d'Ayala, being a true South American, had his hands well
above his head, in the customary and practised manner of his
country.

After a short parley, in which Ahmed explained to the
stranger that we were amiably disposed, and not Italians, he let
us approach.

We offered him cigarettes, and food from our haversacks,
since he looked to be on the point of exhaustion, and gradually
wormed his story out of him, after promising that we would not
betray him to the soldiery.

It seemed that he, and a score of his fellows, were in hiding
not far from the well: remnants of a rebel *djich* that had escaped
from the battle of Ubari and had made their way across the
desert in an attempt to reach Kufara and Egypt!

Naturally, we were interested, and persuaded the fugitive to
take us to his companions. A handful of silver, and the promise
of more food, clinched the matter, and we followed the living
skeleton for a couple of miles to a well-guarded camp in the
caves overlooking the gully.

We had our guns and our revolvers; but were just a little apprehensive, as they numbered twenty, and we were only three. The remainder of our party was away exploring elsewhere.

Never have I seen such relics of human misery and privation as that group of Senussi. Several of them were wounded. All had their feet bound in bloody rags. Very little ammunition remained to them. Three of the fugitives were too weak to move.

We had no right to succour them, of course. Half a dozen men of the camel corps could have accounted for them without dismounting. How they ever hoped to reach Kufara, I could not understand, and my first question was why they had not sought French territory.

The leader, a tall, gaunt warrior, explained that they would be shot on sight by the French, since they were known to have taken part in the campaign of 1917. They were between the devil and the deep sea: chased by the military, and without food, in the heart of a pitiless desert.

I decided to send a confidential note to Captain Johnston-Lavis, who had charge of the convoy, asking him to send food privately by Ben Ahmed.

He returned with a note saying that the Captain thoroughly understood, and was with me in this slight breach of the rules.

It was terrible, to see the orgy that followed; an orgy on the plainest of food. How those poor devils ate! What thanks were expressed by their tired, bloodshot eyes; our only common language!

Ahmed explained that nobody in the camp save the Captain knew of the encounter; but he little expected the meticulous care of Rosselli at the next halt, when stores were checked and our poor guide was threatened with imprisonment for the theft of the stores we had commandeered ourselves and hardly dare explain. However, we persuaded Rosselli that everything was in order, and Ahmed went free.

Meanwhile, he was translating their tale. Fourteen of their company had died on the trail. The rest had fought on, day by day, steadily growing weaker, until they reached their present position. In all, they had covered several hundreds of miles on foot, across a desert hostile and dry, patrolled by alert enemies.

I was sorry for them; but my thoughts occasionally went to those other travellers, whose lives had been forfeit to just such as these.

As we left, they implored us to give them some of our cartridges; but that we could not do. We could not, by our kindness, commit another handful of friends to death, for that is what it would have meant. One cartridge; one Italian! That was their allowance. Yet I shall never forget the farewell as we left those haunted, hunted, hunger- and death-ridden independents who had done little greater wrong than to fight for the country that had been theirs, and their fathers' before them. One hates the idea of Empire at such a price, civilization or no civilization. There they were, hungry and athirst, separated from their homes, their wives and children, doomed to be wanderers on the face of the earth because once they had fought for liberty.

That night, Hector and I had a distinct bit of *cafard,* wondering whether we ought to have betrayed them. Where does loyalty lie? Does it really conflict with humanity?

Following the trail again, we came upon a group of trackmakers working south to join those moving up from the forts: a company of prisoners under the supervision of Arab foremen. They were just in the act of destroying a Roman mausoleum to provide direction stones for the trail. This, naturally, we prevented, threatening them with all the penalties of every law that had ever been passed in North Africa since the destruction of Carthage. Since it seemed to be an enormous weight of responsibility, very wisely they refused to shoulder it, and found their markers elsewhere.

The next day we were at Bir esc Sciueref, where the Italians were building another fort. Our route lay exactly along the old Roman trail: all we had to do was to follow the posts of Roman legionaries to come upon a Roman fort.

This fort stood on a great precipice, overlooking a river which swept across the northern part of the desert, on the banks of which were clusters of palm trees; and immediately adjacent to the Italian fort. The Roman arches were still standing, and we located in the sand an inscription which we took to the new fort for transhipment to Tripoli by the first available truck. Down below in the valley we found tombs of the Garamantes and Libyan inscriptions. Proof was accumulating of the authenticity of this ancient trail.

Thereafter, our route was towards Mizda and back to civilization. We had nearly completed our exploration of the old routes. Our search for prehistoric man had not been unsuccessful, and we had made one or two other finds which should prove of value to the painstaking expeditions that will surely follow. Yet we were not to leave the desert without one final expression of its crime and its horror.

Traveling up from the outpost, we hit on one of those dramas which still make the Sahara to be regarded with dismay. We had not seen a speck of life all day as we raced along a flat, monotonous stretch. Our only diversion was to line up on the flat floor of the desert and race hell for leather for ten or twenty miles, with our last drinks for stakes. Johnston-Lavis, being commodore of the fleet, won most of the heats, it may be mentioned.

At about two o'clock in the afternoon, that most deadly hour of the twenty-four, while we were traveling with the wind roaring past, I noticed a tiny speck, no larger than the head of a pin, on the horizon to the east. Small it may have been; it demanded investigation, just the same. It was the only mark between sand and sky that broke the circle.

Signaling the other cars, and making for the point, I travelled straight. After some miles, we got our glasses on to the objective, and the Englishman shouted "By − − ! It's a car!"

Rosselli was inclined to disagree.

"There are no cars unaccompanied in this desert," he said. "Unless..."

His voice tailed off. We knew what he had in mind. The sentence was left for ever unfinished. We were off, with our chauffeurs clanging the gears through the gates in their haste to be there.

Car it proved to be, with three men stretched motionless underneath, and ours had hardly whistled to a standstill through the sand before we were dismounted and dragging the poor devils out from their hiding. One was already gone, and it took us two hours to bring the others round, with rum and injections.

The survivors were almost skeletons. The dead man was practically mummified.

We saw that the truck contained many cases, of which one had been broken open. Its contents, perhaps, had lessened the sufferings of the three Arabs. It contained hashish.

They were drug-running. That night, one of the Arabs regained consciousness and could talk lucidly. The other roused also, but he had become a raving maniac, and we were compelled to bind him for his and our safety.

It appeared that they were on their way from the coast to Egypt. Egypt is what the Arab said; but we did not believe him. There were other and nearer avenues for the disposal of drugs in the *cafard*-ridden desert!

The cocaine and morphia had come from Germany. The hashish was local. The runners had struggled on as far as they could, but breakdown had left them stranded. One man had started to walk across the desert for help when the water of the radiator was exhausted; but where he anticipated finding succour no one could say.

We sent Escande, with number four car, to follow in his tracks, while we buried the dead man at sunset with his face towards Mecca. The long night we spent waiting for Escande to return, while we worked over the sane Arab to bring him back to some semblance of strength.

The maniac was past our help mentally, but we did what we could. His screams were so terrible that we had to establish him almost a mile away in the desert; his thirst-harassed body and his drug-sodden mind had reduced him to the last stages of insanity.

Escande returned at four o'clock in the morning, having buried the fourth victim about thirty miles away.

The two survivors we carried to Mizda; one trussed and flat in the back of the car; the other supported in the chair. What happened to them after we turned them over to the authorities, with a report of the encounter, we did not stay to see. One already had a life sentence. The other?...

So we returned to contact with advancing civilization. The trail was good; the sea not far distant. We had satisfied ourselves as to the reality of another of the great caravan routes of the dead past, and a little while ago yet another Professor had the satisfaction of publishing the documented account of that discovery.

PART III

MEXICO AND THE POISON TRAIL

PERSONNEL OF EXPEDITION UNDER THE AUSPICES OF
THE MEXICAN GOVERNMENT

COUNT BYRON DE PROROK Director

RODNEY SADLEIR co-Director

PROFESSOR J. SOUSTELLE; Ethnographical Institute, Paris

DR. O. VON SCHMELLING

H. ROTHERMEL

CAPT. F. BIELER

MARQUIS CASA Y MIER

JOSE SERABIA

W. HAYMAN

P. MARTORELL

DON PEDRO LOPEZ

Chapter 1

After fifteen years of African exploration, it seemed imperative that I should cross over to Mexico and Central America, to
see if there were any links, good or bad, with that strip of country which seemed to bear out certain theories concerning the lost
Atlantis.

For a year I travelled through the country, among the various
tribes, and found sufficient of interest to move me to organize an
expedition for the exploration of little-known areas on the Atlantic seaboard.

The real spur came when our preliminary scouting brought us
to the tremendous experiment of the Carnegie Foundation at
Chichen Itza, which we reached from Merida, the capital of
Yucatan, and apparently the Divorce Capital of the world. It was
thick with litigants, who smiled and smiled, and paid their fees,
to depart again on a new and swift adventure. They were good
for hotel-keepers, and added a certain amount of local colour.

It had nothing whatever to do with archaeology, of course,
but it added a certain spice to life, particularly on one occasion,
when a litigant of a certain race passed the hat round among the
fellow inhabitants of his hotel to raise the necessary price of
freedom. I believe he got all that he needed, so sympathetic was
the world with his plight.

Chichen Itza lies well away from the end of the railway, and
a terrible railway it is, cutting through almost incredible jungle.
We were met at the railhead, Dzitas, by the usual *fotingo,* and
were rattled and jolted along a rough trail to the camp.

Camp? Rather call it an archaeological paradise, for it must
be the happy hunting-ground to which all good scientists go

when their work on earth is done. Money is no object. There is no financial depression evident. The flight from gold means nothing to Chichen Itza. There, the scientists have their own world and, dressed like a corps of medicos in a millionaire's hospital – thoroughly bleached, and as thoroughly aseptic – they advanced by companies on us, by way of reception, headed by Dr. Sylvanus Morley, the leading authority on Mayan civilization.

Round the great hall were bungalows; marvellous places, too, and tennis courts, baths, and swimming-pools. The best Bacardi rum was available (but not at the table!) for cocktails. However wet the bungalows are; officially, the camp is "dry."

Our party was lodged in the guest-house, where we were joined by a young man who had arrived at the same time, entirely strange to me, who promptly attached himself to us like a limpet, muttering constantly about something he "had left behind," and which something turned out to be a hypodermic syringe. Dope-fiends in such a place would find quite enough to stir their imagination, for there is treasure, and rumour of treasure, everywhere.

Tradition says that somewhere in the camp enclosure lies a vast, secret hoard. Consequently, every tourist digs a little, and all the visitors leave their mark: a little pot-hole. It is almost dangerous to walk alone in the dusk: there are holes in the bedroom floors, holes on the path to the various places which, in the course of time, *must* be visited.

Is all this shrewd publicity, a clever scheme to rouse interest through cupidity?

It is not all pleasure, of course: there are discomforts too, as Dr. Morley pointed out. An army of marching ants would do the camp no good, and that possibility cannot be overlooked. These brutes move in formation, armies of twenty to thirty million strong, cutting their way like a whetted scythe across the country, leaving nothing behind.

I saw a village they had passed through, before I finished my travels. The people had been driven out, powerless, and I heard that sick children who could not be moved had been reduced to skeletons before the procession ended.

Yet Chichen Itza is the archeologist's finest reserve. I have seen nothing anywhere comparable to it. There was the Casa de Monjas, or House of the Nuns, in course of excavation: a typical temple of the golden Mayan epoch, standing in the very heart of the jungle.

Next to it was the Iglesia, with great carvings of elephant tusks protruding, and my curiosity was roused. I wondered how this symbol came, since there were no elephants. My mind went to Hannibal. Did the idea come with the ancestors who had known elephants, or was the earth only waiting to be turned, to demonstrate that the animal was known on these shores?

On our own exploration, we did later discover massive and unidentifiable bones of lost animals; what they were we could not determine; but the specimens were shipped to the Smithsonian Institute for identification.

Another amazing spectacle was to see innumerable columns which were strongly reminiscent of Greek architecture, and some "Atlantean" sculptures, so called because of the representation of a short, massive figure supporting an immense load on his upturned hands, in the conventional fashion of Atlas.

At Caracol was the first known astronomical observatory; a giant edifice, clearly designed for the study of the heavens; circular, with a pierced dome.

And there was the ball court; a quadrangle with low, smooth walls, where a game was played with a ball against the walls, similar to the game surviving in Havana, and perhaps to be identified with the Basque game. In antiquity, it was called Thlachli, and was played somewhat in the manner of a primitive game of "fives."

The ball court was commanded by the royal box. It was evidently the Wimbledon of Chichen Itza, with stone seats in tiers, capable of accommodating thousands of spectators.

Particularly interesting to me, since I hold the Basques as being not very different, ethnologically, from the Berbers. Perhaps I am always ready to see possible links; but this did make me wonder.

Chichen Itza is called the city of the Plumed Serpent. The god Quetzalcoatl took the name "feathered serpent": a white god, who came from the east, and taught the Mexicans the use of the plough – a fact in keeping with the statement of Montezuma to Cortez that his ancestors came from the Orient. And there was a singular identification, significant in its completeness, of the sign of the plumed serpent with the signs of Egypt, and the traditional delineation of the serpent in the Garden of Eden.

Another link was found in the great pyramid of Chichen Itza, which is distinctly like the step pyramid of Sakkara. Associations were growing very interesting. Whether this old civilization ultimately proved to be without relation to other economies or not, it was a vastly rich field. In one spot it resembled Egypt. I walked round a corner, and could have believed myself back in ancient Greece.

I wondered why it was that these evidences of a highly developed civilization were found on the Atlantic side, and had not continued that little distance north, to the United States.

The most amazing archaeological find of this century, perhaps to the exclusion of Tutankhamen, is the sacred well of Chichen Itza, where maidens and children were sacrificed, in a manner not far removed from the sacrifices known to have taken place at Carthage.

They were dedicated to the god on the pyramid, and then led through the groves, along a defined road, to ultimate sacrifice at the well. It was like the sacred way at Karnak. There was, as has been learned, a great procession along the route lined by Mayan sphinxes, no less enigmatical than their Egyptian counterparts, to the well, headed by priests and musicians. The victims, perhaps, were drugged, or excited by wine. It appears that the sacrifice was not refused but gladly accepted because of the belief that such a death meant instant translation to paradise. At all events, the victims were led to the side of the well, and thrown in.

Although the water in it is sixty feet deep, the well was explored and thoroughly searched some years ago by Edward Herbert Thompson, who succeeded in establishing the certainty of sacrificial rites by recovering a large number of skeletons, sacrificial weapons, votive offerings, and incense.

The wealth of the civilization may be judged from the fact that the intrinsic value of the gold alone, which he recovered, amounted to several hundred thousand dollars.

Over three hundred separate gold objects were found, some weighing more than sixteen ounces, and two hundred and fifty pieces of finely worked jade; besides other objects of a value beyond calculation. Thompson must have been a genius as an explorer and archaeologist. He had his pump and dredge brought from the United States, and refused to abandon his work until he had searched the whole of the floor of the well with his own fingers – for he was an experienced diver. Hard; but it brought an incalculable reward.

He lived in the golden age of archaeology, before there were laws restraining the adventurous, and the removal of material so discovered.

Naturally, this place acted like a match to a fuse, and when we returned to our quarters I was decided. From Dr. Morley, I learned that the best place for us to attack seemed to be the hinterland of the states of Tabasco, Chiapas, and Campeche, crossing the border into Guatemala. It was an unexplored region, but known to be rich in ruins, and there were some strange tribes to be investigated on the side.

In the guest-house, sleep was slow to come. Even when I fell off, it was only to be roused immediately by the young man next door, who had lost his syringe, and screamed the place down, sure he heard lions roaring. Actually, I regret to say, it was my snoring he had heard; but he was off, and not to be calmed without his dose. We filled him full of stiff Mexican liquor, and held him down until he was quiet.

The next morning, he made another attempt. In sheer, insane craving, he set off, to walk back to his syringe.

Walk! A hundred miles through the jungle for a shot!

We collared him, two on either side, sandwiching him like footballers, and locked him up until the visit was over. In the train, as we returned to civilization, he sat eating raw eggs, which he extracted from his hat, conjurer-wise, Flick! – an egg! Flick! – it was opened and swallowed!

The wealth, financial or archaeological, of the Carnegie camp was, of course, utterly beyond my dreams; even with all its luxury there was no little sign of boredom in some of the members; but I felt it was time to move on with preparations and went back to Mexico City, and arranged my company, laid down the lines of communication, and went to see what could be done with the Government.

As usual, as soon as permission was needed, the trouble began. It is easier to work independently of the law, and many people find it quicker; but permission in my case was essential.

What caused us greater trouble was sanction for our guns, since groups of revolutionaries had disappeared into the jungles we were about to attack, and the authorities had some fear that we might be in the position of having to let them share our arms and ammunition. That is how they put it.

Moreover, our real point of departure was from the capital of the Red Governor of Tabasco, the formidable Canibal Carrideo.

Permits were promised, and ultimately the Government took an active delight in the expedition, which definitely eased our way.

Preliminary stages had to be covered by air. There was no other practical means: the roads were time wasters, and we could not get up the rivers; but immediately we almost crashed our hopes, and ourselves also, for we had the bright idea of trying out our plane over Popocatapetl, which was then in eruption.

The two other planes we sent on with our equipment and provisions, and, leaving Mexico City, making for Vera Cruz. Fritz Bieler, who was a German war ace, did not baulk for a second when I suggested that we might try to get a picture of the volcano in action.

Our idea was to fly as near as possible, and try to take a film of the crater; but we had forgotten the fumes, and, after we had risen to the enormous height necessary to top the mountain, we drove straight into what seemed like tear-gas. It was so heavily charged with sulphur that before we knew it we were choking and coughing and blinded by our tears.

Bieler shouted, "It's finished. I can't see!"

None of us could; but it wasn't finished, because Fritz was a genius as well as a hero. Still, we were nearly sacrificed to the Mexican gods at the very beginning. Bieler told us to keep our eyes closed, to hold our breath, and not to look down under any circumstances, while he tried to fly through that cloud, rising still higher as he went.

It was an incredibly long cloud of gas, that breath of the fire mountain; but he held on, and got us to Vera Cruz. We were almost blind, and took hours to recover.

We had left early, to avoid the danger of air pockets in that region as the day warmed up, and we were at Vera Cruz for breakfast. Over the Gulf of Mexico, we had spent most of our time clearing our lungs and stomachs of the foul, biting gas, and our ears were nearly bursting because of the suddenness of the descent. The others thought we were drunk; but we knew better.

At the aerodrome, the members of the staff revived us with all they had, and two hours later we hopped off again, on our way to Tabasco, and there at Villahermosa we really did begin to take an interest in life.

Villahermosa was the headquarters of the Red Governor, an almost legendary figure, although still alive...perhaps that accentuated the legend: the man who had wiped out religion.

Our expedition was the first of its kind that had ever happened. It was heralded by the entire press of the country, and most of the town had arrived at the aerodrome to meet us. We had reached the town at precisely the right moment, and were hauled off to participate in the national sport: priest-hunting.

Every Saturday was a holiday. They had changed from Sunday as a further mark of their dislike for religion, and every hol-

iday was the occasion for the destruction of a church or the
torture of a priest. The enthusiastic vandals carried us off as
speedily as possible, since not even the arrival of an expedition
could compete with the destruction of a cathedral.

The objective on this occasion was the Cathedral of St. John
the Baptist, and a ludicrous procession formed ahead of us. I
have never seen, nor shall I ever see again, such enthusiasm,
such abandon, such lust for destruction and blood as character-
ized those ignorant people of the revolution.

We were in their midst, in Ford cars, naturally, and there rose
one steady chant, if chant it can be called, sometimes low and
muttering; sinister; the murmur of a mob certain of its feast; at
other times ribald, hilarious; as genial as the laugh of a mentally
deficient giant who has received a tasty bonbon.

"Mort a Cristus! Mort a Cristus!" they sang, or shouted, and a
devilish surge would twist the procession until it resembled
nothing so much as the living, plumed serpent of their ancestry.

On the walls were posted quotations, crudely lettered, from
Zola and others. I remember one, which seemed to be the most
popular:

*"La Humanidad no llegará a su perfeccionamento
hasta que no ciaga la última piedra de la última iglesia
sobre el último cura."*

*"Humanity will not reach perfection until the last stone
of the last church crushes the last priest."*

It was a spectacle unbelievable in its intensity: as though we
had landed right in the heart of the French Revolution.

Naturally, our camera-man was not too disturbed by the
excitement. He was a cinematographer, and he turned steadily
away, getting his shots home.

Arrived at the cathedral, there was a momentary halt. The
Red Governor was ready to make a speech and for ten minutes

he harangued the crowd, to their frenzied delight, calling on them to remove every vestige of the old and foolish religion.

He cursed God and Christ, the Virgin and the saints, in a tirade of the most violent Spanish it has ever been my lot to hear. His arms were as expressive as his tongue. There was no rest; no pause; no faltering. Religious observance was infantile. The priests were humbugs; bleeders of the people and oppressors of the poor.

Finally, to drive home his point more conclusively, he shouted: "And don't forget this! After all, Christ never existed. He's only a legend!"

This was the signal for rounds of applause, which could have been equaled only by the lusty throats of Rome, when thumbs were turned down and the slaughter went on.

The crowd was nervous, edging closer to the building; but the Senator, too, had a speech to make, which was only a poor echo of the Governor's, save that he had his last ace up his sleeve.

Cunningly, as one who confides great news, in secret, he leaned forward.

"When you have pulled out all the bells, and the walls are down, then I will tell you something. It is of the utmost importance. It is epoch-making. Do you know that across the river, hiding in a house I will tell you of, there is still a priest? To your labours! When you have destroyed this building of iniquity, I shall ask you to chase that last priest from our borders..."

A new wave of enthusiasm swept over the crowd. This was real red meat. There was a wild fusillade of revolvers, and rockets exploded. The Governor rose, to take the last curtain, as principal actor.

"Now," he commanded. "Pull down every stone!"

And how they went to work! They were inexpert; but willing. Ladders were brought. Some disdained the ladders and made straight for the belfry by the inner staircase. Others followed to begin work on the altars. These were smashed with hammers. The statue of the Virgin was brought into the centre of the square, attacked, and shivered to bits.

The Reds were like ants; eager, enthusiastic, tireless if not so very efficient. They wasted much effort; but they accomplished much.

As each bell crashed to the square, a new cheer was raised. The walls began to lose their solidity as block after block of masonry fell to earth. There were figures on the top, walking, almost dancing, from end to end. Ropes were anchored to the obstinate supports and a thousand hands laid hold, with an enthusiasm that could not be denied, and with terrible effect.

The zealots came along to us. Our camera-man was still working. They were not satisfied that we should remain purely spectators, and demanded that our representatives should also strike a blow for freedom, by way of doing a little demolition. The newspaper-man obliged.

There was a retributory side to all this vengeance. It was the Conquistadores' bill being paid. Those people who had burned all the priceless documents of Mayan civilization because they were afraid of them; the church that had held its own bonfire of "vanities," which destroyed works of art and other unseemly things; the steady dominion of nearly four centuries: all were being repaid. The venom of untold generations was spilled on those stones. It was brutal, bitter; a terrible revelation of reaction and rage.

The bonfires of "vanities" were now lighted by other hands. And, when we were weary, and a little terrified by it all, we returned to our hotel, to achieve some composure before we went on to see the Red Governor in person.

The hotel was little better, by way of introduction. We wondered if they were giving us these displays to intimidate us. It seemed possible, for the manager of the hotel was a formidable giant, booted and spurred, and carrying more fire-arms than one man could possibly use. He stood facing us, his sombrero on the back of his head, a huge and stinking cheroot between his teeth: a vile-looking half-breed, whose Indian blood certainly predominated.

"Sign there!" he commanded, pushing the register towards us.

We signed. You would!

"Don't forget," he said. "I am the manager of this hotel, a Revolutionary General, and the friend of the Governor. I command the troops. And I must be respected!" We felt sure he would be respected.

Behind him, hanging on the wall, were portraits: on one side, Lenin; on the other, General Calles. Between the two pictures was a scrawl, "Death to Christ." It looked like some fantastic and obscene parody of that hill with three crosses. But the centre Cross was vacant. Only the malefactors remained.

Lunch was arranged in the *patio,* and he came to join us, his artillery clanking. He could not sit comfortably because of his gigantic revolvers. Everything was flavoured with pepper in that meal; inclusive of the General, who recounted his adventures with no girlish modesty. He boasted of the priests he had hounded, of those he had joyfully accounted for with his own hands. His laughter was immense.

"We're smoking out another rat this afternoon!"

Once, he informed us, he had been a peon. Now, thanks to the Sacred Revolution (why "sacred"? I wondered, since they were dispensing with all the formalities and formalisms of religion), we could see what had happened to him.

He cast a complacent eye around. Once a peon, now a General.

"And everybody is equal!" he affirmed, inconsequentially fetching a servant a hefty clout, because he spilled the coffee a little.

The meal finished, we broached the possibility of interviewing the Governor, taking strict care to observe an injunction on the wall:

"A los Pasajeros del Hotel. Sirvase no Apoyar ni Ponar los Pies sobre La Mesa" –

with which we fully agreed. Even in Tabasco it is better not to put your feet among the dishes on the table; it is simply bad form – and dangerous.

The Mexican Robespierre considered a moment, and thought that an audience would be possible.

He spoke excellent English, incidentally, which he had picked up in the course of his revolutionary activities. He had been engaged in fifteen risings, and, as each failed, had escaped across the border into the United States and continued his studies.

It seemed incongruous that such a man should be in the hotel business. We asked him how it happened. He was terse and to the point.

"When the Sacred Revolution took place down here, with the result that men became equal, I found the proprietor in the way, being a Conservative. He lies buried in the dining-room, under the floor. Since then, I have done well. I fix my own prices. It is not too difficult."

Word came through from the Governor that audience would be given to the expedition. Perhaps it was made a little easier because we carried letters of introduction from General Calles, who hated the Church as much as did the Governor himself.

The Governor, it appeared, had never heard of archaeology before; but was very interested in it, and highly delighted to talk it over with us.

We were still a little apprehensive of meeting him face to face, since the tales of his prowess were pretty terrible, including the violation of all the Catholic women of an entire village: they may have been only laudatory rumours.

On our way, we passed the prison, escorted by Robespierre, who suggested that, as we should certainly have to wait for audience, we might as well look at a few murderers.

There they were, caged in a dingy cell, the heavy, latticed door letting in a little air and light, and their women folk seated outside talking, or bringing them food, which was passed in through the openings.

Among the prisoners was the famous Tiger of Tabasco, an ex-candidate for the Governorship who had lost the election, and was here awaiting the day of his trial, when he might also lose his head. He claimed eighteen notches to his gun, and the only thing really against his record was that he had robbed the churches just a little prematurely.

He was quietly playing cards in his corner; a peaceful, inoffensive creature to all appearances. But, as we approached, he remembered that he had a reputation to uphold, and rose to pace the narrow den, scowling terrifically, imitating the beast from which he took his name.

We passed along. The Tiger quietly resumed his game. "That," said our General, "is what trouble with the authorities means!" and he gave us a prodigious, terrifying wink.

The Plaza of Villahermosa is like all the squares of Mexico, save that the church has now disappeared. There were trees surrounding the open space, and a bandstand in the centre, where the town band was playing revolutionary airs.

The bandsmen, we were told, were murderers now enjoying the Governor's pardon. There seemed to be no crime below murder in the State, so perhaps they were to be regarded as decent citizens. Still, they were watched by armed guards, stationed at each corner, whose duty seemed to be the maintenance of their revolutionary enthusiasm, and to see that they played lustily, as the Governor wished.

The names of the tunes, we learned, were "To Hell with the Church!" "Mort a Cristus," and "Off with the Priests." To these strains, we marched up broad, sun-drenched steps to the Governor's Palace, and, as in the good old days of the French Revolution, there were groups of his desperadoes right and left, exercising to the full their authority and his favour, spitting in cunningly devised curves, to demonstrate the beauty of brotherhood and equality.

We were led by a swashbuckler into a reception room, all red and gold. There were holes all over the place, and Robespierre explained their origin. Once, there had been a fight here. A Governor had been deposed by a reception committee – which explained why the guards had showed so much interest in our hips and armpits, before they fell back to drowse against the wall.

Patches framed in the accumulation of stain and tarnish showed where the portraits of conservative days had hung. A few disreputable prints took their places: all of Reds; here and abroad. The chandelier had been shot to bits for practice.

Here we waited until, suddenly, the major-domo flung open the door. Canibal Carrideo was ready, and would see us.

Chapter 2

We trooped in, to see a powerful figure, dressed in the costume of the poorest peasant, surrounded by his ministers. There was a lot of Indian in him, too, and it showed plainly enough; but he was not unhandsome.

He looked us squarely in the eyes. His handshake was something to remember o' nights when the wind howled. He held his position by personal magnetism and force, to which he added a few flourishes in the manner of Mussolini; but, differing from Mussolini, Canibal made no outward display. Display cut no ice. He preferred to be taken for one of the people; one of his poor, down-trodden people; people who had suffered under bondage and had nothing but their lives to call their own.

We wondered about his wealth, safely stored away, in countries other than his own. We readily understood that he could trust no Mexican bank. He was the bank.

"So," he said. "You have come to study the antiquities of this ancient land. You are the first party of men that I have seen on such a mission. I am delighted to help, and have something of real interest to convey to you..."

He broke off abruptly. This was too formal. A straightforward smile appeared.

"How did you like the show this morning...the church business?"

We kept quiet, not knowing how to answer; but our newspaper-man was with us, and came out boldly.

"You have driven out Catholicism. What are you going to put in its place? Protestantism?"

Canibal smote the table a mighty thump, and we knew the secret of his oratory.

"No Catholics! No Protestants!" he screamed. "No religion at all!"

We were knocked flat with the blast, but he calmed down and explained that, according to his view, there was no need for any kind of religion. He gave us statistics: of the priests hounded out, or dead; of the churches, statues, and pictures destroyed; of the prohibition of simple crosses, even on the tombs of the dead; of the attendance at the Saturday festivals, when rosaries and sacred pictures, medals, and shrines were burned in public, and ended with a boast that began with a truly formidable Spanish oath and tailed off into a friendly bet that we could not find a drawing of the Virgin in any part of the State.

The fanatical moment passed, and he began to talk like the orthodox revolutionaries. He was a man of vision. He really did have a programme of sorts. He admired Lenin and Trotsky; but finished by calling them pikers, compared with his idea of progress.

He would be glad, he said, to take us to the schools to see what was being done. He had a great map on the wall behind him, which showed how Tabasco had been apportioned, county by county and village by village. All property belonged to the State. It looked well on paper. He had the logic of it. There were no unemployed. The noble State of Tabasco was prosperous and self-supporting. He was doing so well that he had actually been invited to Russia, to see how it could be made to function on the grand scale necessary before he could tackle the problem of the whole of Mexico. He was an ultimate candidate for the Presidency.

That candidature, he confessed, seemed a little way off, which was only natural in a country where every guttersnipe believed himself fit to rule; and had the chance, too, which was worse. The national ambition seemed to be the Presidential chair.

But he was growing tired of bolshevism and religion as small talk. There were other things afoot. We caught him looking anxiously out of the window. The crowds were gathering again for the afternoon's excitement.

He returned to us and our mission.

"I am the only man," he confessed, "who knows the burial-place of the last Emperor of the free Mexican nation: the tomb of Guatemoc, who was carried down by Cortez as a hostage. They strung him up in the middle of the jungle, on the banks of the Usumacinta river. I have spoken to the Indians down there, and they still venerate a great mound at a place called Canizan. When you come back, I'll fly over, and meet you there, and we'll excavate the tomb ourselves."

I was delighted by the suggestion; to think that the great hero might be discovered by our expedition; but the "Red Flag" suddenly blasted out on the square, and the audience came to a sudden end.

Outdoors, cries of "Long Live Mexico!", "Long Live the Revolution!", "Long Live the Governor!" greeted us, and he waved his hand gaily to the plaudits of the rowdiest, dirtiest, most devilish-looking mob it has been my lot to see.

Not too closely, some of us followed the maniacs to the river. We were not enthusiastic; but we were in Tabasco.

It is not very amusing to see a maddened crowd spit on Jesus and Mary, even in effigy; but they undoubtedly enjoyed it, and stampeded on their way. almost swamping their boats to be across the river in time to share the hunt; routing out some poor devil of a priest who had had courage enough to stick it until then. Landing on the other side, with a crashing "view halloo," they were gone, and we returned to discover one other sign of the deeps of the new order in Mexico.

Calles' great slogan was "no re-election"; meaning to throw open the succession to supreme power in the Republic to any who could earn it. No man was to possess the right to prolong his term of office. He, therefore, could not establish himself openly as dictator without term; but he could, and seemed to be intending to, make himself dictator behind the scene.

Canibal's nephew was taking a name for his offspring. There was no Church, only a civil rite, and this is the name they engraved for him, which seems to be worth recording: "Lenin, No re-election, Liberty, Article 36, Carrideo."

Our stores were gradually collected and loaded, and the next day we spent at the aviation field, tuning up for the flight across the jungle; which proved to be one of the most memorable flights of my life, as we made our way to Ocosingo in the State of Chiapas.

Bieler, myself, and Soustelle, ethnographer from the University of Paris, made the flight in the light plane. The others were to follow immediately afterwards, in the service planes.

Even to hint at the truth of that flight is almost impossible. It began with a beauty that was superb, with the dense foliage spreading like a carpet below us, and the mountains rising in awful majesty ahead. From time to time, we crossed the frightful swamps that are the constant danger to all travellers, swamps which had only recently swallowed two Spanish aviators, flying from Madrid to Mexico City. They came down here, almost within sight of their goal, and were not recovered.

For over an hour after leaving Villahermosa we flew over the swamps, and when we approached the mountains of the southern Cordillera we saw that clouds covered the heights, and that a tempest was ahead. A storm over the jungle is no light thing to encounter, and Bieler turned south as it broke, in an effort to skirt it if possible, but there was an apparent break. He changed his mind. The little rift closed almost immediately, and we were completely lost with the full fury of the wind buffeting us off our course, and below lay only the pestilential, almost impenetrable jungle. Occasional glimpses, as the clouds parted, showed us stupendous canyons with roaring torrents and carpets of trees; trees that looked as smooth and inviting as grass. Currents of air would play with us like a shuttlecock, rock us like a feather.

I called to Bieler to make an attempt to rise above the storm, and he asked me what the hell I thought he was doing, anyway! The rain beat down on us, a dead weight almost impossible to be borne. Lightning seemed to strike right through the plane. For a while our bearings were lost, and the solid mountain-wall grew rapidly nearer. We tried to rise with it. Soustelle was violently air-sick. Our troubles were perhaps more mental. It became as black as night, but it was actually midday; we were in the heart of unbroken cloud that seemed to stretch for mile after interminable mile.

One gust more terrible than the last lifted us so that we seemed poised like a bird, but on the tip of our wing. The next moment there was no air at all round us; we fell like a plummet. Bieler was magnificent; beyond words.

I have had my camels sink under me. I have been pinned while diving in a submerged ruin. I have waited for a fanatical tribe to complete its deliberate ritual before attacking. But never have I known greater anxiety.

Bieler said he would give it up, and try for the sea, to make a landing on the shore, as the engine was coughing and he thought there was water in the petrol. He was just completing a bank, when that uncanny extra sense of his operated. There was a momentary rift; the faintest, feeblest sign, and he went for it. And ultimately he won. With the engine missing treacherously, he reached Ocosingo, and we caught sight of the rough landing-ground.

We had been told that there was a fair landing-place, and that, failing all else, we could come to earth in the main street. Bieler gave the field a miss, and came down in the heart of the half-deserted old town, making a miraculous landing on the bumpy paving-stones.

We had come through. The others had turned back, unable to get through the storm, and we were shocked to learn later that one of the supply planes had crashed, killing the splendid young Mexican pilot Serabia.

Bieler, with four years' experience of war, confessed that he had never known anything worse.

At Ocosingo, Dr. von Schmelling was waiting for us. And let me at once pay the tribute that is essential. He, an old German doctor, who had lived among these people for many years, was the real nerve-centre of the expedition from that moment. It was he who led us from ignorance to a certain skill, he who made our passage possible, who did all that was necessary to be done.

My good fortune has been in the weathered pioneers who have been available for my expeditions. Baron von Schmelling was one of the best the world can have known; but that you will discover for yourself, as the tale develops. This was no joy-ride.

Ocosingo consisted of about two hundred stuccoed white houses with flat roofs, set about the plaza; of muddy roads, and the remains of ruined churches. Von Schmelling, in addition to curing, when he could, the ills of men and beasts, worked his tobacco fields and coffee plantations, and very calmly he informed me that since there was no other room available in the town he had booked accommodation for me at the local brothel. There were at least beds there.

He hoped that I should be peaceful; but he warned me against the bugs. So I took my own camp-bed, and found my room, partitioned off from the rest by a thin wall which was anything but sound-proof. Sleep was impossible.

I heard for the first time the music of the marimbas, not particularly amusing, and listened to the Mexican visitors raising their particular hell.

Von Schmelling arrived in the morning, apologizing for his forgetfulness; but I had more to upbraid him for than the omission of tins of alcohol to put around the legs of my bed against the invasion of bugs. During the night (and I have a trick of sleeping with my mouth open, sometimes – ill-trained I know; but habitual) I had an experience I do not wish to repeat. Something clammy fell from the roof with a sickly, inert plop on to my face: the dead body of a snake.

"Probably died of old age," was all that Von Schmelling had to say before explaining that, after all, he had come to the conclusion that it would be better for me to sleep in the open.

I was feeling anything but gay, with the thought of Serabia's death, but we faced the Indians. After all, our poor pilot meant little to them, and they could not be expected to restrain their celebrations. This was an event such as had never happened in their lives: men descending out of the air. They crowded round our plane, and decorated it with flowers.

We had had news by wire, and awaited the arrival of the others, during which interval Von Schmelling took me on a little jaunt to the "hot pools"; his sole amusement; where the native maidens disported themselves in a state of nature, while the older women attended to their washing, at a little distance. He called it "chez Maxime," thinking back over his youth in gayer capitals.

"Since we have no dancing girls," he confessed, "I like to come and watch these lovely little monkeys."

Not so little, sometimes, it seemed to me. And sometimes not so lovely; but there we sat in his particular seat, among poinsettias, hybiscus, and wild orchids, watching the seal-like girls with their glistening bodies darting like mermaids in the warm water. Around were a ring of mountains, tropical groves, ancient ruins, and gay, parasitic flowers. The sun shone throughout the day, the temperature was even, since Ocosingo lies high, and is not overburdened with humid heat. I began to think that, after all, the doctor did not greatly regret his home on the Baltic, its cold and its austerity.

The storm had abated, disappeared from the tops of the mountains. We knew that we should soon see the others; but were still a little anxious, and that night we sat up late, talking about old times, and I gave the doctor all the news of his old haunts that I could think of, so that it was nearly dawn before we turned in. I was hardly asleep, it seemed, before there were cries from the populace. Out of the opalescent skies we could see our two service planes slowly appear, to circle round over Ocosingo and raise the unanimous cheers of the Indians. We were reunited.

For our edification, the Indians staged their traditional dance, very similar to the games of children. It represented the coming of Cortez, and the participants split into two groups: the Mayas and the Conquistadores. Cortez duly met the Mexican ruler, all the dancers wearing fantastic masks to represent the epoch; but the dance ended in a squabble.

Play became serious, and there was a reversion to strife, very one-sided, because all the Indians prefer to be Mexicans, and candidates for the role of Spanish invader were few indeed.

The local idiot is invariably cast for the part of Cortez, or for the priest who accompanies him, and the priest in this case wore the traditional black robe, and came in for a terrible drubbing, so that Von Schmelling and I had to rescue him. He really did look like a priest, and perhaps the mob forgot that they were playing, and took him for the real thing.

As soon as was practicable, we took off again, to make our way to the ranch of El Real, where Don Enrique Bulnes had prepared a rough aerodrome for us.

Bieler, as chief pilot, gave the others their instructions: on arrival, they were to circle round, watching his landing, and then wait until we had cleared the scout out of the way.

We had no further ill-luck, and rose easily enough, to clear the mountains, roaring ahead, watching the little Indian villages in their clearings, whose inhabitants rushed to the centre to see the giant birds flying overhead. It was a new experience for them, never having seen an aeroplane before.

Like a hawk, Bieler manoeuvred until finally he caught sight of the signal, a huge white cross on the open space of a pasture, roughly flattened by Don Enrique's peons.

For all his labour, it was a terribly bad landing-ground, and Bieler had to go into the wind carefully, as he came over the tops of giant mahogany trees, to land as best he could on what must be the strangest aerodrome in the world: a little patch surrounded by almost virgin jungle.

We dismounted quickly, to drag clear away and give the others a chance to come down, slightly rattled, but elated by the conclusion of still another stage.

Don Enrique had a group of youngsters with a flag standing by, announcing that this was the Prorok Aerodrome, and came forward to embrace us in true Mexican fashion, which means to be locked in strong arms and kissed soundly on both cheeks.

A collection of magnificent horses, gay with trappings, awaited us, to carry us to the hacienda, where a lavish meal had been prepared for us – at the expense of surrounding tribes, for Don Enrique was king in his dominion.

The contrast was staggering, for there had been no revolution here, and the old Don was praying that he might end his life in peace before it did arrive; but he was not a man to run before the storm.

One concession he had made; for the safety of his chaplain. The priest had been sent across the border, well supplied, and when we were led to the little chapel on the estate to offer thanks for a safe journey, and to seek a benediction for our new undertakings, the service was recited by an old Indian woman, who mumbled the prayers in correct Latin.

The meal we enjoyed was a wonderful flash-back to ancient times; compliments were exchanged in fine and sonorous phrases.

"My home is yours, señor! My home is yours!"

With every course, the Don's gracious daughter found some new politeness. We, who had been treated as roughnecks and equals by the Reds of Tabasco were treated as gentlemen and superiors by these last remnants of a fiercely proud aristocracy.

The courtyard was put at the disposal of the expedition. While Don Enrique's servants were busy twisting cords and ropes for us from the fibres of the wild *maguy* plant, Indian women were remaking our mosquito nets according to his instructions, and men were braiding hammocks to be carried on the way. Our stores were taken from the planes and dumped in a convenient place, ready for sorting and assembling.

Another group was busy preparing *mangas,* the famous Mexican waterproofs: rubber capes which stretch in a seamless piece from the neck to the ground, so that, in the torrential downpours that we were bound to encounter, we should walk each in his own impervious tent.

During our stay at the hacienda, Bieler and I went off in the scout to map and photograph the route we were intending to take, while Don Enrique and Von Schmelling haggled and bargained over the hire of mules and porters.

We made flights of about three or four hours' duration, trying to locate the villages of the elusive Lacandon tribes, and to map the temples, rivers, and lakes to be encountered on our way.

There is no doubt in my mind that the aeroplane is the finest contribution mechanics have made to archaeology. I had used it before, several years earlier, in our work at Carthage, and had traced hitherto unsuspected outlines. Now, with fine cameras and expert observers, the time saved was incredible. Our expedition could never have succeeded otherwise.

We made a detailed map of the region we were to cross, and calculated the equipment necessary to reach the Lacandons, who were definitely located by the aeroplane; and, incidentally, we discovered lakes never before charted, which were communicated to the Mexican War Department and Geographical Survey, and named Lakes Calles, Rodriguez, and Marcelle Prat.

Also, we flew over Lake Pelja, and later learned that the Lacandons of this region were so frightened by the appearance of the "great bird in the skies" that two of their tribe died of shock. They were the descendants of the Mayas, and their traditions spoke of "flying dragons that heralded the end of the world."

When we reached them later, we found some villages on the point of packing up, preparatory to migration: a thing they do easily, and on the slightest threat.

The Lacandons have long been known to exist; but the Spaniards never succeeded in conquering them. At each attack, they would retire farther into their jungle, poisoning the trail behind them. Expeditions that have sought them have perished in similar fashion. Even priests who attempted to visit them as missionaries failed to return.

The tribes are completely isolated and utterly independent of outside civilizations, save that occasionally some of the smaller groups of the northern tribes would seek Indian settlements, trying to bargain for salt, of which normally they are deprived.

We hoped to make contact with them by means of double interpretation. Von Schmelling spoke the language of the Tzeltal Indians, and we were taking one of this tribe as a guide who had some knowledge of the language of the nearer groups.

Very rare and very brief were their appearances out of the jungle. Don Enrique, a living encyclopaedia of all things concerning his country, told us that occasionally stray members of the northern communities would drive as far as his ranch, seeking protection, alcohol, or salt; but that they were gone immediately. They communicated nothing of their life, of their numbers, or of their habitations.

They had their own religions and customs; but what they were he had never heard. They had their sacred temples. They were afraid their women would be stolen. That was the sum of his, and apparently anybody's, knowledge.

Considering that his ranch was ten days' march distant from the nearest group for a Lacandon, and fourteen days' march for anyone else, this ignorance was, perhaps, not so surprising.

However, we knew now where their villages were. We had seen them from the air. We had had a glimpse of that innocent-looking, beautiful territory, which lay below us like an emerald glowing in the sun; its silver streams and sapphire lakes. We had seen the squares and tree-grown pyramids, definitely identifiable, and had marked them down.

While one of the planes flew back, to fetch a larger supply of antiseptics and medicines, and Von Schmelling closed the last bargainings over mules and porters, Soustelle and one or two of the others visited the near Indian villages, to take measurements of the Tzeltals. Sadleir and I tried to follow up a rumour we had heard that there was a lost city somewhere in the mountains towards Ocosingo.

We had, incidentally, seen something that looked like a group of three buildings, which served as a clue for this minor excursion.

Don Enrique lent us a small armed guard, and we took a Tzeltal as guide, making for the ruins that were located after riding all day through trails at which we guessed.

We camped in a small Indian village, and found three pyramids and a courtyard in the ruins, hearing also of gold to be found in the streams. We collected specimens of quartz, to be analysed later. There is little doubt that the country is rich in valuable minerals.

The villagers told us that if we visited the ruins we should be under the curse of the *pishans* or Mayan ghosts, which, like the ghosts of the Arabian and Saharan deserts, are reputed to walk at night, to lay their malediction on those who disturb the ancient stones.

A singular thing we noticed in the village was that most of the inhabitants were pot-bellied, which we could not understand until accidentally we came across some of the children, about seven or eight years of age, scooping up the soft mud near the river and eating it. They were earth-eaters, the first I had seen in America, although I had seen them at Siwa and in the Fezzan; but there they mixed white worms with the mud, and made a sort of sandwich.

Caves were reported in the region also, and were equally accursed. Trying to find their location was like hunting for a needle in the proverbial haystack; but we were ultimately successful, and were surprised to find that they contained traces of Neolithic man, in the shape of fine obsidian flints.

The caves stood midway up a hill, and as we followed them we found a waterfall cascading away in the very heart of the rock; but what was more singular was to discover that an overflow of lava had covered a number of ruins in the vicinity, which was particularly interesting, as we saw embedded flints, which gave us a date to work on. Geologists place the date of the extinction of the volcanoes at about 6,000 years ago; which supported research we had done some time previously near Mexico City: at Pedregal, where a volcanic eruption had created the Mexican Pompeii. A pyramid there was almost completely covered by lava, only the summit standing clear. Under the lava were skeletons and ruins. The geologists of the Smithsonian Institute put the destruction of that early civilization as being coeval with the earliest civilizations of the Nile basin.

We found the natives apprehensive of the caves, saying that they were the home of vampire-bats, and that the whole place was accursed. And we saw the bats, which were certainly sufficient to raise fear in the villagers, who produced individuals who had been attacked.

On our return we ran into another strange sidelight of native life. On the banks of the river some Indian women were busily crushing the bark of a tree, or rather a large bush, and pouring the resultant juice into the stream, across which it spread, like a reddish soap solution, and floated down-stream to where the men were standing, evenly spaced from bank to bank, throwing fish ashore as they drifted on the surface.

This was the easiest fishing I had ever seen. The juice, which the natives call *pati,* acted as a drug, and was, we learned, much used throughout the country. Its effect, which was only temporary, was not ultimately harmful.

Arriving back in camp, we found everything nearly ready. Don Enrique had collected mules from the ranches in the neighbourhood; he had selected the guides and ordered the preparation of something like fifteen thousand *tortillas,* or pancakes, to serve as food for the porters on the trail. We were anticipating a journey of about two hundred miles to the river Usumacinta, and another two hundred on the river itself. Food was likely to be a serious question.

The Don, however, was a little disconsolate. There would be no more long evenings of talk, talk of his schooldays in England and his reception by Queen Victoria. We should no more see his excitement and pleasure on being taken for a joyride when work was finished over his jungles.

The mules were there, and forty Indian porters. The Don went to his secret store, and produced for us a thousand silver dollar pieces: half-pay in advance for mules and men, and we went on our way after a farewell meal, when the oldest wines in the cellar were brought out for us. For the first fifteen miles Don Enrique rode with us.

Our Indians went ahead. Twenty of them, in groups of threes, began to cut a path through the jungle, keeping a steady pace so that our progress was never halted. Their sabre-like machetes flashed rhythmically. They were the most important people of all, with the exception of Domingo, our sturdy, indefatigable guide.

All they were there for was to cut and slash the line of our course, mapped and oriented from the air. With never a pause, hour by hour they cut away. We had said good-bye to the sun, and almost good-bye to the earth itself, for the green of the jungle made a vault over our heads, through which the sun rarely penetrated, and the foliage made a carpet for our feet. We moved as though we were in an aquarium, with a great, green wall ahead, of enormous umbrella plants, and a myriad lianas and bamboos. Yet the *macheteros* went steadily on through the oppressive, humid heat. We were soon dripping from every pore, although mounted on our mules.

Chapter 3

Every now and then, the great bellow of Von Schmelling would shout a warning. "Achtung! Achtung!" or "Poison! Poison!" and we were taught to pass with hands raised high above our heads, so as not to touch the plants on either side. The poison trail had begun. Nor were the poisonous plants all we had to fear. We seemed at times to be fighting our way through a concentrated attack of every kind of thorn, which simply ripped our clothes. Every bush seemed armed with lances, daggers, fishhooks, bayonets, hayforks, and harpoons. The jungle fought our passage at every step.

Suddenly, Domingo came to a halt and called us over. Schmelling, too, thought it would be interesting. I had my first glimpse of the vampire plant which, two or three days earlier, had trapped a bright little bird on its treacherous leaf, and now was in the process of taking its meal.

We all wore gauntlets to our elbows for protection, since it was natural to put out a hand to ward off the leaves and plants that threatened to brush back on us, and woe betide the victim if he touched poison or thorn! My own first encounter was not so bad, simply a thorn which struck above my eye, and blinded me until the doctor patched it up.

The camera-man was in worse plight. He had taken off his gauntlet, the better to take a particular shot, and touched a plant. Half an hour later, his arm was covered with huge water-blisters, and the pain was agonizing. Yet it had been such a beautiful plant; with fine, red flowers. We heard him cursing with pain as the doctor attended to him also.

He was seldom free from practice, the doctor, for the first few days. One after the other we had to fly to his medicine chest.

Later, we learned a little caution.

It was Soustelle who gave us the laugh, to end our first full day on the trail. Of course, it was not laughable for him, for he was such a methodical, scientific fellow – perhaps a bit too academic for the trail; but not so absent-minded as he seemed. Absent-mindedness can be an excuse for forgetting (and therefore borrowing) essentials sometimes; but not as a habit.

He was riding, entirely free of burden because he must take notes, on his mule, when suddenly one foot was caught by a great tendril that seemed to snap round his ankle like a spring. The mule, all unconscious, plodded on and we watched Soustelle slowly lift one leg into the air, in the manner of an acrobat. Next we heard his anxious voice, and next we saw him slowly, deliberately, forcefully hauled from the saddle as the liana stretched to its limit, and held on. The mule still trudged forward. Soustelle described a nice are through the air with an effortless grace that Mowgli or Tarzan might well have envied, and came to rest; a smart, white-clad figure, hanging head-downwards by his heel, while we cut him free and restored him to equilibrium and dignity.

We laughed. We should have expected to be laughed at ourselves; but I am afraid he took it ill. He was not used to the give and take of expeditions. Perhaps, after all, we were not so sorry as we might have been that he got a mild sort of baptism.

That night the doctor showed us how to make camp. He knew all there was to be known about the art. Deserts are one thing, jungles another. It is no easy matter slinging a hammock and fixing a mosquito net in the open. In Mexico, that is.

The hammocks, which had been made for us at the ranch, were slung between trees, and disks were fixed to the ropes, soaked in a concoction of Von Schmelling's, to prevent the approach of bugs and snakes, or other pests, and the hammock was encased in a thick mosquito net which fell all the way to the ground, making a sort of tent. Over all, our waterproofs were stretched, so that we were sealed against the dripping moisture. To retire, we climbed up inside the net and clambered into the hammock (when we had mastered the trick), and drew the net up after us. That was the only practicable thing to do; fewer precautions would have been as useless as none at all.

Our camp fire was lit. Von Schmelling began to move, and the Indians climbed the trees to find wild honey, while the *macheteros* produced their daily miracle: building us shelters so quickly that it was almost impossible to follow their movements. First they lopped off palmetto leaves and cut stout poles, ran natural cords from pole to pole, and with leaves made walls and roof to shelter us.

We had our evening meal of red, luscious Mexican bananas, fried, with tortillas and honey, and after dinner discovered just what it was that had occupied the doctor on his journey. We had watched him pulling leaves, and twisting them into shape, tying the ends with thin fibres. He was making the *cigares de voyage;* and they smoked exceedingly well.

We found that the natives had also provided themselves with an abundant supply, and the air was thick with a fragrant smoke. We were at peace for some time, and quite still; but I noticed Von Schmelling casting amused glances at a few members of the expedition, who shifted their positions more frequently than the others. Before long, we were all just a little restless and, manners forgotten, began to scratch.

Scratching was not enough. First one and then another moved off on some private examination of his own, and the doctor was the only peaceful member. Almost to the second there was a unanimous yell. When we had dragged off our shirts, and dropped our breeches, we discovered a girdle of *garapatas* which, more efficient and more sizeable than their European counterparts, the ticks, had chosen the softest part of our respective anatomies and, according to habit and sense, had taken good hold and were rapidly bloating.

It was amusing, if not pleasant, to see the explorers turn their backs on the rest and dig away with their fingers, trying to extract the ticks from parts which, by all the rules of propriety, should have been immune.

Von Schmelling came when we yelled, and stilled our fears, assuring us that there was no real danger, only pain and annoyance, and smeared us with a mixture of oil and tobacco juice which he had ready. Then, with an expert touch, he went about us all with his tweezers.

"This is nothing," he consoled us. "Wait till the worms get to work. Then you will have something to excavate, real practice for archaeologists!"

The jungle was still. The trees dripped constantly. There was a steady, warm rain from the leaves. Everything was hushed, blanketed. To me it was a great contrast, after desert travel. We seemed imprisoned. The voices of the night were myriad. We had the feeling of a host of ill omen camped round about us. Some of the cries were so unearthly that one or other of the crowd would awake and call to the doctor to ask what it was.

"Animal about the size of your thumb," he replied.

By about three o'clock the jungle quietened and we were at peace, save for the intermittent falls and consequent curses, as the tenderfeet found their hammocks too much for them. Ultimately, the inexpert were bound in, and their only ill was occasionally to lie face downwards, as the hammock responded too freely to their sudden movement.

There was scarcely any change in temperature; it was a steady bath of steam, and the sultriness was increased by the waterproof stretched above us. The mosquito nets were like gags.

Just as we were all unanimous in sleep, the cry, which became historical as we progressed, roused us.

"Vamonos! Vamonos!" shouted the doctor, making his round, and banging at every hammock like a sergeant-major. So, we tackled the job of loading up again, and the *macheteros* went ahead, slashing steadily at the jungle wall.

Our route lay across mountainous rises, which offered but scant foothold for the mules. The damp stones were moss-covered and seemed safe enough; but, once the usually secure feet came down, the slide began. The first casualty was the doctor himself, who disappeared down the side of the mountain with a crash and a roar and all the choice Prussian profanity of which he was excellently capable, to take a header into the jungle, from which he emerged with his nose bleeding and a face like that of a prizefighter who had gamely qualified for the short end of the purse.

He was the first; but we were all similarly afflicted. None of us was secure in the saddle and we all took our tumbles and bruises, for the descent had to be made, whether we liked it or not. The mules were badly battered by the time we finished, because we dared not trust the low ground; the swamps were too well disguised and too treacherous. Even so, we found patches where the earth was nothing more than thick slime, and our legs went down, without resistance. If we grabbed at a bush to save ourselves, as likely as not we would clutch something that was no better than a saw, and would tear through our gauntlets.

The stench of the swamps was terrible. The Indian name, which is excellently to the point, is "stink water."

On the hill-side, we came ultimately to a Bajahon village, which was quite unexpected, and had almost decided to make our camp there – it seemed deserted; but, as we approached through the *milpa,* or clearing round the hutments, we saw a dog traveling uncertainly, leading a man who was evidently blind, who, in turn, was leading a cow which stumbled at every step.

It was a terrible, accursed place: a village left half-deserted, whose inhabitants were suffering from a disease of which we had heard some mention before leaving Mexico City, caused by the sting of a gold-fly.

Bieler, Von Schmelling, and I were riding ahead, and came first into the clearing. Von Schmelling said there was not much danger to us, as the victim needed to be well inoculated by the flies; but all the inhabitants whom we saw were blind, or nearly blind. They looked as though they must ultimately starve to death. The stronger members of the community had evidently deserted, leaving the stricken to their fate. There was nothing to do for them; they were hopeless. Even though we had prepared ourselves against every sort of sting and bite (we had antidotes for all the poisons), we were helpless in this case. Von Schmelling could do nothing! All we could do was to push on, and we came to camp on a mossy, elevated spot.

So we blasted on, for day after day; it is useless to describe the regularity of the trail. The more it varied, the more it was the same, only differing in contour and seldom in character. From time to time our mules would give out, and the ailing animals had to be left in charge of porters, to be picked up on the return.

The porters sank into a hopeless melancholy, moving monotonously forward, without smile or song, their wicker baskets on their backs. They, too, were crushed by the jungle, stealing along on padded feet, looking apprehensively from right to left; relics of a hundred years of serfdom and Spanish oppression.

They seemed glad enough when we left them with the mules, to recuperate while we pushed on to Lake Pelja; and, later, they simply disappeared into the jungle. How or where they went we did not discover. They had had half their pay in advance, and were probably fed up.

One day, as we toiled along, Domingo came to me with a complaint.

"Señor," he said, "we are being watched..."

"How do you mean?" I replied. "What makes you think so? We have seen nobody, heard nothing..."

"It is the little men," he protested. "They are following us on the trail, on either side, and they have been there for days."

"You mean the Lacandons?" I asked.

"Yes, señor. They go through the woods faster than any man..."

"But how would they know?"

"Seen fires, señor. Camp at night. Or perhaps we pass one of their villages, and not see it. News gone ahead!"

It seemed doubtful, for we were not near the point which we had marked from the air; but we were a little more alert as we pressed on, and later, on the shores of a lake, which we called Sapphire Lake, for its extreme beauty of colour, we had the first touch of what may have been their animosity.

Bamboo grew around the shores of the lake; bamboo of all sizes, from the thin graceful wands to giant "organ" bamboo, whose poles strongly resemble the pipes of an organ, and during the night the jungle was fired. The bamboo burned and exploded, the blaze chased out all the animals, big and little, and we had an hour of quick work to save the stores.

Von Schmelling was half inclined to believe it was "the little people," and he did not add to our sense of security by telling us of a party of *chicleros* (hunters of chicle gum) who had gone to the west of a Lacandon village and had been wiped out by poisoned arrows. The Lacandons had come on the party and picked them off, one by one, from ambush. The disaster was only discovered when the people who had financed the expedition sent out a search party.

It was time, said Von Schmelling, that we began to try to make contact with them, for we were now approaching Lake Pelja and there we could camp on the shore, and he would take Domingo and try to bring them to peaceful terms with alcohol and other presents. Alcohol, apparently, worked miracles with them.

He imitated what he believed to be their call, on a conch horn, and went off with Domingo and a few runners.

The following day one of the runners returned saying that we were to move up the lake in small groups, and we were so anxious to see these mysterious little people that we drew lots to see who should be in the first party. We were compelled to travel two by two, with a fair interval between, lest we scare them off altogether, when the doctor would have all his work to do over again.

Obviously the camera-man was the first to go. Whatever else failed, we wanted a picture. The rest of us filtered in in turn, and it was wise that we were as careful as we were, for we must have seemed like an army to the pygmies. We had forty mules and porters, in addition to our riding animals.

When we reached the doctor, he was sitting on the ground, with all the presents spread out in front of him; but quite alone. I asked him where the Lacandons were, and he laughed.

"They're here all right," he explained. "They're in the trees over there. Act casually. Get out the phonograph."

But first we covered the moving-picture camera with leaves, so as not to scare them, and Von Schmelling told us that two of the old people had died from shock, following the sight of our aeroplane.

We waited; but still there was no sign, although the doctor was sure they would return. He had given four of them enough alcohol to make them drunk, and they liked that. I asked him what he thought about it, and he replied that they might have stolen back to their village or across the lake. In any event, they had promised to bring the chief to-morrow, to replenish their store of rum.

For all his certainty, we did not see them again that day. They had disappeared into the jungle, without a sound, leaving no trace.

The next day they came again, approaching in dug-out canoes, about twenty feet long, pointed at either end, and propelled by crude paddles. But they were efficient, those canoes, hollowed from a straight mahogany trunk by fire and flints.

Our camp was on the very edge of the lake, with little runnels and creeks near. Behind us was a magnificent forest of giant mahogany trees and the earth was carpeted with brilliant flowers. Giant poinsettias made an enormous splash of colour, and orchids such as I had never seen before added their exotic touch. It was amazing, from such a setting, to watch the short procession of tiny folk coming to meet us, in their great canoes.

Von Schmelling cautioned us to control our excitement, to pay absolutely no attention to them, for they were raving with rage against us, and as venomous as the devil.

We pretended to be busy about our own affairs, although the camera-man was tirelessly turning away in his shelter. He was never known to miss a picture. Soustelle was for rushing them as they got out of their canoes and circled round us. His instruments were ready and he was eager to take measurements. The doctor held him off.

Since this was to be our permanent camp, we had plenty to do if we needed it, and little by little the ugly, sly, more-than-malicious men of the Stone Age crept closer, dressed in a primitive, one-piece gown of home-grown cotton, that hung to their knees. Their heads were covered with matted, slightly wavy hair, that came almost to their shoulders. Their faces were almost devoid of intelligence, and sometimes eaten by disease. They seemed somewhat Mongolian in type, due to their bulging, almond eyes; but ultimate examination discounted that first impression. They were white, with a tinge of brown.

If anyone spoke, they darted off like rabbits in a field. They were as wild as monkeys, and obviously degenerate.

We ate a little food, so that they could see us, and put the rest down where they could see, and reach it if they felt inclined. Animal-like, wary, they drew near. The daring ones tasted the food. There was a smile on a cunning face, and a hurried withdrawal. One movement on our part, and they were gone. We could discern easily enough that they had no welcome for us.

That first night, a strange thing happened. Of course, Von Schmelling put it down to the Lacandons: he had not much use for them, anyway, saying that there was nothing but evil in their make-up, and however important the study of this disappearing tribe might be, the sooner they disappeared from history, the better. They were rotten right through!

Still, we felt secure. We had guns and sentries posted. We slept with the water rippling peacefully near, and had a sight of the sky again, where there were stars and a bright moon. Out in the lake were the islands with their sacred temples, and occasionally we heard the splash of a fish or an alligator. We were actually happy to have reached our first objective. There were days of rest ahead. We licked our sores and nursed our bruises. We had achieved something and were encamped in beauty. Lake Pelja spread like a silver disk; there seemed to be no menace any more, only beauty.

But, in the early hours, there was Von Schmelling rampaging like a wounded hippopotamus, shouting and cursing.

"Tzojorine!" he cried. "Get up! Get up, every one of you!"

His imagination was never at fault. He was sure that the Lacandons had laid a trail of honey from our camp to a gigantic mound, and that the giant ants had followed the trail as intended, to reach us and our provisions and equipment lying around.

At his summons we tumbled out, and must have made a fantastic sight, there on the shores of the lake; for we wore the most brilliant pyjamas ever made. We had bought them in Villahermosa as a rag: vermilion, sky-blue, petunia, mauve, magenta, and lemon-yellow. A spot of colour that was so cheering that I have ever afterwards repeated it when on expedition.

We began the slaughter, and were nearly slaughtered! The ants were almost an inch long, and even before we had taken a step, most of us were hopping about on one leg, trying to free the other of the devils that had caught us. And their bite is nothing to laugh at. They really do nip!

Von Schmelling cursed us for not putting on our boots. We repaired that omission as quickly as we could, although some of us were actually screaming with pain. Then we set to work. The ants had attacked everything. They were even trying their chances with tinned provisions. And ultimately we won; by Von Schmelling making a line of fire round the camp, and setting the Indians to work cutting trenches round the tents, which were filled with water from the lake.

Later, the doctor did discover honey on the ground: the Lacandons had extended their welcome.

We had bites by dozens, and were dying for a swim. We were under orders from the doctor not to be fools; there were alligators.

The next day the Lacandons came again and we learned the cause of their apprehension. Domingo explained that of course we had not come for their women, that we had thousands where we came from. The Lacandons are short of women; even grand-mothers were precious in their settlements. Rothermel said that their best protection was their looks; but these pygmies must have regarded us as the Conquistadores were regarded. We were a strange and alien race, and the sensation we roused in them must have been unbearable, comparable to the arrival of the invaders at Mexico City, when the natives thought that they were centaurs, that horse and man were one, and gasped with fear when one fell from his horse and remounted.

He was a god, who, though broken, could repair himself! Sadleir wanted to put a shot through a duck on the lake, to bring the Lacandons to their senses; but Von Schmelling protested that after such magic they would disappear for ever.

Little by little, fighting for every particle of their confidence, we succeeded in obtaining permission to visit their village on the morrow; but even that was nearly wrecked by two of the *carga-dores,* who later complained that their feet were poisoned.

Von Schmelling was after them like a shot, extracting the confession that they had actually tried to follow the Lacandon trail, and cursing and curing them. Fortunately the poison was old, otherwise there would have been no chance for them, for the Lacandons are past-masters in the art of laying traps. In this case, it was giant thorns hidden under moss.

We later found that they use poison only against men, and that it is obtained by cutting the bark of the *echete* (which may be the manchineel tree) and moistening the tip of the weapon in the sap which flows. The effect is almost instantaneous, and annihilating.

Those porters will be unlikely to take such a journey again, for the doctor went after their feet with a thoroughness of which he was traditionally possessed, and in the fashion of a horse-doctor; which method, incidentally, he employed with every-body.

The next day, true to programme for once, we made our way to their village, voyaging along the lake. Von Schmelling had the paddlers half-drunk before we started, lest they should change their minds, and, if that treatment did seem to assure continued performance, it almost brought about a sudden discontinuance of the mission, for the craft are not of the unsinkable variety, and the oarsmen were erratic, to say the least.

We crossed in single file, threading our way through a series of swamps, and, as we passed, between two canoes, a giant wild fig tree crashed to earth. The roots had been loosened by the water. That meant turning back, and helping to haul the following canoes over, before we could continue. We certainly had no intention of arriving in sections this time.

We were well armed, and carrying our own food, Von Schmelling insisting that we should touch nothing that was offered to us in the village, and be on the alert the whole time.

Coming to the jungle-wall, the leader in the first canoe separated the hanging lianas – another example of their cunning. There was absolutely nothing to indicate a waterway behind that curtain; it looked like the edge of the jungle.

When we were through, the curtain was closed again.

We came to a halt. The movie-man was the first ashore, mounting his camera and taking a picture of the landing, which was almost the cause of another panic; but confidence was growing just a little. They were readier to listen to Domingo and the doctor than they had been, and we were led forward to the village.

Until we were almost on the top of it, we could see no sign of a settlement. We could not have found it without the Lacandon guide. It was in the most terrible, inaccessible part of the jungle, and the village consisted of a very small section which had been cleared by burning: the stumps of trees were left charred in the ground. Round that space, scarcely recognizable, were their houses; simply poles standing upright and draped with giant leaves. Their crops, little patches of tobacco, maize, and cotton, grew right up to the huts. Dried shells of pumpkins lying around were their water-pots.

The tribe was very small indeed; we could only trace about thirty members of this northern group, of whom ten were children. There were eighteen males to fifteen women, living in eleven establishments. So far, however, we had not seen any women. They were hidden out of danger, for the great fear of the Lacandon was a raid on his women.

They were definitely pygmies, not more than four feet six inches in height, and some much shorter than that.

We had them at that moment; but they stood around nervously alert; we could not be sure for how long they would stay.

The recording machine was produced, and kept manned, to make records of their speech and music, and Von Schmelling made a parade of the drinks. Chen Tan, their chief, sat on the ground, carefully tucking his single garment between his legs as he sat; the very soul of modesty.

The scientific hunt was up! Soustelle went after his facts without pause, digging into the past of their history, the nature and number of their gods, the reason for their flight into the jungle, and their refusal to trade with the people of the north. He asked questions easily; it was not so easy to persuade the hideous old man to reply.

We discovered, however, that they were nature worshippers, with local gods: sun gods, gods in the earth to prevent the spread of earthquakes. Their religious ceremonies were simple and few. They had a feast, and a pilgrimage, and the chief feature of it all was that they daubed their smocks with fruit juice to stain them red, and drank themselves into a state of complete abandon, when they were capable of chanting their religious songs.

These songs were sung independently, every man for himself. Words were few, and unintelligible. The chief effort in the propitiation of the gods was a long, mournful wail.

For history, we learned that the white men had hunted their ancestors, and that the tale had been handed down from generation to generation. For which reason they kept to their jungles, and had nothing to do with the rest of the world, lest they lose their women and their lives.

Of the Christian religion they had heard nothing, although in days gone by men dressed in black had tried to visit the northern villages.

They were quite frank about the fate that attended these men, who must have been missionaries; they were eaten! Asked why visitors were treated that way, the chief told us that it was the will of *Teo;* God.

Chapter 4

All this time, the camera was grinding away, slowly and unobtrusively, and it was obvious that if we wanted further information, more light on their degenerate civilization, something would have to be done about it; Von Schmelling produced more presents, and we proceeded to the little space before the house of the chief, where coloured beads for the women, hunting-knives for the men, alarm clocks, and such things were put out for display.

The doctor made a *faux pas* with the alarm clocks. He wound them up, and left them ticking away, with the alarms set for a few minutes ahead. Then we stood apart, getting the Lacandons to demonstrate the use of bow and arrow.

Arrows were fixed and fired with surprising speed; almost as quickly as a burst of rapid fire on the ranges of a modern army school. The bows were primitive but efficient, and carried the parrot-feather fletched arrows of bamboo for a considerable distance. The arrow heads were of hardwood or flint, and the flints we saw them working for ourselves, much as prehistoric man must have operated. We were living among men of the Stone Age, who wore roughly woven cotton wraps and for needles used thorns.

So much they had shown us when the alarms went off, and the Lacandons with them! They jumped, spun round, and disappeared. We were medicine men, and they were afraid.

Later, when we had tempted them near again, and were still more in their confidence, they wore the alarm clocks round their necks, but never learned to use them.

They were savages; we, presumably, wise men with real scientists among us; but the Lacandons were almost given the spectacle of a full-sized row among us. I suppose we all knew what we wanted for ourselves: our investigations were different. I wanted a picture of the life of the tribe; of their habits and little industries. Soustelle wanted his precise measurements for later study, the record of their voices and their religious chants.

To be exact, I wanted them to go through the performance of poisoning their arrows. We found the correct trees, and we put them through their motions in the traditional manner; but the season was not correct. The poison was not potent in the sap, or something, so Soustelle raised a highly academic protest against filming the scene.

The rest of us protested that he was pushing science to the limit, was being too technical; so technical as to be absurd; and we took the picture, since we could not wait in the village till the sap turned poisonous, and anyhow the poison would not show a different colour in any film we could take, whatever the season. But he was annoyed; more annoyed later when we made them hunt fish that were not running. Again it was not the season, so we ought not to dream of taking the picture. Yet we were determined to get pictures of how they used their flint-headed lances, and got some of them into their canoes on the lake, and they went through their actions and made a good picture, while Soustelle growled on the shore: the real scientist who had never a thought beyond his own study and could not understand that there were people who would find the answer to many questions by seeing even what we could get in the shape of a film.

Later, glory be! we took our academic revenge, for he was hot on the trail of the religious festivals and the chants must be recorded. He put his apparatus to work – a heavy load we had carried through the jungle, just for that purpose.

It was not the time of year for singing, so what was he going to do, scientifically, about that?

Scientists arguing are marvellous! He would get the real song. It would be scientific. We could reproduce all the necessary conditions and he would vouch for their authenticity. I suppose we couldn't for our scenes!

The question was: what were they going to sing? They had several chants (much the same to our ears); funeral songs, melancholy and eerie, and songs to the rain god and the sun god. Still, there was no funeral, and the gods were perhaps on a journey; or perhaps sleeping.

Records were taken just the same, after we had encouraged the singers with enough drink to achieve the requisite spirit.

They made it clear that their songs were copied from nature. In the evening, when the wind came from the lake, it sighed and moaned in the bamboos and among the trees, and, when the wind did rise, we saw that the Lacandons had produced quite a fair imitation.

Their song of the departed souls was similar: a song which, they said, was carried by the spirits from the sacred temple on the island.

Naturally, we wanted to see their temples, the one in the settlement and the one on the island, and we thought we could go straight away; but found that they held their present-day rites inviolate. There was nothing doing. If we were to make that investigation it would have to be by strategy, so Von Schmelling persuaded the chief to summon the women, that they might receive their presents, promising them immunity from attack.

He showed the necklaces, which must have seemed brilliant things to the Lacandons, for they made a grab at them; but the doctor joked with the men and held them out of reach until Chen Tan raised his shell trumpet and gave the signal.

As if by magic the women filtered through from the jungle, and made a timid approach. Terrible specimens they were: haggard mental deficients for the most part, utterly primitive and unbeautiful. The only difference we could see between the men and the women was that the women wore their smocks longer.

Still, they approached; more specimens for the scientist, and the whole village sat around, smoking cigars and looking at the presents Von Schmelling dangled before their eyes. When they were all amused and thoroughly interested, he gave Soustelle and me the sign to disappear silently, and we crept off to look at their village temple.

It proved to be nothing more than a sort of skeleton barn, without walls, before which, somewhat raised from the ground, was a hollow tree in which were the ingredients for their *balche,* or ceremonial libations, and under the flimsy thatch of roof were crude shelves which bore the pots of the cult, arranged according to the various families of the settlement and decorated with crude drawings. They were used for the burning of incense.

There was little of art; everything was of the crudest and most primitive character.

Further examination at that time was prevented by the quiet and unsuspected approach of some of the men of the village, who stared at us, arrows in hand, to see what we were doing. We smiled innocently, and Soustelle and I pulled away, wondering if we should get something in the back as we went. Later, we were able to make a fuller examination, and the scientific reactions of our professor will be published in full, with measurements, in due course.

Thereafter, we sat down to our meal, which the Lacandons watched. They provided us with a fireplace, which, to our surprise, proved to be made of fossilized bones of prehistoric animals; a discovery in themselves.

We asked where they came from, and were told that in the *milpa* of another settlement there were many such bones.

The village was described as being up the lake, near the shore, and near waterfalls, so Sadleir and I went off with some of the Lacandons to investigate, while the remainder of the population submitted wonderingly to the indignity of anthropological measurements as Soustelle got busy with his callipers.

We had some difficulty in getting to the prehistoric stores, for in the centre of the lake were sacred islands which we must pass, or else go round the entire shore. We did what we could, and ultimately persuaded our guides to take us straight to the spot; but when they passed the islands, they steadfastly refused even to look at the sheer walls, although we, who had no scruples, could distinguish the crude red hand of the god, which looked like the hand of Fatma, painted on the face of the rock.

This, they told us, was the finishing mark of creation. When the gods had done all their work they put their sign there to say they had finished. In addition to the hand, the plumed serpent and the dragon were also visible.

We made several trips to the field of the prehistoric animals before we had done, and collected a considerable number of bones, which were delivered to the authorities in Mexico City, since they were not released for export; but we were promised that they should later be shipped to the experts in Paris. Some day, I hope, we shall succeed in persuading the authorities to issue a final report.

Even at first sight, it was a real discovery, and would be a marvellous field for a fully-equipped scientific mission, with all the necessary apparatus.

Having cleared it as best we could, we left Soustelle in camp, taking measurements, while we explored, on our own, the sacred islands that had been pointed out. To do this, we borrowed the canoes of the Lacandons, and Sadleir, Rothermel, Hayrnan, and I risked their wrath and that of their gods, since we were absolutely prohibited from making the journey.

We stole round the other side, however, and felt our way along the face of the rock, not knowing what we should find.

Ultimately coming to an old stone staircase, roughly sculptured in the rock and rising from the level of the lake, we saw ancient drawings and carvings, mostly of the alligators we had heard about as being guardians of the holy place.

These alligators are, by the way, the present-day guardians – the lake is full of them – and the drawings may be a survival of totemism. Perhaps it is too much to hope that they may be associated with that cult known to have existed in Egypt.

The Tuaregs say their ancestors are personified by giant lizards. The Lacandons informed us that their ancestors were alligators, and they showed us huge skins – evidently of man-eaters.

We tied the canoes down below, and in great excitement made our way up the old stone staircase, to reach the heights and the interior of the island, where we found a mass of Cyclopean ruins, covered with the jungle growth common to all Central America, and were compelled to leave traces of our visit, since we had to cut our way through with machetes in order to obtain photographs.

So we laid bare a great central pyramid and some circular edifices with vast walls.

Digging with our alpenstocks in one of the chambers, we found several heads of idols, and numerous prehistoric flints among a mass of broken pottery. Sadleir made a collection of incense-burners which he sent to the British Museum, and I found three marvellous arrow heads worked in opal, as well as jade adzes.

We had made our find, and were highly delighted. So far we had traces of Mayan and prehistoric civilizations, and returned with our trophies, going on to the fossil-fields, covering our flight and our subterfuge as well as we could.

One of the most beautiful sights of the entire jungle was the approach to the fossil-field on that occasion. Around the edge of the creek were laburnum trees, with their vivid golden flowers, which had dropped their petals on to the cascading water: we paddled through a stream literally plated with these spectacular blooms, the sun catching them and the multi-coloured flora on the banks.

Returned to camp, we were in time to hear the sad tale of the raids and of the dearth of women. It is a terrible economy, that of the Lacandons. The males varied from one year to about forty-five years of age, the women from five to sixty-five, and the women were in the minority; but the richer members of the community sometimes had two wives. Consequently the others either had to share, or to be content with marriage to women old enough to be their grandmothers, or young enough to be their grandchildren. The old women were past child-bearing; but still were not pensioned off. One boy of eighteen was married to a woman of sixty-five. A man of thirty was married to a girl of ten.

The chief said that the last raid for wives had been unsuccessful: two grandmothers and three infants!

In a few years, probably in two generations, the Lacandons seem destined to disappear altogether. They are the relics of a once numerous tribe; fast-fading remnants of a population that could be counted by millions.

Having seen the central temple, and hearing that other islands were also sacred and possessed of ruins, I wanted to continue exploration; but this time it could not be done in secret, as the tribe was fully aware of our movements.

Therefore, after much trouble and many presents, I persuaded one of the Lacandons to act as guide and canoeist, to take me to an island somewhat remote. It might not be the best; but I thought it would be something, and I was assured that there were ruins to look at.

Passing the great island which we already knew, I saw that the Lacandon kept his head turned from the rock face; but not from me.

He was either malicious or afraid. It is impossible to exaggerate the extreme reverence with which that island was regarded, but his awe seemed to diminish as we left it behind, and I had less trouble than I expected in getting him to land me on one of the smaller islands.

I had hardly begun my investigation when he threw himself into a fury of gesture and pointed frantically to the sky. There was a storm brewing. I gathered that he was more afraid of the gods than of the storm, and that he took this as their message to us to clear out. He was on his way, anyhow, and I had no alternative but to follow.

Soon we were afloat again, the little devil behind me muttering his incantations as he paddled furiously out of range of the island. I could not see him, but I could hear him, and suddenly, without the slightest warning, the canoe took a sudden list and I was overboard. My first impression was that he had deliberately thrown me out, a present to the guardian alligators.

He was out of reach when I came to the surface, and I began to swim as straight as I could for the shore; for the alligators were no fable. I thrashed the water, believing that they did not approach a violently moving object. Whether they followed or not, I was never positive. I certainly felt that they were there, close behind me, when I reached the shore and had the pleasant sensation of standing on rotten stumps, which simply gave way under me and left me still compelled to swim and stumble to a real foothold.

With alligators behind and swamp ahead, snakes in the trees, and the Lacandon gone, myself covered with slime, I was not in the best of positions. And my worries increased when I realized that I could not work my way round the shore of the lake, but should have to drive through the jungle in an uncertain direction.

I had hauled myself out of the swamp, and clambered on to a branch to regain my breath, when tumult broke out behind. Two of the amiable guardians of the temples were fighting it out between themselves. I saw their strange, tearing, twisting manoeuvres, and shall never believe again that they are anything but efficient, nimble creatures.

It was a horrid spectacle: tails flailing the mud and slime, jaws cracking in fury, and a dreadful, fetid odour rising, they fought to a standstill.

My machete had gone overboard with me, and my way through the jungle was blind and blundering. I envied the Lacandons their skill, their expertness in direction-finding, and particularly their ability to travel silently.

I could not tell the difference between solid and swamp sometimes, and went through to the thighs in the horrible mixture of the "stink-waters." I saw a procession of snakes, any one of which could have ended me; but luckily they slank away, more afraid than I was.

Happily, the homeward journey was cut short by the others coming out to meet me, cutting their way in all directions through the jungle. It was time enough; for three hours' fight with swamps and lianas are quite enough to take the joy out of life, especially when the very plants take a hand in the battle and sting and lash for the sheer pleasure of doing mischief. Gurra blisters were showing on me from wrist to neck, my shirt was ripped, and there were the evident traces of the strength of the thorns in every part of my clothing.

The Lacandon never returned to camp. I have often wondered, but was never able to discover, whether it was by accident or design that he tipped me over. Was he defending his gods, or just hating the white man on principle?

He had only given me first-hand experience of the swamps that protect the tiny tribe; and they are efficient to their task. I doubt if there is anything at once so beautiful and so foul as these remoter pitfalls of the jungle. Evil-looking certainly, in their cruder features, they are not without a strange and gigantic natural art. Water condenses and drips from the leaves, like a continual march of little men; the surface of the water is covered with a green scum that is not infrequently iridescent, catching the ghostly light and throwing it back in broken rays. There are pockets of gas which, suddenly released, throw an irresistible attack into the air; some dead creature has been caught and held, to inflate and distort itself to twice its natural size. I saw an alligator that might have been the world's greatest saurian, had he been alive. He was only preparing to disappear altogether from sight. A little longer and the pressure, even on his tough, dead hide, would be too much and he would go up in smoke and down in deadweight to the bottom of the ooze.

The humidity, of course, is insufferable, and pendent from the branches are strange little balloons; black balloons for the white ants, and white nests of the poisonous jungle wasp. Everywhere are bees and butterflies and the richest colourings of parasitic plants, with flowers that are the wreaths of the dead. Trees, uprooted, stand on their heads or lie on their sides, their stumpy roots showing above the surface like decayed molars. In the shadows, alligators lie in wait, and snakes in the patchy light.

Not until they are travelled alone, in a failing light with weariness creeping on, do the swamps show their real worst. I was glad enough when that particular bit of exploration had become only a memory.

After that, we had to pack up. We had had quite enough of the Lacandons, and I am sure that the feeling was mutual. We got on our way, and began the struggle back to the base camp, to receive a surprise that was almost shattering in its completeness.

Our pack animals, left to recover from their bruises and sores, had been ignored by the porters left in charge, and the real pest of Mexican travel had made rapid headway. The colymotes were tucked away in the sores of the mules, and Von Schmelling went berserk for a while.

The colymote is a white worm, with hairy bristles, ever on the look out for a kindly host, in the shape of man or animal, to give him refuge. He settles, when occasion serves, in a sore, and burrows down, until only his beady little eyes show, and there he stays, feeding on the animal, growing bigger and bigger, and breathing visibly in the sore, Three of the mules were a mass of the brutes; utterly useless. They would have been dead before long, had not Von Schmelling, with characteristic decision, made us turn to, bind and throw the animals, while he heated irons and began to work.

The worms had to be burned out of the poor devils' backs, and the doctor wasted no time: it was the choice of two evils for the mules, and the worms went. After the operation, he applied a balm, and the mules slowly recovered.

We were pretty well exhausted, all of us, and showed all the signs of what had been a hard journey. The porters were beginning to be disgruntled, and abandoned their customary silence, to move about, muttering among themselves. We made our way back, along the same trail, in a monotonous retreat.

So far as we knew, we were free from the threat of real rainstorms; but on the third day of our return march the evening was perhaps a bit too clear and fresh, yet nobody anticipated the downpour that hit us in the night, when everything was pitch black. Von Schmelling had roused at the first sound of rain, and only a few drops – but what drops! – had so far penetrated the foliage. Before the actual deluge, we were out and struggling, with our lamps belted to our foreheads, carrying the material to higher ground and covering the perishables as well as we could: at first in organized parties, and later every man for himself; for a solid wall of rain struck us with titanic force.

Sadleir and the camera-man collected their photographic apparatus. I trailed along loaded down with guns and ammunition enough for a small Mexican dispute. The rest came with stores, all ploughing knee-deep in water, so fast had the floods come.

When dawn broke we were only just finished, sitting disconsolate on the higher ground, waiting for the floods to subside. We had lost a certain amount of food, and some of our objects, and there we stayed all day, like tropical birds on their rocks; although some had courage to go swimming after saddles and lost articles among the undergrowth, while the porters scrambled among the lower branches of the trees, fishing for cases.

For eight hours the rain pelted down without pause, to vanish as suddenly as it had come: as though some heavenly fireman had turned it off at the main. Now, it was no joke traveling back, for the trail that had been just bearable became absolutely impossible. The downpour had turned the lowland into a vast morass, and we were driven again to the mountains, trying to reach the remains of an old Spanish settlement.

We still had to fight through the swamps for the better part of two days: desperate labour, with *macheteros* working in double shifts, while we dragged the pack animals through the water.

The porters came out in open revolt, saying that they would carry no more ammunition, and certainly not the heavy bones that we had collected in the Lacandon settlement. All they wanted to carry was food. Von Schmelling squashed the revolt, for a time at least, and we plodded steadily, if slowly along.

On one part of the trail that looked moderately solid, in patches it was necessary to take occasional jumps. One of the mules missed his take-off, perhaps because he was weary, and fell short into the slime, where we saw him disappear before our eyes. Although we halted immediately and cut poles and slung ropes, he was gone. That first slide was the last we saw of him. After that, all the animals were roped.

The owner of the mule instantly demanded payment. Cash on the spot. No promises, no arguments were availing against his obduracy, and he found ample support from the porters and *macheteros.* Failing payment, all animals and men would be called off and we could go to the devil in our own way and our own time. We paid, and ultimately gained the heights and followed the chain, resolved that there should be no more swamps if we could help it. The risk to human life was too great.

Mud-covered, we came out at El Capulin and its old chapel of the massacred priests – a pitiful monument, after two hundred years. It had been a mission station for operations among the Lacandons, more powerful and numerous in that day, and was now on the fringe of a village of the Bajahon Indians.

We were foul with slime. Martorell had malaria and dysentery. I got off lightly with malaria. Rothermel had hookworm. Sadleir was a mass of poisoned sores from the different bugs that had bitten him. The others were in little better plight, save Von Schmelling, who seemed capable of resisting anything. He was a man of iron, miraculously efficient, and as brutal as hell in his thoroughness. Like the rest of us, of course, he was a mass of wounds; but brisk and healthy. We were nearly flat.

Camp was made. Our clothes strung out in a line. Chickens and eggs and a pig or two were bought from the Bajahons, who had taken over the old chapel.

Von Schmelling saw to the damming of a fine, crystal-clear spring, to make a bathing-pool for us, and prepared his medicines.

When we were sufficiently recovered we began to take a little interest in the Bajahons, who were sufficiently in touch with the outside world to be quite different from the Lacandons. They were powerfully built: a hunting, fighting, thrusting tribe of fifty or sixty people, situated about four or five days' march from their nearest neighbours.

Every little while they went off on the trek to Ocosingo to carry their wares, which they exchanged with that most ubiquitous merchant of the world: a Greek trader. Failing the Greek, they went to an Armenian, and returned with the equivalent of their labours in alcohol, either consumed or to be consumed. Ocosingo was well over a hundred miles from their encampment, through thick and difficult jungle; but that was nothing to them.

We visited the chief, and although we had been announced, he seemed amazed to see us. Lying around in his tent were priceless skins of leopard, puma, and snake, numbers of idols in jade, and platters of gold.

I asked him if he considered it safe to leave such possessions unguarded, and there was not even a change of expression on his face as he replied "Why not? There are no white men within a hundred miles that I know of, except you..."

Naturally, I was interested by the sight of the gold. So was Rothermel, who was a keen speculator, and had ideas of developing the country. The Indians, secretive people, take their gold to Ocosingo and exchange it for a few supplies and a lot of drink.

From the chief we learned of ruins in the mountains, and of caves reputed to be the haunt of the dead. Caves like that always fire me. I have enough experience, by now, to know that when the natives talk of the haunts of the dead it is likely that some unexplained relics are in the neighbourhood.

So, naturally, we went afield, and lost one day in a wild-goose chase. The Bajahons took us slashing and cutting our way, without pause, for eight hours over the rough country to the top of a mountain, just to see a sheer wall of rock, perfectly natural in formation, which they called the "Iglesia."

Our disappointment may be imagined, and a little of our rage; but these things happen from time to time. Not every trail leads to a goal.

We did, however, circle the rock, and climbed it, to find nothing more than stones that perhaps had served as a sign in days gone by. Or, it may have been a sacrificial mountain. There was no means of determining the actuality. It did, however, serve to suggest that there might be something better in the vicinity.

The next day we asked to be taken to the caves, and we told the Indians that if there were no caves we would treat them as the Spaniards had treated their ancestors; but they only smiled. The caves turned out to be authentic.

The entrance was masked by creepers and a riot of gorgeous flowers, before which there was a small lake, fed by a natural spring. It would have made a splendid foyer for prehistoric man, and our hopes rose a little

Parting the curtain of creepers with our machetes, we were about to enter, when a *tomagoff* snake preferred to leave, to which we made no objection, and shot it; but ruined the skin with the shot.

The interior was covered with bat-dung in a thick layer, which meant no sleeping-quarters there!

Penetrating the cave, using our torches, we came to the most marvellous spectacle of natural beauty that any man could wish to see. Passing along an opening for about thirty yards, we looked through stalagmites and wild flowers which half-veiled the lake and the vivid carpet of jungle growth. Then, working with our alpenstocks, we cleared a space of the floor, and came upon Mayan remains, with thousands of pieces of pottery, among which were some jade beads. In a niche of the wall were bunches of torches of henequen fibre, which still functioned when we lit them. They must have been centuries old. But we saw that the Mayas had lived there. It might reasonably have been a cave of ceremonies. The ceiling was blackened with the smoke of a thousand fires. So, our appetites whetted, we decided to stay and explore the cave thoroughly, sending back a written message to Von Schmelling that we wanted other tools and supplies sent to us, sufficient for several days.

When the messengers had gone, we scouted around, and cut a few *sondages* below the Mayan stratum, finding several flints of the Neolithic period. Then Rothermel made a real discovery: a typical flint of pure solutrian workmanship. This was followed by laurel-leaf flints, with marvellous patina.

To me, it was a terrific moment. I can be roused to an excitement, by flints, comparable to the Spaniard's enthusiasm for a good bull. Here was something not too dissimilar from the stuff we had found in the Dordogne, and in Africa. I whooped with joy, and doubtless our remaining Indians thought I had gone completely crazy. The cave was a find. It had been used and lived in from time immemorial. We could hardly wait for the return of our men with implements and stores.

They, however, had six miles each way to travel; but towards evening they returned with a reply from the doctor, who said that other members of the expedition were on the point of departure for a settlement of Lacandons on the Rio Jetja: a three days' trek. So far as I was concerned, they could have their Lacandons! I had seen enough of the little people.

We, however, had prehistory, and found a considerable number of rock-drawings around a lagoon at the back of the cave.

Chapter 5

It was no fun working, however satisfactory the rewards, since the humidity was stifling and the mist oppressive, while the odour was such as would have moved Hercules to yet another feat. We worked in the gloom, with our lamps on our foreheads and our handkerchiefs round our nostrils and mouths.

Some bits of the writing bore a distinct resemblance to the Tifinar inscriptions of the Hoggar. Also, we recognized the Solar disk, and thought of Ammon Ra.

Below this disk had been placed a stone table, with a duct clearly visible, while above the disk was a badly-damaged head. The altar, which it assuredly was, had been cut out of the living rock, and was probably sacrificial.

As soon as we had our collapsible shovels, very like trenching tools, we got to work in earnest, with some of the Indians excavating and the remainder making us a suitable camp. Our hammocks were slung outside the cave: we liked neither the bats nor their perfume.

During the following days we uncovered the different layers. It was the first stratified cave discovered in Mexico, and included the Maya, pre-Maya, Neolithic, solutrian, and Mousterian civilizations. We found more than two dozen typical Mousterian *coup-de-poing* flints, which we have called "Chiapian," from the name of the State in which they were discovered, and hope that that name may ultimately be accorded to the type.

It was known, of course, that Engerrand and Urbino had found, and brought back to Europe, specimens of stone hatchets from the shores of Lake Peten in Guatemala, similar to the Chellean period of palæolithic man in North Africa; but these seemed to me to offer a closer identification.

The theory of Mexican civilization often put forward is that the Mongols came down from China by way of the Bering Straits, traveling south through the cold and waste of Alaska and Northern Canada; but why they should leave warmth to travel through inhospitable regions, leaving practically no traces on the way, and then appear suddenly in another warm climate, thousands of miles from their original haunts, seems to ask for more explanation than is usually given. To me, it does not seem exactly reasonable.

However, finding palæolithic flints here showed that man, in this region of America, was much older than had been believed, and that the possibility of an independent, autochthonic civilization is not entirely to be dismissed.

When we had finished our work in the cave, we loaded down the mules and obliterated as far as possible the traces of our work, leaving only a cylinder, with a report of the discovery, buried under the bat-droppings of the floor, marked the cave on the map, and took bearings, for our report to the Mexican Government.

The gifts we gave to the Indians for their share in the work roused their friendliness to such an extent that as we travelled back to camp they told us that "if we were interested in stones" they would show us others on the mountains.

So, instead of going directly back to El Capulin, we made a detour, and sure enough found pre-Maya ruins on the mountainside. Here is country good enough for a permanent archaeological camp for ten years or more, thoroughly equipped. The ruins were pre-Mayan without a doubt, and in themselves traced much of the history of mankind. Man was emerging from his fear, becoming more courageous, more skilled in defence. Evolution was plainly at work. Just as we had seen in the Atlas, and in Tripolitania, there were camps on the hill-tops, with comparatively huge edifices.

Before we returned to the camp, we had found traces of cave-man, cyclopean, and Mayan constructions, followed by the mud-brick period and the degenerate hovels of the post-Mayan people, who built in the lightest possible fashion; namely with leaves. The Lacandons, it would appear, are in the direct line of descent, and of degeneracy.

We photographed the ruins, and made our way back to El Capulin, just as the other half of the expedition came in from their visit to the Lacandon settlement.

They had had enough, more than enough, and were nearly all-in. Soustelle, Casa y Mier, Don Lopez, and Bieler went back on the homeward trail, with their half of the animals and stores, and we were sorry to lose Fritz. He was a real companion of the trail. As to the others, they were not so accustomed to the demands such travel made.

The camera-man was as dead-beat as the rest of us; but he definitely refused to show any signs of weariness. His job was to take pictures, and he certainly did his job. He was splendid. It takes real guts to work as he did, with his eyes nearly closed from weariness, and that massive camera to operate.

So we were left: Britishers, Americans, and that rugged Prussian who would have died without a murmur, to carry on without a representative of the noble Red Republic. But we missed Fritz.

We gave him our letters, and took a sad farewell, after having spent a day in writing to everybody we knew, and dealing with a strike among the Indians, who all wanted to go back with the return party, preferring the easy life of the hacienda, and asking nothing better than a chance to spend some of their wages.

Even so, Von Schmelling managed to drive a little light relief into us, who were secretly somewhat envious of the returning travellers.

He lifted our spirits, by one means or other, and we were again on our way.

But what an effort it cost to respond to his familiar "Vamanos!" We were tired men already. We knew more or less what faced us, and what might reasonably be expected; but we did not expect the half of what we found. Our mules began to give out, to be abandoned in the care of their Indian owners. Our porters filtered away in the silence of the night, or even on the march. All that could happen, happened.

Our route was to a small lagoon which we had marked from the air, lying, as far as we could judge, two days' march from the monastery, and, as we went, the Indians showed us the traces of their gold-washing.

Riding down a canyon, leading to the jungle below, we saw many places where the gold was definitely identifiable by the points of "colour," and Sadleir, practical as ever, marked out different claims, and mapped them, collecting specimens and carrying them with him for analysis in Mexico City. They proved rich in gold content, and he may yet profit by his foresight.

It is not a difficult matter, prospecting for gold in this part of the country. Nor is it even necessary to go to outlandish places. Prospecting is one of the joys of Mexican life, and all that seems necessary is to find a few thousand dollars, hire mules and Indians, and send them on scouting expeditions, camp in the dry season in these gullies, and collect the spoils. The ore is crushed secretly, to escape Governmental tax, and, after the season's work the prospectors reappear, to make the traditional "whoopee" in Mexico City or Havana. Preferably, in Havana.

We camped ultimately on the shores of our lake, which we had named Marcelle Prat (the discovery and charting belonged to the expedition), in a situation difficult to beat for beauty. The jungle, heavy behind us, waved gently in the breeze. The placid water reflected the glint of a thousand stars, the air was alive with fireflies, and as the darkness deepened we had the added joy of the night-flowering jasmine.

The only discordant note – and it was enough – was the cry of the howling monkeys, who were excited by our arrival and persisted in raising their bedlam of sounds: the hoarse cough and snarl, which sounded very like the roar of the puma.

Next day storm-clouds seemed threatening. I asked our guide what he thought of the weather. His answer was so typical of the country that it is worth recording.

"Perhaps it will rain, señor. Perhaps it will not rain. Most probably maybe. But who knows?"

We were spared the downpour, and the only incident of the day's march was that a falling tree knocked me out. The trees, sometimes, seem to be strongly rooted; but often it is only pretence. They are held up by others, and when our *macheteros* cut a way through the jungle this particular tree lurched forward, and I happened to be in its path.

Thereafter, our way lay across undulating hills of vivid forest, with no sign of human habitation, save that, occasionally, and very rarely, we passed an abandoned Lacandon village whose people had either seen us afar off, or were on a raid to their neighbours, ten days' march away, hunting for women.

We were beginning to suffer from saddle-sores and the continual jolting made us occasionally take to our feet. Sadleir, who was on foot, ahead, looking for game, suddenly turned about, and began to race for the company, his face fully expressive of his fright. He had been walking along in a dream when a "bush-whacker" snake had attacked him.

This is one of the few snakes that does not hesitate to attack, and its attack is with its tail, which acts as a powerful flail and whips its victim into insensibility.

Sadleir was no coward; but he had heard enough from the Indians about this snake to make him take no chances. And sure enough, it followed.

Some of us shot it with our revolvers, while others gave the finishing touches with alpenstocks. It measured between seven and eight feet in length; no giant, but certainly an uncomfortable fellow. Thereafter, Sadleir kept to his saddle, as did the rest of us, despite our sores; but just the same, there were times when we had to dismount, and I, perhaps a little hurried, trod on a grey fellow that I had not seen, to receive a smashing blow just above the ankle. I was wearing boots, so the blow was harmless.

Of these boots I was a little vain; they had belonged to a Mexican General, and had been bought for me in the thieves' market of Mexico City. What I did not know until later was that they were the boots the General had worn when he went to his death against the wall. Still, they were lovely boots!

Day by day, our only experiences were the monotonous clearing of the path, and an increasing weariness, until one day while we were still camped among a beautiful chain of water-falls and tiny lakes, fringed with a mass of wild flowers and orchids, we heard a loud roar overhead, and saw our planes cir-cling, looking for us. Fritz had come to say "goodbye," with Casa y Mier.

We fired our rocket, to indicate location, and the planes dipped and circled, until they were not more than a hundred yards above the forest, and we could see Fritz waving.

Then, traveling up and down, following the undulations, we began to strike the vast timber forests, with every day's march offering variety. Sometimes we would be among great cotton-woods and at others traveling through aisles of gigantic, majes-tic mahogany, with Rothermel and me bringing up the rear, hunting orchids for his collection.

Altogether, on his journey, he found fifty specimens of dif-ferent characteristics, to him more precious than gold, intended for the University of Pennsylvania; but, such is the waywardness of life, when he finally reached the Mexican border on the way home, all the specimens were impounded by the United States Customs, for fear that he should introduce some new plant dis-ease and ruin the crops.

Thousands of orchids lay on our trail; blooms worth real money to the florists of Fifth Avenue or Bond Street; not exactly waste, for we enjoyed their beauty; but lost to people who would have been delighted to wear them.

For some days we had discovered practically nothing, and drove on in dead monotony, on and on to the Usumacinta and, we hoped, to rest; but one night we camped on the top of a hill as we thought, and the next morning were beginning to pack up and take the trail again, when suddenly Hayman, who had been nosing about, gave us a call.

A giant mahogany, blown down by some gale or other, had brushed a clear space in its fall, and had uncovered a section of wall that was evidently of human construction. Unawares, we had actually camped on the mound of a pyramid. There was no thought of continuing that day. The men and mules that had already started were recalled. Hammocks were slung again, and camp re-established. Pickaxes and shovels were soon at work, and we found that we had a whole city at our feet, with temples, houses, and stone walls covered by jungle growth.

One temple, nearly a hundred feet high was mapped, and we passed to another on the side of a hill. We found that there were actually three temples, and decided to dig into one as far as we could, to make a sectional investigation.

While the men were put to work removing stones and debris, to see if there were chambers or tombs accessible, I went to the base of the hill, and had the thrill of cutting away jungle, cactus, and thorn, to uncover a frieze with figures, heads, hands, and eyes of a high priest of the Mayas. The colouring was still visible, in red and blue and green.

We stayed on the spot for three days, cutting down the jungle to right and left, so that the site could be properly photographed. From the massive trees that were growing on the ruins, they must have been in that state for three or four hundred years.

The small temples were opened, and we found rooms about fifteen feet square, in which we decided to work, discovering that one of the rooms must have been coated with opals, flattened and embedded in cement. One small section of the wall-covering I was able to preserve and carry away. I judged that the walls had been so covered in order to reflect the light during the ceremonies of the temple, and to throw it, possibly, on to the god of the central altar.

In that room also we found a skull, badly rotted and powdered; the teeth had been replaced by opals. Whether this had been done in life or after death it was impossible to say.

There was a jade mask of a face, intact: there must have been many at one time, for we found fragments; but whether they had been destroyed willfully or not, when the city was abandoned, could not be determined. Some clay figurines, which were intact, we were able to remove, and found that they included most of the Mayan gods: Chacmool (the Mayan Bacchus); Tlaloc (the god of rain); and Huitzipotli (god of war).

Vases and vessels lying about proved to contain the remains of ceremonial libations, and there were sherds of well-worked pottery whose colour and design showed perfect art.

Painted peacocks, headdresses and plumes of the priests were equal to anything that has been discovered in the Nile valley, and one object in particular was of exquisite workmanship: a small skull in crystal, similar to the one now preserved in the National Museum in Mexico City.

The place must have been abandoned hurriedly, and late into the night we sat round the camp fire working it out, each advancing his own theory. What had happened to the Mayas? Where had they gone? What had wiped them out so thoroughly?

Perhaps the frieze on the walls of the temple of Uxmal at Chichen Itza may hold the secret: the picture of a mound of dead, and men taken with the plague – the black vomit.

Certainly the edifices seldom look as though they had suffered at the hands of the invaders. Breakages seem to be the deliberate work of the inhabitants.

We dug down into two more mounds, which were clearly burial-places, and recovered flints which were strikingly like those of the Fayum, and almost identical in form and workmanship with those of the Sahara. One especially magnificent object, which would have brought joy to any collector's heart, was a beautiful obsidian sacrificial knife, found on the top of a ruin next to a stone basin. Certainly it must have been used for the sacrifice of prisoners of war taken by the ancient Mayas.

Finally, having an eye to our stores, we were compelled to leave the site, although regretfully, and took the trail again towards the Usumacinta, plodding on day after day, and finding the ruins ever more numerous, with mounds right and left, impossible for us to excavate. All we could do was to mark them on the map, and occasionally, when we were fortunate, dig into one at the halts and find an approximate date.

Of the Lacandons we were unable to find a trace, beyond their deserted camps, and one old man who had been too feeble to run at our approach. He was too utterly senile to give us any information. These southern Lacandons were more fugitive, more frightened; unapproachable in the time we had to spare. We tried; but failed, leaving gifts and food in the village, before the house which seemed to belong to the head man. The next day, when we returned, nothing had been touched.

All we could drag out of the old man, and that very uncertainly, was that for days and days they had known of our coming, and had fled.

Then began the tedious crossing of the tributaries of the Usumacinta river, which necessitated the constant unloading and loading of the mules and the slow cartage of our cases, with men and animals roped. Sometimes, by chance, we would find that a great tree had fallen, to make a natural bridge.

The signs of a vast and departed civilization increased as we made headway. There were mounds on either side of our trail, all, doubtless, worth close investigation; but which had to be ignored, for we had not provisioned ourselves any too liberally and it was necessary to keep going towards the river with some attempt at speed. We might have been fugitives ourselves.

Not only an ancient, but a modern civilization had suffered. We passed through the abandoned camps of the Indian mahogany-cutters. Everything seemed ready for their return, as though they were simply gone on a journey. Great boles of trees, fine logs, taken to the trail ready to be hauled to the river; saws, machinery, stores, and even banjos had been left lying there, haphazard.

World crisis, changing taste, or some other little-suspected calamity had descended on these wood-cutters. One day, they found that there was no demand for luxury woods, and they just had not come back; their money was exhausted.

It may not be altogether an evil thing, for the Indians were being spoiled by the money they made. Chicleros (gum-hunters) and Monteros (wood-cutters) had made a relay race to the dogs. They would work for high wages and a little time, then would "work one season and lay off three" because they could afford it. Drink and high living, in imitation of the whites, was killing them off. Some of the villages had been depleted of their women, because the women preferred to follow these "million-aires" into the woods.

Finally, a perceptible increase in the abundance of natural life indicated our near approach to the river. The trees were full of brilliant birds of wonderful plumage; flashes of scarlet, indigo, vivid yellows and blues greeted us whenever we looked up. The parrots chattered and screeched. Camp at night was infernal, with the many voices of the jungle. Monkeys of all sorts, jaguar, pumas with their snarling cough, otters, raccoons, tapir, and, of course, deer were abundant, and we had some good night hunting, both for the pot and for sport, bagging one or two jaguars and a fine puma.

We came through to the bamboo, and cut our way out, to see the magnificent expanse of the river Usumacinta, across which lay the country that is in a state of perpetual revolution: Guatemala, where lay our next stage, the Piedras Negras camp of the University of Pennsylvania.

It took us the whole of the next day to cross the river with our animals and stores. Seeking along the banks, we came to an Indian village, from which we borrowed two dug-outs to which the mules were tied, three or four at a time, and ferried across.

In camp on the other side, we wondered how Cortez with his army had crossed the river, somewhere to the south of us. It was inconceivable that men in armour, with horses, equipment, and small cannon could perform such a feat.

We were anxious to see Piedras Negras, the wonderful city that was being excavated and has been fairly well advertised, and to gain time made an attempt at night marching. Our stores were fast diminishing anyway, and speed was imperative.

The whole trail was lined with relics of that past age. We seemed to be traveling through the suburbs of a great metropolis, with a wide frontage to the river; but the trail was long and uncertain, and the leading party arrived in camp while we who came later were still examining a mound that seemed more interesting than usual.

We were beginning to believe that we had lost the trail when a search party sent out by Professor Satterthwaite met us and led us home. The others had arrived hours earlier, and had dined in comfort; but as we rode into camp we were received with shouts and cheers and the many drums of the Indian workmen, helped down, and whisked away to a well-laden table where dinner was awaiting us. Everybody was hilarious. The effect of a couple of drinks of the real stuff was overwhelming. Then we realized how tired we were! So tired that not even this magnificent excavation could rouse us until we had slept ourselves out.

Piedras Negras is the site of a truly spectacular city, spread in a semicircle facing the river, with the jungle behind. It seemed almost incongruous, there, to receive news of depression, tragedy, and crisis, We had come to the ruins of the old world to hear of the collapse of the new.

The city was wonderful enough by day, with gigantic pyramids, temples, and palaces of a strange and faery beauty, fine architecture and historic significance, with the forest all cleared and controlled; but by moonlight, when the great curve of a past civilization swept indomitably to the river, softly illumined, the shadows vibrant and the walls gleaming like beaten metal, it was unreal: the fiction of a happy, but disordered brain.

Day by day the work went forward methodically, almost monotonously, and the boredom of the "regulars" must have increased with dissociation from the world and the inability to do anything unusual and a little strange. Half – no, more than half the joy of it all lies in discovery, in acting as a sort of pathfinder to the serious, solid, useful, accurate people who tabulate and tabulate and sketch and photograph, and wring the last drop of juice from the archaeological orange for the possible benefit of future generations and the acquisition of another academic distinction. Occasionally, of course, there are archaeologists of the greatest, most stupendous standing, who have not yet forgotten the thrill that comes to eye and heart, and can bring the dead to living reality. But how much we ordinary mortals miss because the account of these massive, majestic monuments is presented to the world as so many stones, measuring so many centimetres, covered with inscriptions engraved to a depth of so many millimetres!

Piedras Negras was all that it ought to have been, in science and in beauty, and I left it reluctantly, feeling that I had been lifted. But we had to go, there was still a long way before us.

We had forgotten that we were in a new country, that we had come from one storm centre to the birthplace of all political storms, and before we had travelled far we were under arrest. Our passports had been overlooked! They were somewhere – but where? That was a question we asked and could not answer. The local Guatemalan official – booted, spurred, and silver-plated, with silver ornaments even on his sombrero – twirled a nasty moustache and spat questions at us. We had not guessed the answers.

We tried, however, to explain that we had been exploring the Lacandon country and making an investigation among the tribes. That was like powder on the fire. It was so unbelievable that the real story must be that we were incendiary revolutionaries or escaping murderers. We were promptly booked for prison in the capital, where there would be people capable of taking care of us.

Von Schmelling, as usual, came to the rescue with his unfailing and successful bluff.

"Do you know who this is?" he demanded of the bejeweled half-wit, dragging me forward. "This is the son of the King of France...and you know what would happen if France laid hands on the son of your President..."

The embryonic General scratched his head. This was a serious moment. He had the keeping of the welfare of Guatemala in his hands.

"No," he said, slowly, deliberately, ponderously. "I don't suppose it would be profitable to us to go to war with the King of France..."

We were on our way, to the old cry "Vamonos!" down to the river and across it again; that boundary of the shuttlecocks of revolution. And it was high time, for our men were deserting in increasing numbers, some for fear of the revolutionaries who undoubtedly were in hiding in the neighbourhood and lived as they could, waiting for their misdeeds to be forgotten or to bear fruit and another battle to begin. Some were paid off; others simply decamped, taking the mules with them.

There we took our farewell of the doctor. Never was a man more blessed by companionship than I had been by the presence of Von Schmelling. I should like to pay my tribute to him here. Men like him are rare, they come singly. He had been doctor, guide, encouragement, and rest to us. He had cursed us all; but he had cured us all, and asked for little enough in return. Bellicose, Prussian, downright; but gentle on occasion; when extremes had to be accepted, he did not flinch. I have seen his drawn face tortured by want of sleep while he thought for the rest of us, and any sympathy was met by that reiterated cry "Vamonos!"

With him went the last handful of mules and porters. He was to fight his lonely way along the trail, a little more directly perhaps; but still not agreeably, back to Ocosingo.

We tied our instruments into canoes, and went down-stream, shooting the rapids as we went, to the first outpost of civilization, Tenosique, which we reached after passing through gorges which confined, cramped, and enraged the river.

The country was a virgin paradise for hunters; the river was alive with fish. We did not trouble even to throw a net or line for food, but potted the big fellows with revolvers. And they were obliging. If we missed, they came again, to see what it was all about.

We expected news of the Red Governor of Tabasco at Tenosique, for he was coming to take us to the tomb of Guatemoc; but none had come through, so we went on to Monte Cristo (now renamed Emiliano Zapata), and there we heard. The Governor had put trucks at our disposal to take us to Palanque, the Athens of America.

We were about six hours on the outward trail before we came suddenly upon what looked like medieval walls, as though a castle had been dumped down here by Simon de Montfort; and thereafter followed a panorama of temples, one of which we chose for our headquarters, leaving the trucks in an Indian village not far away.

Palanque proved to be of surpassing beauty and interest. One of the most amazing things of Mayan civilization was there: a complete canalization through the city of the clear waters of a stream that came from the mountains above. The narrow canals flowed past the very doors of the houses, and through the squares. The drains were intact in many places.

Our temple was covered with sculptures, and there was a native guardian, whom we asked to pose (and insulted by the request) alongside the frescoes: his face was almost a duplicate of the grinning, hook-nosed god, even to the receding forehead and lantern jaws.

There we lived for several days, thrilled one evening by the sudden bursting of a tropical thunderstorm. Before the rain fell, solid clouds banked behind the ruins; thick, ominous, like a distant velvet curtain. Lightning reft the clouds from time to time; but they fell back again, still whole. The ruins glowed in the spasmodic light. The jungle beyond waved like a slow sea beginning to stir in anger.

The forest had been cleared to some extent from the ruins, but there were still great trees which had kept their hold and were splitting monuments that may well prove to be priceless relics. It was heartbreaking to see the impending ruin. Works of great art were in grave danger. Frescoes were being scorched to a colourless monotony by the glare of the sun.

Fortunately, our report to the Mexican Government resulted in the dispatch of a well-equipped expedition, three months later, and, whatever else our exploration may have accomplished, for one thing we can take a little credit: Palanque will fall into no greater ruin.

Having surveyed and photographed the city, which was all that time permitted, we returned to our cars, to find that in some mysterious fashion they had all broken down, and were useless for the return journey, which we made on horseback, taking thirteen hours on the trail to Monte Cristo.

The cycle was almost complete. We were lodged in Monte Cristo as I had been lodged in Ocosingo, in a bawdy house. But we were unaware of that. As soon as we saw a floor, we slept on it, oblivious of all that went on round us, and in the morning suffered the wrath of the proprietress.

"You come here," she said. "We take you in. We give you tea and wine to drink..."

Had she? We wondered. I had no recollection of drinking any tea or wine; but it might have happened.

"And you do not look at my beautiful girls. They are the nicest, the most loving girls in all Mexico..."

That meant nothing to us; but in her protests she had mentioned fetching ice. Ice! We learned that there was an ice-plant in the city, and promptly paid our modest bill and vamoosed, to guzzle ice-cream like schoolboys until, like them also, we felt a little ill.

The people of the town were terrified when we came back without the cars, fearing the red vengeance of the Red Governor when he heard about it; but we sent back a mechanic to put them in order and bring them safely to town, while we were waiting for the Governor's yacht, which was to take us along the river to Canizan, to the tomb reputed to be that of Guatemoc.

It is probably the tomb of that Mexican hero. The boat duly arrived; but not the Governor. He was attending a conference of the various State Governors, and sent us word that he would like us to survey and photograph the tomb and make a report on it.

Magnificently we floated down the river, guests of that most excellent man of the people. Everywhere we touched we found that our advance had been well notified. Fiestas and dances and glorious hospitality awaited us.

In two days we reached Canizan, and found an Indian chief waiting to act as guide, and we went to the historic mound, not risking to make an excavation in the absence of the Governor, who clearly regarded it as his own property. The natives, however, produced some splendid statuettes in jade and other stone, which had been found in the neighbourhood of the tomb, and explained that its size was due to the fact that Indians on pilgrimage brought stones to add to the monument of their hero.

Every indication seemed to point to its authenticity, and our disappointment at the absence of the Governor was real; we should have liked to spend a few days opening it up. There ought to be real treasure in the tomb.

We had completed our tour; when we returned we were received with great cordiality. There was a banquet, at which even the wine was red.

Our finds, documentation and stores, our cameras and photographs, and, finally, we ourselves, were packed into a plane sent by the Pan-American Airways, to take us back to Mexico City; and again the scientists are preparing to publish the detailed report of our finds. I believe there will be something to write about, in that same detail; but my eyes most frequently seek the splendour of the sacrificial knife, which paradoxically links so many threads in that old land, and has at once the touch of beauty and the threat of a merciless cult.

PART IV

IN SEARCH OF KING SOLOMON'S MINES AND THE LOST LAND OF OPHIR

PERSONNEL OF THE EXPEDITION, UNDER THE AUSPICES OF THE IMPERIAL ETHIOPIAN GOVERNMENT

* COUNT BYRON DE PROROK Director

ING. T. "PASTOLINI "   CAPT. N. HILLIER
* W. H. KHUN   DR. P. CHADOURNE
* W. HAYMAN   M. DE JOUVENEL
* H. ROTHERMEL   M. P. AGID
 * N. ELLSWORTH-BROWNE

* REACHED ADDIS ABABA

Chapter 1

One trail crosses another. I had found gold ornaments in the excavations of Carthage, Utica, the French Hoggar; gold in Jupiter Ammon; gold at Oueddan in Libya. The question was now one of origin: could the source be traced?

There are no known gold deposits within easy reach of the Saharan regions; but ancient historians spoke of the Land of Ophir. Moreover I had covered many of the old trails whose indications seemed coincident with those of the historians, and I judged that an expedition to Ethiopia might be productive of results. The logical site of Ophir and the gold deposits seemed to be there: in the region of the Blue Nile and the mountains of Western Ethiopia.

Before leaving Paris, through the Ethiopian Legation the projected expedition was officially detailed to His Majesty Haila Sillasiei, since there were two great obstacles to be overcome.

The first was the closed area of the British Sudan bordering the Ethiopian frontier. The second was that we proposed entering Ethiopia by the back door. Other expeditions had gone by way of Addis Ababa, traveling by rail from Djibouti.

We were compelled to wait until the Abyssinian Government had gone very thoroughly into the project before we could even begin the organization of the expedition, for no one may travel through the realms of His Ethiopian Majesty without a personal passport issued by the Emperor. This meant that passports and a military escort would need to be sent to us on the frontier, a thousand kilometers from the capital.

Permission was finally given, and we were assured that passports, permits for our guns, and a military escort would meet us at Kurmuk, the British frontier station.

We travelled up the Nile by private boat to the Sudan, well furnished with documents from the officials and a personal letter of recommendation from Lord Tyrrell. They were all needed, since all previous expeditions, including those of the French, German, and Italian explorers, had been refused permission to cross the closed area.

Reaching Asswan, trouble began, on account of our guns and ammunition. We found that a treaty was operative which meant that no guns were allowed to pass from the Sudan into our projected territory except under permit. All our arms were sequestrated until this permit came from Addis Ababa.

We also learned that there was trouble on the frontier, due to raids, of which we received more details later.

The British authorities told us that the Ethiopians were great on promises, if a little weak in performance; delay was inevitable, although arrangements had been made six months in advance. Guns would certainly not be allowed; the promise of a permit was not enough. The escort was guaranteed; but as certainly would not arrive. And, as a final sinister warning we were told that the last expedition of the Trocadero that tried to get through landed in jail for three weeks, simply because they got tired of waiting for passports.

So, I lost half my expedition, people who would have been happy to continue had things been "different." The rest of us decided to take a chance of blasting through. We would have a shot at it, get as far as we could, and see what happened.

The raids complicated things for us, for the Abyssinians are constantly trying to get guns, and there is, perhaps naturally, some illicit effort made to supply the demand. Moreover, whenever a body of game, particularly elephants, crosses over into British territory the hunters also try to follow, for ivory is a precious commodity. And, should a batch of slaves make a breakaway for freedom and the British flag, that old man of the

mountains, Ghogoli, sultan of the Bani Shanqul, as naturally
makes an understandable if not particularly successful effort to
prevent their escape.

For this reason, the area from Roseires to Kurmuk is a closed
military area.

However, having decided to go through, we busied ourselves
during our enforced stay in Khartoum with the practical details
of organization.

I had been put into touch with a Greek, who happened also to
be a hotel proprietor, and he, not without two eyes to the main
chance, dilated on the delays that were essential. Delay meant an
augmented hotel bill, and his greatest trouble was to find mules
and bearers. These, he insisted, could not be obtained on the
frontier; but he could find some for us, given time and a price.
That meant a long stay in Khartoum, and Khartoum is an expen-
sive city.

We were in the hands of the Greeks. War began. Thoroughly
exasperated, I applied to Mr. Coxen, the editor of the Sudan
Daily Herald, and a man of real friendship. Through him, I
made contact with a character who ought to have existed certainly not later than Prester John.

I have had some tremendous fellows on expedition with me,
men of all nations; but never have I seen his like. Nor shall I
ever again. He was a miracle.

Let us call him Pastolini. That is not his own name; but for
certain reasons let us leave it at that. They who need to know his
name, know it well enough. For the rest, any name will serve
equally well.

To meet him, since he was not at that moment desirous of
undue publicity, I was escorted to a small cafe in a by-way, and
there learned what "electric personality" means. He was a com-
bination of most of the virtues of a pioneer; he was respectful of,
without unduly respecting, the law; he was cunning, wiry, elusive, full of wiles; but I liked him on sight.

Small, with the most penetrating eyes imaginable, he was a
mixture of condottieri and vandal attributes; a Don Juan and a

Don Quixote, with more than a touch of the fire of a Garibaldi and a way with opposition that was final, if not always charming.

At that moment he had nearly all the city against him because of his various activities in trade and in love. All the women loved him: he was legendary in a pioneer country. He would disappear broke to the wide, and reappear temporarily as rich as Croesus.

All the men hated him, because he could not only charm the women, but could play the men's game in trade. The Greeks and Armenians were roused to fanaticism by his mere presence. For body-guard, when I was presented, he had three huge negroes standing by, brandishing murderous shillelaghs, and explained that he was so much adored by the ladies that the men were not above making a combined attack on him, and, since he was somewhat short of stature, he felt it advisable to have protection. I wondered: were we in Chicago, or in a disciplined British possession?

I had been told, probably at the instigation of his enemies, that he was suspected of every nefarious trade and habit man could devise, and I mentioned these reports to him. He did not trouble to deny the imputation; but merely shrugged his shoulders, and the charges simply fell away.

He had a decided manner in trade. The Greeks had showed me a telegram saying that there were neither mules nor porters at the frontier. He discovered that instructions had been sent to the agent to dispatch just such a telegram.

I was out of the hands of the Greeks almost before I could turn round. He was a cyclone and a tidal wave. What he could not blow up he submerged in a flood of speech that could not be dammed save by agreement.

Mules materialized on the frontier; but the Greeks still smiled as they approached, washing their hands. We should need trucks to carry us on our first stage. They had the trucks, which we could hire at twenty-five pounds each. I told Pastolini.

"No! No!" he ejaculated. "I can grab three cars for no more
than the cost of the petrol"

"You are not joking?"

"I nevaire joke!"

It was no joke; they were the cars waiting for some prospecting party, which would be arriving in three weeks. Our trip
could be made and the cars returned before the need for them
arose.

Back to the hotel again, to explain courteously to the Greeks
that I should not need their cars. They scratched their heads and
sniffed. Was it possible that they had already scented the air of
Pastolini?

They tried again. I should need rations for my party. They
had arranged to get me a fine price, guaranteed to be a 50 per
cent. reduction on list prices. It was all because they liked to deal
with such a nice gentleman, who was going to take a long journey and might never come back.

Once more to Pastolini, with the list and prices. He did not
bother to comment. After he had run a grimy finger and a keen
eye down the list he tore it up.

"I'll get them on credit for you, if you like, at half those
prices..."

We compromised between credit and the Greeks, and I paid
half their price; but this refusal to trade had them frothing at the
mouth. A better price was impossible. Half-price was robbery: I
had bought stolen goods.

They were thoroughly suspicious by this time, and I was
given to understand that they sent messages to those in authority
that my expedition was not all it seemed to be; but had an ulte-
rior and sinister motive. Wherefore I was invited by those
authorities to discuss the matter officially, since every member
of the party would need a special permit to go through the closed
area, and the inference was that if I were taking Pastolini there
might be...doubt.

Still, they confirmed my own idea that he knew Ethiopia
well; none better. There was not a pass through the mountains

that he could not find. He was a great explorer; a fine man in a crisis.

So much was immediately conceded; but I could see that there were other thoughts, not altogether without humour, behind that official mask of a face. I was advised to be careful, and I replied that I was between the devil and the deep sea, and of the two I preferred the devil that I knew to the deep sea of the Greeks, which I did not want to know too well. And I had a strong feeling that Pastolini *was* the man to get us through.

Officialdom relented. They have a fine sense of adventure, and a better sense of sportsmanship, these marooned Britishers on the frontiers, and I was simply told that if Pastolini went it would be on my own responsibility; that whatever he did would be my look out...and all that that meant. So I got my permit for him, with the strict injunction that I was to be careful not to be employed by him for his purposes. He was to be my man.

All this I related in detail to Pastolini, and he did not raise even a murmur of protest. Certainly, he had done some things in his time that men might regard with unkind eyes; but he was my man, reserving only a remote and doubtless profitable corner of his loyalties for his own affairs.

Finally, after spending about a hundred pounds in sending telegrams all over the place seeking our passports and permits, we left with everything in order save the most important things of all: the Emperor's passport; the announcement that the escort had arrived at the frontier; and permission to go armed through a wild country.

So we departed, with the world laughing slightly, and the Greeks mysterious and annoyed. In the night we loaded our equipment, and pulled out at about one o'clock in the morning, to escape the attention of any who should want to take a last look at Pastolini.

We were worried by the absence of guns; but there was nothing we could do about that, so we put up a good show, even to the hotel proprietor who presented our bills in person, and smiled.

"All right, all right," he murmured. "See you back in ten days. I'll keep your rooms for you!"

Our first stage was Sennar, where we made a detour to visit the mysterious Djebel Moya, where again I did something that I ought not to have done; but it is impossible to keep always within the narrow channel marked by two lines of red-tape.

In Khartoum I had heard talk of strange happenings at Djebel Moya. It was a favourite topic of speculation; but not a shred of real information could be got beyond the fact that it was a site of secret excavations.

Djebel Moya is a sort of Rock of Gibraltar standing out of the Sudanese desert to the north-east of the Blue Nile, and it seemed that digging had been going on there, at enormous cost, excavating a whole city if rumour were to be believed. It was commonly said that at least two thousand sealed cases of objects had been shipped down the Nile to England, and nobody knew what was in them.

Hoping that persuasion would suffice to obtain permission to view the excavation, I had obtained an introduction to the guardian from the Museum authorities in Khartoum, and a letter had been sent on, stating the approximate time of our arrival.

I was in greater hope of success when I learned that the curator of the site was a Venezuelan Revolutionary who had been rescued from a firing party in the very nick of time and transplanted to this safe place. I could tell him at first hand some of the things that were going on. He might be interested in the progress of ideas in South American Republics.

We crossed that land that Kitchener called "devastation, desolation, and damnation" and, traveling through the Sudan brush, up from the Nile, we saw the Djebel Moya standing boldly out in splendid isolation.

At the base of the mountain we were met by an armed guard, who bristled like a brigand, and whom we informed that we were going to see the General. The first guard signaled another guard, also armed to the teeth, and we followed a stone path carved out of the rock, suddenly to find ourselves facing an amazing edifice like one of the houses of Oz.

They had collected together enormous boulders, and built them into a mighty fortress. Each stone must have weighed tons, and I rubbed my eyes, to be sure that there was no distortion, that such a building really did exist. It did; and then I thought of the cost of it all.

There was a narrow doorway, with an iron grill through which visitors were examined before admission. We suffered the gaze of beady eyes and the door opened, whereupon we were greeted by the South American "General," who was an excellent specimen of the Revolutionary type: squat, sunburned, dark-eyed, with charming manners and 75 per cent. Indian blood.

He swept his sombrero across his chest and bowed, saying that he had had word from Mr. Coxen that an explorer coming from South America would be passing that way.

Contact with his own country had worked! It was my passport to the serene presence of Uriburu.

Imagine, in the heart of British Sudan, being greeted by an exiled Revolutionary!

He ushered us into a great room, with a vast, high ceiling, which might have been inspired by the monumental ruins of Karnak.

The room was dim. Perhaps our eyes would get used to it; it might have been only the contrast, for the sun was blinding outside. At the moment, there seemed to be a bluish light pervading the building; but I distinguished sculptured stone tables and leopard skins, a few chairs, comfortable if roughly made. We were seated. A meal was in preparation for us.

I noticed a great staircase, leading down to the bowels of the earth. Pretending that I needed to absent myself, for purely natural reasons, I contrived to reach that staircase, and saw cases piled high in the cellars; but, before I could wander far, our urbane host was at my side, quietly showing me the proper direction.

They were very close, those caretakers; but I had seen enough to tell me that here was a work of the most gigantic proportions. The place was perfectly equipped; the draughtsmen's tables and photographs told their tale.

I proceeded as the "General" indicated, hoping on my way to find another door or two which might gently be opened, for I was burning with curiosity. Every doorway was guarded by a burly negro. This was theatrical archaeology. It might easily have been a stage-setting.

We were all assembled again. A meal in keeping with the grandeur of the camp was immaculately served by gigantic blacks. We were given a taste of luxury: the finest French wines, liqueurs, and mellow Havana cigars: and we spoke of everything except the excavations. When that was in the offing, the "General" met it half-way, and took its wind.

I was plotting in my mind. Somehow or other, I intended to get into the excavations. And I intended to take some photographs; for I was convinced that there was a great treasure being unearthed: perhaps not of gold, although that was quite probable; but certainly of art, and of historic significance.

In ancient times, Ethiopia had been the cradle of the arts, if the historians are to be believed, and, after covering a great deal of North Africa I was convinced also that it was the cradle of the religious cults, including those of the Sahara and of Egypt.

After the marvellous dinner, on the pretext of fetching my camera to take a photograph of the "General" (which, incidentally, I did; he was an archaeological "sport"), I scouted to the north to see if there were an unofficial way in; but I found myself confronted by a great stone wall. The work reminded me instantly of the prehistoric walled city of Garama, that we had found in 1930. There were the same huge blocks of stone, stone that must have been handled by giants, one on top of another, rising to a height of nearly twenty feet. Mentally, I called it the "Great Wall of Nubia." It seemed intended to prevent invasion; but I followed it until I came to a spot that seemed scalable, and carefully hoisted myself to the top.

Everywhere, in a great circle of rocks and walls, were hundreds of mounds, and what appeared to be mausoleums. Was this the royal burial-place of the Kings of Nubia and Ethiopia?

Crawling through thorns and cactus, the hot sun cracking the rocks, and my head, I was able to get a close-up of the remains, and, painfully and quietly, on hands and knees I got down to the central area. Quiet was essential, on account of the dogs I could see near the workmen's huts in the distance. Luckily, the guards were taking a siesta.

Most of the important tombs were shrouded in great sheets of tin-plate, to serve as roofing against the sun; but the form of tomb was new to me. I snapped away as quickly as possible, and would have given much to know what had been found inside.

Further I dared not investigate, although in an adjacent valley other edifices were visible. The dogs and huts of watchmen seemed too numerous, and a South American General is...a South American General.

Some day, perhaps, the outside world will benefit from this great, secret undertaking. To me, it seemed rather a pity that archaeologists and historians should not be allowed to study this certainly important find of an ancient Sudanese city, on the spot.

My return journey was more awkward than my advance, for the rocks and crevices were a paradise for snakes and scorpions. Black and yellow reptiles slithered into their holes, but I was able to get a thoroughly theatrical close-up of a giant scorpion at a distance of two feet.

I was outside again. Rock-sculptures on a sun-blackened rock attracted my attention, as I made my way to the truck, hidden among the bushes at the bottom of the hill. It was the old trade-mark of the Sahara, the Baal-Ammon Ra symbol that I had seen in the far-off Atlas, in Carthage, Garama, Jupiter Ammon, the Hoggar, and in Mexico: a sun disk with horns.

Was this, then, the boundary of the great Libyan Empire? Was it possible that the Nubians were of the same race as the Libyans? The inscriptions, pottery, flints, and beads I had seen in Khartoum, coming from the region of the Djebel Moya; the relics of Meroe and Napata; the prehistoric drawings discovered by Count Almasy in the Wady Hawar and recently studied by Professor Frobenius, are astonishing links in a long trail that stretches right across North Africa.

As I carefully copied the ancient drawings on the stones beneath the citadel of Djebel Moya, the old hypothesis of the Libyans being the descendants of the lost Atlanteans recurred. If there is any definite evidence, it will be discovered ultimately by the accumulation of all the signs that may now seem to be in the world of coincidence. To me, however, the pyramids of Meroe and those of the district round the river Usumacinta, the identical workmanship of stone implements, the same designs of sun cult and astronomy, the human sacrifices at Carthage, Meroe, among the Aztecs and the Mayas, are all potential links.

Chapter 2

Our next halt was at Singa, where we fought our last battle with officialdom, in the persons of the District Military authorities. There was news neither of our guns nor of our permits; but there was considerable activity on the part of the Greeks, who had obviously heard from their fellows in other places.

Whenever there was anything to discuss, Pastolini would hurry me out of earshot of the Greeks, and he invariably kept out of the picture when there was anything "official" afoot.

The authorities were friendly, without being favourable. Evidently, they had been warned that we had a "character" with us. The Greeks would have seen to that, in any event. Part of their business is the purveying of information, which sometimes may be useful to the administration. To us, it was distinctly wearying.

"Has Pastolini any arms?"

"Certainly not!"

That seemed the customary question. It was certainly the habitual answer, and whenever I had occasion to talk with Pastolini, I used a negro as intermediary.

Getting away, still apprehensive, but still determined to go as far as we could, we camped at Kariba on the other side of Roseires, now in the closed Military area, nearly exhausted. It is one thing to say "we went"; the going was another matter. Still, we reached camp, and the sight of the inviting waters of the Blue Nile and the firm little beaches were too much for us. One or two took the plunge; but almost before we had reached the water, there was a terrific din, as the natives rushed to the river's edge, and began throwing stones into the water, and banging tins and drums.

We had forgotten the crocodiles. And what crocs they were; we saw them swimming, with their ugly snouts on the surface. And we retreated while we could.

The natives told us that, on an average, they lost about twenty people by death among the crocodiles each year. Not that the crocodiles caused them any fear when they went for them; they had a delightful little trick of lassooing them and dragging them to a convenient place to be skinned. It was the unsuspecting people who suffered, blissfully ignorant until a flail-like tail sent them spinning into the stream.

The Blue Nile negroes occupied a village opposite our camp, and they had seen our caravan arriving, and our tents being erected, so they made it an occasion. We heard the drums sounding; strange and exciting on that first occasion, and the population rallied. A little later we saw the chief man making a stately progress towards us, followed by a large retinue. Messengers announced the imminence of a "fantasia," and we got out our collapsible chairs and the phonograph.

The musicians advanced; great, glistening blacks, quite nude, with their "hippopotamus" horns and other instruments. The "hippopotamus" horn is a huge, hollow pipe, similar to the Alpine horns used for the benefit of tourists to awake the Swiss echoes and the visitor's generosity, except that this horn gave a very clever imitation of the gruff snorting of the cumbersome beast itself.

Arrived, they broke immediately into their formal dance: the death of the hippo.

That presentation was a thorough diversion. The calm waters of the river, the green and rustle of the jungle, the soft air and pulsing light made a wonderful setting, and the dance was excellent mimicry.

One of the more massive negroes played the hippopotamus, and he was eminently suited for his role, being gigantic of stature and rolling in fat, with enormous jowls, three layers of stomach and ham-like arms, which he waved as he pranced into the midst of the circle, grunting like the beast he represented, while the hunters, with flashing spears, to the rhythm of the drums and flutes advanced and retreated in ever-narrowing circles.

The realism was almost perfect, so exact that sometimes it seemed as though the spears of the hunters had actually pierced the victim, when he rolled and twisted, and screamed and grunted in his death agony.

He recovered miraculously, however, when a drink made its appearance, and to return the compliment we put on records that we thought would rouse and amuse them.

On the assumption that jazz was of negro origin we tried the latest examples and they scoffed at it, considering it decadent and unmusical. So it was; but not more so than their own drumming and bleating. They asked us to take the devils out of the box, and we gave them Caruso. He fared no better, and the chief asked us how we could stand such a din.

We returned to type and played negro spirituals. That was worse. The Africans finally decided that the white men could not make music, and disappeared to their tukuls: those little houses whose pointed thatch rose to the sky, outlined against a full African moon and reflected in the river.

It was a malarial region. Mosquitoes were a pest. We fixed our nets and prepared for sleep as the night quietened.

The camp was still under the moon when suddenly, in a nearby tent, I heard a startled question.

"What's that?"

I had heard nothing, so I did not trouble to get up to see; but the question was repeated, more loudly and a little angrily. From another tent another voice asked for information, and from yet another a loud string of oaths proclaimed that all was not well. I was compelled to get up, since it seemed that everybody else was up already.

There, outlined in the light of the moon, were real hippos, who had invaded the camp and were lumbering, like slow tanks, here and there among the tents.

They looked terrible enough; but there was no real danger, and our attendants ultimately scared them away by shouting and

banging on cans, while the American added to their fright and
our amusement by becoming entangled in the folds of his mosquito netting and prancing about like some devil or ghost waked
from the lower regions.

The next day we moved on to the Tabi hills, and did we curse
the authorities for their punctiliousness in the little matter of
guns? We did, for we could not travel a hundred yards without
starting wild game. There was everything under the sun to
delight a hunter's heart: this must surely be his paradise.

The hills held our attention for a couple of days, since, con-
trait to advice that was almost a command, we attempted to film
the natives. Our operations had to be in secret, for the people
were nervous; but it is seldom that one sees such perfect specimens of humanity in any part of the world. Men and women,
practically naked, moved with the grace and freedom of ebon
gods among the hills of their paradise; a race completely
unspoiled.

Their beautiful hills covered with forests, the strange, unreal
rock formations, the vivid colouring of earth and sky, and the
clear streams made a setting fit for those apparitions of dark
Venuses and Apollos, who could be seen playing like true children of nature.

There seemed to be not a care among them. Their picturesque
villages knew never a beggar; sharp contrast with Egypt. No
tourists had penetrated here.

The climate was almost perfect in the shelter of the hills during the dry season, save for a certain warmth about midday.

Strangely indifferent to sex, they played together, boys and
girls, young men and women of that absolute perfection of form
that is only to be found among such people; played and romped
and laughed, and swung each other to and fro, their arms around
each other, in the game, their smooth forms often interlaced.
They were dynamic enough, ebullient enough for anything to
happen, and I remarked on the freedom to Pastolini. He laughed.

"Why not?" he asked. "But it is not always so. They are men
and women, not gods. At other times, other amusements."

Obviously, it must have been so; but on this occasion there was no visible serpent in Eden.

We moved on to Kurmuk, where we found the District Commissioner anything but optimistic about our passports and permits for the guns, and definitely pessimistic about our going on unarmed and unwelcomed.

His life was being lived in a beautiful situation. The house, with a fine lawn and shady trees, seemed just a little incongruous in such a place. There was a stone walk, like that of Tudor England, the table was set for tea, there were whiskies and soda for such as preferred that refreshment.

Incongruous, that is, to those who had had little experience of the British official abroad. They know what they like, and how to get it. The officers were as freshly turned-out as though they were just back from the King's levee, with spotless uniforms, shoes highly polished, and servants in immaculate white and treading softly; but jumping to obey the word of command like drilled guardsmen. And, of course, since it was not yet sundown, the Union Jack floated from the top of its pole in its own particular little breeze, and the ceremonial gun was clean and neat on its tidy spot.

Beyond, rising as beautifully as the Swiss Alps, we saw the majestic panorama of the great mountains of Abyssinia, and we wondered how we should get through without running foul of Ghogoli.

The District Commissioner told us that he had heard some hard tales about our friend across the border, and about the Bani Shanqul. As for Sultan Ghogoli, he was afraid that we should have trouble with that gentleman. We pressed him for information.

The look on his face was sufficient answer; but he added a little detail. Only a short while ago they had had a gang of slaves, numbering over a hundred, who had escaped to British territory in a terrible state of hunger and distress.

"And our worst job," he said, "when we have got rid of their fetters, is to find them some means of getting a living."

Even while we were there, after the rest-house had been put at our disposal, the District Commissioner was called off by the news that there had been an incursion of ivory hunters into British territory, chasing a herd of game.

I got the impression that the British officers were simply straining at the leash, and that they would have welcomed any legitimate pretext to try conclusions with their neighbour.

"Besides," said one of them, "just think of the tales that come through of his way with the women of his territory. They say the old devil has a thousand wives. And he's reputed to be a hundred years old, anyway. He's got even Solomon beaten!"

Meanwhile, there we were. The District Commissioner asked me if we were determined to go through, and I said we were, after which he became quite human, and said that as soon as the passports and permits came he would send a special convoy to follow our trail into the Bani Shanqul, which region we intended to explore first.

As soon as our reception by the District Commissioner was complete, we were assailed by the Greeks who wanted to sell us food, arrange for mules, procure guides, and so forth; but we knew that we had a pretty good man on the job, and so fought the Greeks, who swarmed like flies.

When we were established in the rest-house, however, it seemed propitious to invite the Greeks to a parley, and they came, bringing their cognac, and when they saw that we were not at all interested in hiring their services they turned to another form of trade, producing little bags from their pockets.

This they did with every evidence of secrecy, for the bags contained gold, and there was an obvious rivalry between the British and the Greeks, for the latter have a special way of trading, and make about 300 per cent. return on the price they pay for their gold; yet it is dangerous for them to be caught by Ghogoli on his territory.

Pastolini had not yet appeared on the scene in person; but was doing a little scouting in nearby villages, and, after we had entered into a little speculation with the Greeks for their gold, we settled down to a well-earned rest. We were on the very threshold of Abyssinia. Our adventure was about to begin.

During the middle of the night, my window opened, and the noise brought me upright in bed. Mephistopheles Pastolini was presenting himself in his usual dramatic fashion, and was swinging through my window, dressed like an Abyssinian dandy in white cotton; swathed, veiled, mysterious.

"Signor!" he announced. "I am here!"

And he swept his hands to the ground, bending almost double. He loved effect, and had come over the wall, eluding the guard. We were the guests of the British, and they took no chances of our safety, locking us up at night and posting a guard; but Pastolini was cast for theatrical puffs of smoke and trapdoors.

In his self-laudatory fashion, he came to announce that he had found animals and guides: the best in Africa. He had found an interpreter: the best in Africa. To hear him tell it, nobody but Pastolini could have discovered them. All, he said, was arranged. The caravan, complete, would arrive in the morning to await my commands.

"I, signor," he declaimed, with another bow, "will meet you across the border..."

I asked him about mules and porters. He had forty mules and thirty porters, with guides for the secret passages through the mountains. I could trust them. He, not being sufficiently esteemed by the authorities, could not appear in person.

"But the prices?"

"They are cheap, let us not talk of prices," he replied with a smile, and added, in a voice that Tree might have envied, "We meet at Dul..."

I was insisting that I must know about prices, but he gave me no reply. Turning to face him, I found he was gone.

The next morning, I saw that he had accomplished the impossible. As promised, in came the mules and the silent Abyssinians, looking as though the fear of God had been deeply implanted in their hearts.

Actually, there was no shortage of transport on such a frontier. Beyond it lay slaves, ivory, gold, and platinum, and on the nearer side illicit commodities in much demand and exchangeable at great profit. Pastolini knew where men and mules were to be found.

What he had also done, so thorough (and dependable, to me) was he; was to collect cases of the great silver thalers of Abyssinia. Six mules appeared, ostensibly laden with tinned goods; their cargo was silver coins. Another six carried cases of cognac: the real secret of barter over the border.

We formed caravan, and mounted, moving off like a small army, beginning our winding way down, passing, in some wonderment, the Union Jack, last symbol of order and civilization, with myself in the van and the others, on Pastolini's suggestion, keeping close to those conspicuously labeled cases of tinned goods which were our passage money.

Three or four miles away lay the dread boundary. It seemed only so many hundred yards, so apprehensive had we become. The dried river-bed was ominous. Abyssinia's worst might lie in waiting on the other side. Every second we thought we saw a sinister shadow. The glint of the sun on a leaf was the flash of a spear. We expected to be confronted by a ferocious band of men whose sole purpose in life was to bar our entry.

We crossed the river in a compact body, looking and feeling scared as we climbed the farther side. We were in Abyssinian territory, without passports, without arms, really afraid although we would not admit it, and the only living thing that we encountered on that dread boundary was...a goat straying.

It was a ridiculous anticlimax. Abyssinia is the maddest country that ever was. The frontier post had been moved on, for a hundred miles. Our crossing was unmarked and unattended. There had been no guard there for ages, and we had expected trouble. We might have been held up for weeks, on the pretext of paying customs dues, but actually held to ransom since the customs authorities are not much more than brigands. And some of our party had turned back, because of these same frontier dangers. Meanwhile, we were met by the goat of Abyssinia, which we promptly photographed, before we continued our way to the Werka Warka, the river of gold.

All day we travelled, with never a sign of a human being until in the distance a figure suddenly appeared, outlined against the sky, Napoleon-like, on a boulder. It was Pastolini again, in his customary role.

"Bravissimo!" he cried, coming to meet us. "Marvellous! You had no danger?"

There had been only a goat! And Pastolini had made a long detour with his own mules to avoid a frontier post that did not exist.

Since he was with us, there was no need to continue all the way to Dul and declare our presence; but he told us that there was something afoot in a nearby village, and that night from our camp we heard the rhythmic beat of drums high on the mountain-side. The hot air seemed to beat with the pulse of Africa's mysterious heart.

I asked Derissa, our interpreter, what was going on, and he replied hurriedly that it was better not to inquire; but that we must leave before dawn, and get away as soon as possible.

Since I had not come to Abyssinia to "get away as soon as possible" from anything, his uneasiness served only to increase my curiosity, and I said we might as well visit the village. "No visit village," said Derissa. "Bad night."

Ultimately, with Pastolini's aid, I got out of him that the priests of the Bili cult were in the neighbourhood.

These fanatics, I thought, had been confined to the Kordofan, and repressed by the British; but Derissa assured me that they had been driven out of Kordofan and now practised among the Bani Shanqul. I had vague memories of the mad cult that took its toll of the virgins of the tribe: semi-fanatical, and not altogether dissociated from black magic. But it was a surprise to find Bili here.

Here or not, I determined to see it; but the increasing excitement of the drums must have driven deep into the heart of my guide, as it came from the secret places of the mountain, and he showed great reluctance.

"I am a Christian," he said. "They would be killing me, those pagans: a lot of negroes raving drunk on *merissa*."

Pastolini suggested that we might safely go the following morning, when the excitement had given way to stupor; but it was not the aftermath I wanted to see. It was the feast in progress.

"Very well," I said to Derissa. "Lend me your *shamma* (the Ethiopian burnous in white cotton), and I will go alone."

Seeing that I insisted, and for pride not refusing the challenge, he said he would show me the way to a sheltered rock, from which, if I were quiet, I could look down on the village.

The early hours were dark, but an electric torch shining on the ground helped me to avoid the cactus defences of the villages, and when we approached reed instruments were adding to the clamour of the drums, while my heart beat an uncomfortable accompaniment. The feeling that I was about to witness one of the little-known rites of these strange jungle negroes developed into an almost unbearable strain.

Ultimately, Derissa brought me to a rock that seemed to hang suspended over the village, and I slowly snaked myself up and peered over.

A great fire lit up the centre of the clearing, before a great thatched *tukul*, which, I presumed, belonged to the chief, and at that moment it seemed as though I looked down into a negro inferno. Swirling, naked figures pranced round in a serpentine procession, while a ring of musicians made an unholy din.

The great hippopotamus flutes beat the steady undertone of threat, and I noticed a chain of young females, bound, and yoked together in the centre of the festival, obviously terror-stricken.

I knew that the cult of Bili included the violation of virgins by the priest, and I looked for Derissa to see if I could get some word of interpretation from him, some idea of the programme of the feast; but he had withdrawn, leaving me alone on my rock. Even so, I felt tolerably secure, since all the inhabitants of the village, which must have included about two or three hundred people, seemed to be absorbed in the ceremony.

Even at a distance of two hundred yards, the night air was heavy with the odour of human bodies and *merissa,* which was constantly offered to the dancers, and poured over their shoulders. Great horns were in every hand, full of the drug-like drink.

When the dance reached its climax, a masked figure came from the main *tukul,* and a silence fell, as if by magic, on the expectant negroes. My eyes strained to see what followed.

The figure of the priest, sharply outlined against the dark curtain of the hut, was chalked in white, and looked more like a skeleton than a human being. Apart from his grotesque mask, he was completely nude, and his twitching body showed him to be in a state of intense excitement. I judged that he, too, was drugged.

On his appearance, two gigantic blacks approached the cowering virgins, and there was a momentary struggle, followed by wailing as the first victim was torn from her companions.

Chains rattled, and two other blacks appeared, to help.

The slim girl, her body gleaming after anointment, and illumined by the glare of the central fire, was held by the four attendants of the priest, who approached with the most grotesque of capers and stared at her, intensely, as though attempting to hypnotize her.

I was wet with sweat on my boulder; but the struggling slowly subsided, screams turned to a wild sobbing and later to an animal grunting, while a gorged sigh rose from the throats of the entranced spectators who had all risen, like wet ebony statues, and stood regarding the priest and the virgin.

The priest advanced, his white body now streaked and gleaming, to sacrifice the girl to the cult, and a shrill scream rose on the air. With its crash, the silence was shattered. Men howled in delirium. Women shrilled hysterically, and the instruments began again their discordant notes.

Utterly ravished, the girl was thrown aside. The negroes released their hold. Women devotees approached to minister to the hysterical victim. The priest retired to the *tukul,* to be restored by his medicine-man with drugs, and the dance continued round the minor priests of Bili, while a sort of sexual frenzy pervaded the whole population as the fumes of drink and the clash of instruments rose, and the savage love-making of the priest was sung and celebrated in a crescendo of devilish, barbaric, pagan excitement.

Restored, the priest reappeared, and the performance continued, with the people increasingly stirred, until the scene developed into an orgy which is beyond words, and almost beyond imagination; certainly beyond description.

That introduction to the rites of Savage Africa from my rock can be witnessed by any writer, and particularly by such as seem to be intent on *debunking* the country, only provided that they are willing to travel far enough into the country, and take the risk. Provided also, that they do not try to mix with the participants; that might be really dangerous.

The origin of the scene I had witnessed goes back to the darkest pages of antiquity, and is only a cruder, rougher form of the sacrifice of virgins to Venus and Tanit, which has persisted from the dawn of recorded history.

It is a ceremony which has an even crueler manifestation in the Congo, where the virgins are initiated into the cult by being offered to a wooden statue, life size or greater, on which they are impaled by the priests.

Chapter 3

The trip back to the camp was difficult, since Derissa was not there to help me through the rough underbrush and cactus. I had a sneaking feeling that friend Derissa, Christian though he might have been, when he had satisfied himself that the drunken orgy had reached safe limits and would preclude recognition, had himself enjoyed the camp-meeting of the fanatics of Bili.

Next day, his hang-dog expression spoke for itself.

"Very interesting ceremony next village to-morrow," he mumbled, apologetically.

"With you as high priest?" I replied, adding iodine to my scratches.

"No, sir, quite other affair. Circumcision girls," he answered quite happily.

"I've heard of that; but only women are allowed," I retorted.

"Perhaps feringhe dress as woman!"

"Nothing doing," I replied. "Look at my beard. But I should like to get near enough just the same..."

Pastolini, who was standing by, said that he knew all there was to know about it, and that he had ample documentation already; but in any event he could arrange all that was necessary.

Meanwhile, he thought – since the inhabitants of the village would be quite drunk – of our getting photographs of the people who had just been visited by the priests of Bili, and it was unlikely that our luck would last much longer.

So we got out gifts and baksheesh, collected our company, and made our way up the slope to the overhanging village, whose houses, in the daylight, seemed to be composed half of mud and half of straw, and stuck to the face of the rock.

When we arrived, the village seemed to be completely deserted; but Pastolini got busy, and went into the huts. Very soon afterwards, we heard scuffling, and out came the high priest, still in his white war-paint; but more dead than alive, with not a stitch on him beyond his coating of whitewash. Pastolini got him, grinning dazedly, into line, to pose for the cameras and cinematograph. And so we had him, before he knew what was happening. I doubt if ever he realized.

Pastolini then started to hunt up the women; but found it impossible to approach the violated victims, as they were under very necessary treatment, being somewhat badly wrecked. He was able, however, to get hold of the women devotees of the cult: those women who go from village to village with the priest, to work up the excitement and to drive home the fetish, its blessings and terrors.

To them we presented cheap bracelets and ear-rings, necklaces, and bangles, of which we had several cases for distribution *en route.*

Bottles of the fiery cognac supplied by the Greeks were also produced, to soften the regards of the attendant minor priests.

The old priest, who seemed to be nearing the end of his tenure of office, brought forward his nominated successor: a mighty and virile fellow, who seemed to promise well for his allotted term of seven years, and him also we photographed in all his naked pride, with one of the votaries, who seemed inordinately proud of herself. Not having jewellery for her adornment, she had had recourse to the paint-pot, and had painted stockings on her legs, and drawers round her rump and thighs: a crude and comic imitation to us; but of more significance to the blacks.

At this village also we were given *merissa* to taste, by Pastolini – a joke whose import did not appeal to us until much later.

Merissa has an etherish odour, and tasted to me something like hard cider, with a honeyed bite. Pastolini laughed immoderately as we sipped the drugged stuff, and then explained.

The beverage is made from grain which is put into a watertight basket, with water, honey, and hydromel. That was not so bad; but the basket was sealed and made watertight with cow dung, and the fermentation ripened in stagnant water that was actually the village cesspool. After fermentation, it was strained and put into pots or other containers.

Well, he had his joke, and we had our photographs and our experience; but still Pastolini owed us something, and, to make up for the omission, since he seemed to be aware of everything that was happening, or about to happen, within a radius of fifty miles, he told us that we should not travel that day beyond the next village: about five hours' distance. There, he said, since the moon was right, and other things were favourable, the rite of circumcision was to be performed.

Therefore, we camped below the village of Goha, after traveling through a region of blazing heat, climbing to the Abyssinian highlands.

For two reasons, we camped at some distance from the village: the first being that the natives reach a certain pitch of excitement during the ceremony, and it might not be altogether humorous to be too near their *tukuls;* the second was a reason which might have applied equally to any village: the danger of ermoli and tapeworm, those scourges of Abyssinia.

Pastolini went ahead to investigate and arrange, while we made camp, putting up our tents and mosquito netting, for we were still at an altitude where the mosquitoes were ravenous; but the men of the caravan went nearer to the village, being unwilling to sleep in the open for fear of Ghogoli.

If he should make a sudden appearance, they counted on the people of the village, and especially the dogs, giving due warning, when they would silently disappear.

Our camp was near the half-dry river-bed, and the animals were put out to graze among the thorns and elephant grass, while the cook continued his nightly psalm of misery. He had been brought up among British officers, he said, and was already itching to get back to civilization, since the Abyssinians were all thieves, and he could never rely on having for dinner what he had laid out in preparation.

We had taken him because, being of Abyssinian origin, he could speak some Amharic: but he hated Abyssinia. There was no water in Abyssinia; but plenty among the English in the Sudan. He prayed nightly that the English would take the country as quickly as possible.

We had to dig down a yard into the bed of the river before we struck a brown and disagreeable water, since it was the height of the dry season, and this water we flavoured each one to his taste with vinegar, rum, or lime juice. Actually, everything was secondary to chlorine.

After several hours, supper was ready. The sun went down, and, as if by magic, the flies went with the sunset. That is a phenomenon noticeable throughout the continent; but it never fails to excite attention. Before sunset there were literally millions of flies to torment us; after, none. One or two of the hardier souls organized a quick expedition to discover where they went. So far as I know, no one has a satisfactory reply to the question.

Pastolini reappeared in due course, full of admiration for the majestic stature of the belles of the village, and certain that we should have marvellous pictures on the following day.

What we were interested in, however, was the affair on foot in the evening, and that, he said, with a characteristic smile, was also arranged. We had better get out our presents and a bottle of cognac from the case for the chief, together with baksheesh for the operators.

Shortly afterwards, the village band of the Bani Shanqul variety began to approach: a medley of strange and fantastic instruments, of local origin, played by musicians to match.

We followed Pastolini to the village, leaving the caravan leaders and five guards to look after the camp.

The headman of this village, a huge buck nigger, led the way, his glassy eyes indicating that he was already under the influence of *merissa;* but just the same, to make assurance doubly sure, we showed him the bottle of cognac, and he promptly led us to the great *tukul,* where an intense excitement could be sensed. To my amazement, I was pushed in by Pastolini, who seemed far too much at home, with a dozen or so women who were in a state of complete nudity, singing hymns.

Among them were six adolescents, their breasts *en bouton*, lined up before an old woman, and after the hymns ceased she presided over the formal ceremony.

Seabrook says that the operation of female circumcision is not complete. I can assure him that it is complete among the Bani Shanqul, where it is thoroughly ritual, although Pastolini said that it was done in the belief that it assisted fecundity, since enjoyment on the part of the woman minimizes the chance of conception. It is much more probable, however, that the operation is designed to increase voluptuous pleasure.

Actually, the ceremony was too much for some of us; but the rest remained until the whole affair was finished, and the tom-toms began, the signal for the usual orgy and drinking bout.

Following this operation, we witnessed also the ceremony of the cicatrization of adolescents. Boys and girls alike were compelled to submit to the tribal marking, and to this end were bound and thrown to the ground.

The boys were expected to show no evidence of suffering, otherwise they are looked down on by the women, as being lacking in courage. Most of them did bear the operation stoically, not a murmur passing their lips although they were covered with perspiration, and in evident agony.

The bound victims are scored with deep lines in the approved fashion, on cheeks and forehead and torso, and the wounds are sealed with clay, when the victim is left in the sun until the clay is dry.

The girls, being under no obligation to act as heroines, registered their protests, and their screams were terrible; but not terrible enough to prevent our operator taking a film of the ceremony. Much is suffered for art; but more is suffered for the sake of photographic documentation. The operator took it for granted that he would pass that way but once!

Pastolini then entered enthusiastically into the hunt, from a purely ethnological motive, and rounded up the girls.

In the evening, by the light of flares, we filmed the obscene dance, which I named the *danse de viol*, following the ceremony of circumcision, in which the performers danced round in a line, with six or seven women in front and the men behind, while the music rose steadily, and slowly, to its crescendo.

The dancers, growing excited, ripped off their own and their partners' scanty clothes, and began the motions of violation, refreshing themselves occasionally by draughts of *merissa*, until finally there was no pretence.

The dust and din, and smell of *merissa* became almost unbearable. The men were foaming at the mouth. Their mimicry had passed from the semblance of animalism to animalism itself. They grunted like baboons on Monkey Hill, and with a bound sprang on their partners, bearing them face forwards to earth, in a fierce and reciprocated ecstasy.

The following day, our fourth day out, we travelled for our customary five hours, more being impossible because of the heat of the sun. Generally, we were away soon after dawn, having now settled down into something of routine, perhaps helped by the ever-increasing threat of Ghogoli, and our groups followed with reasonable precision and little delay under their various leaders.

The trail led up a wild valley, in which we were astonished to find hundreds of slaves at work, riddling gold in the riverbed. Here, naturally enough, we halted immediately to take a film of the gold-hunters of the Werka Warka.

These were the men assigned by the Sultan Ghogoli to work his deposits, and we had already seen the well-worn trail that was of greater age than modern Ethiopia, following the river and marked by mounds, none of which we had been able to excavate since we were kept on the go by Pastolini, who had a real urge to be out of the domain of the mad Sultan.

Our guns had not arrived; but Pastolini, though urgent, was still confident. He wanted us to press on; but this was a picture we could not afford to miss. The work was continually in progress, and hundreds of men and women and children were engaged: slaves under brutish foremen armed to the teeth and furnished with whips of hippopotamus hide.

These we tried to placate, since we had no desire that messengers should be sent to Ghogoli, informing him of our advance. The thing to do was to tip them well, and play for time.

The workers were digging in the river-bed till muddy water was reached, into which holes they took their washing, picking out the grains of gold.

It was not unnatural, perhaps, for us to hope that we had come across Pharaoh's mines, since we had been in no doubt of the age of the trail. Was this really Ophir?

The slaves were in pitiable condition. Surprising as must have been the appearance of our caravan, they were still apathetic.

I tried the effect of a good hunting-knife and a bottle of cognac on one of the foremen, who produced a bag of collected gold, and Pastolini suggested that we should try to buy it. The foreman wanted thirty pounds for it; but Pastolini suggested ten: then we should have a profit of about 300 per cent. on our capital.

Rothermel, growing excited, said we had better pitch our camp right there, and buy up the river; but Pastolini said that that was foolish. If it had been possible, he would have done it years ago.

"This is Ghogoli's," he said. "And you seem to have forgotten all about him!"

That old ogre had a way with illicit buyers, and if he knew that the foreman did any private trading he would tie him by the thumbs to the branch of a convenient tree and let him hang there till he dropped away from his thumbs. That was his idea of adequate punishment.

Rothermel wanted to know if all the gold went to the old scamp, and Pastolini made it clear that a certain amount found its way to the hands of the Greeks along the frontier. Most of the slaves contrived to collect a little sack of the dust, and with it tried to escape to British territory, where they were freed of their chains and their bondage. For which reason the guards were armed. If a slave were caught trying to escape, the usual punishment – as a deterrent to the rest – was to be flayed alive.

So the Old Man of the Mountains got most of his gold, although Pastolini said Ghogoli paid an enormous tribute to the Central Government for the privilege of mining, and lived under a constant threat of dethronement, since he was a perpetual source of irritation, which sometimes approached international importance, and the British would not be too reluctant to break into the Bani Shanqul.

I told him that I had heard of contemplated "breaking" along the Eritrean frontiers, and Pastolini, in his usual burst of enthusiasm, replied, "Why not? Adua must be avenged!"

Adua, by the way, was a great battle lost by Italy in 1898 when, for the first time, Menilik's warriors made an international reputation, and incidentally inaugurated the "hands off" policy of the Powers. The Italians were ambushed and wiped out. Those who had the misfortune to be taken prisoners were not killed, but emasculated.

"So, you'd better be careful, Pastolini," I said. "Unless you have an ambition to return with a tenor voice!"

"So you know the pleasant custom?" he asked, and we ragged the life out of him, just for the pleasure of seeing him go into the air; but he advised us not to laugh too soon, since that was one of Ghogoli's customs too.

He was growing really anxious. We had lost quite enough time. It was essential for us to get ahead as quickly as possible. So we began to climb the path from the river, through a country in which game was abundant, and that night we heard the roar of wandering lions, without the chance of going after them for a shot.

At the junction of the main trail and this new trail we were taking to avoid Ghogoli, we posted a guard, to give the route to any mission that might be following us with our permits, pressing on as hard as we could.

During the day, the heat in that gold and ivory coloured canyon was intense, and after about five hours, the beasts, to say nothing of the men, were worn out. We longed for the higher altitudes that loomed ahead in the palpitating, purple haze, and the coolness that would permit us to explore the area which promised traces of the gold mines of the ancient Egyptians.

Our trail had been well worn into the rock, and we took a number of photographs that indicated the incessant chain of caravans that had passed through the ages; but, due to our fear of that old man meeting us unarmed, we slipped into a narrow pathway, so as to sneak as far as possible into Ethiopia before opposition began.

On the 6th of February we saw stone mounds on either side of the trail and, naturally interested by these structures, I asked Derissa what they were. He replied that the natives never went near to them as they contained the bones of slaves who died before men remembered. Could they be the victims of the Pharaohs?

We resolved to dig into them, to see if we could obtain a skull or two, for anthropological study, and camp was made at some distance, since the mule drivers were apprehensive of the dead, from whose graves sounds were reputed to come during the night: cries of those dead souls protesting against their imprisonment and slavery, even in death.

It was impossible not to think of the long chain of misery and suffering the world has known, just for the sake of a little yellow gleam.

At night, we arranged to leave camp secretly, and to go back on our trail, to excavate one of the mounds.

The main camp had been pitched on a precipice, overlooking the river to the left, and the plain; and as soon as we could four of us took our hunting-torches, strapped to our heads, and went to the mounds. In about an hour's time we were busy pulling down the stones, and getting a foothold in the tomb, trying to discover the secret of some long-forgotten tragedy.

After two hours' work, our torches showed us a rough chamber in the centre of the mound, with crudely-hewn columns supporting the large stones overhead. With our pickaxes we pried open the burial-chamber, and found it filled with sand, coming finally to a pile of bones which crumbled at our touch, and presently reached a rock, which gave protection to a tolerably intact skeleton, at the north-east corner of the tomb.

Someone exclaimed "There are beads in the dust!"

They could be seen, in the light of our torches, and we collected what we could, after we had handed out the bones. Also we found two potsherds and what looked like a bronze chisel.

Feeling that we had got what we wanted, we made our way back to camp, tired and thirsty, and after breakfast examined the enclosing rocks. They were mostly granite, occasionally diversified, with gneiss, porphyry, clayslate, quartz, and serpentine, containing embedded minerals: cornelian, jasper, and turquoise. The beads we had found came from this point, as well as those found in the valley of the Nile, and in one place I saw what appeared to be an unfinished obelisk, similar to those encountered in Egypt.

Later in the day, we dismounted to examine an ancient quarry, where the stone was of a perfect purple colour, and at some distance along the ridge we came to marble, the *verde antico*. Our trail had certainly been worn by thousands of slaves, who had quarried through this infernally hot valley of the Bani Shanqul, dragging stones, digging mines, and washing gold in the rivers, for hundreds of years.

We were in the district where, I thought, the Greek and Roman authorities had placed the emerald mines of the Pharaohs, and Pastolini added his word to my suggestion; but, before we could investigate, it was necessary to hold a council of war, since the military outpost was reported to be established on a higher ridge.

Pastolini and Derissa began their scouting after we had encountered some natives among the rocks, who said they had seen the Abyssinians on their mules, galloping off to warn

Ghogoli. The natives were really slaves, little better than troglodytes, who lived in the caves of the rocks and spent their days tending the herds of their great master.

They also had a little trading to do; and, while my companions began to explore the reaches of what seemed to be a disused mine, I stayed to discuss with a foul-looking individual what was on his mind. This had to be done in sign language, of course, since I could not comprehend a word that he said.

When I, too, made my way into the passages that seemed to have been sculptured out of the rock, he followed me, indicating that we were to go behind a friendly boulder. There, he made me understand that what he had was worth a bottle of cognac and a gun; but the gun was too much, although I went to the store and got him a bottle of cognac, a can of bully beef, and a hunting-knife, whereupon he passed over the smallest of his little bags, which I noticed contained rough emeralds, particles of gold, obsidian, and rock crystal – which I thought at first were diamonds. The emeralds were light in colour, and have since proved to be identical with those found in the tomb of Tutankhamen. My troglodyte friend had already consumed half his bottle.

Though hilarious, and sitting on the top of the world, I could not make him understand by signs that I wanted to know where the emeralds came from; but at least I could negotiate with him for the rest of his treasure, and it was amusing to think that I was following in the ancient tradition.

Cosmos, the Greek historian, was probably referring to the ancestors of this old ruffian when he said:

"The land of frankincense and gold lies at the farthest end of Ethiopia. The inhabitants of the neighbouring Barbaria, or Senna, fetch from there costly things which they then take to the Nile, or transport by water to Arabia Felix. This country of Senna is very rich in gold mines. Every year the king of Axum sends some of his people to this land of gold. These are joined by many other merchants, so that altogether they form a caravan of about five hundred persons. They carry with them oxen, salt, and iron. When they arrive among the mountains, they take up their quarters and make a large barrier of thorns. In the mean-time, having slain and cut up their oxen, they lay the pieces of flesh, as well as the iron and salt, upon the ground. Then come the inhabitants and place one or more parcels of gold upon the wares and wait outside the enclosure. The owners of the flesh and other goods then examine whether this be equal to the price or not. If so, they take the gold, and the others take the wares. If not, the natives add more gold, or take back what they have already put down. The trade is carried on in this manner because the languages are different, and they have no interpreter. It takes about five days to dispose of the goods they have brought with them."

"Five days," I thought, as I uncorked another bottle. Evidently the traders of old lacked the white man's secret of barter. I got everything from him after that, at a price that was mutually a bargain. He was absolutely cock-eyed with excitement.

One of the bags contained a roughly-beaten circlet in gold, and a little gold statue that almost sent me flat with surprise. It was identical with the golden idols recently discovered at Oued-dan in Tripolitania, and stood about three inches high, of pure gold, grotesque, with hands half raised, in representation, per-haps, of a priest's hands; a caricature of a face with mouth, eyes, and two horns on the head which made me think that possibly it was a rough statue of Ammon.

This was too much. I had to run back to the others, to see what they were doing, and to show them my objects.

I located them about a hundred yards in the mountain-side, along an ancient shaft, and showed them the emeralds, flashing my light on them.

"Emeralds!" they cried. "They must have come from these passages in the *djebel!*"

"But it would take days to work them out," said Dink, our geologist.

Rothermel said, "I'm going to get a concession from the King of Kings, and just settle down here for a few seasons." But he was the son of a banker.

I concluded after that, that there was not much wonder the Abyssinians feared feringhe penetration. There are still some, like Cortez and Pizarro, who would make short work of Ghogoli, if the outside world really understood the extent of the natural wealth lying there. And so I said; but Rothermel was insistent.

"All right," he retorted. "Only keep quiet till the claim is filed!"

We were at the end of the passage, my drunken friend still jabbering in the sunshine, waiting for another drink, when the sentinel whom we had left in the valley appeared at the entrance to the shaft.

"Ghogoli!" I cried.

We tore out of the mine, and looked along the valley to see, coming up the trail at full speed, eight or so mules, led by the giant son of the Mamur of Kurmuk, who was holding aloft a letter in the end of a slit cane.

I did not realize at first, being so excited at the thought of Ophir and King Solomon's mines, that it was the permit for our guns; but in half an hour the panting little group reached us, and saluted profoundly, hand almost touching the ground.

Then I saw that the envelope was heavily sealed, with official seals, and we all cheered. Discretion was thrown to the winds, and we hopped around, unfastening the cases, which also were sealed with the arms of Great Britain and Ireland, extracting our guns, revolvers, and ammunition.

Fully armed, we stood, and solemnly sang "God Save the King!"

The British did things! It was a terrific moment for us when we paid off the men who had carried our guns and wrote a hurried dispatch to Mr. Coxen, reporting the discovery of the emerald mines. Then we grabbed our guns and shouted defiance to Ghogoli.

The amazed son of the Mamur went off down the hill to the tune of "For He's a Jolly Good Fellow," and with the wind in his tail.

Chapter 4

We were able to defend ourselves; but we still had work do in the shafts, and, climbing around, we discovered rough, archaic hieroglyphs on the rocks. Some might have been engineers' marks, which we carefully chalked for relief before they were photographed and filmed. One mark in particular struck me: the ancient sign for gold, with a rough picture of necklace and pendants. In addition there were crude cartouches, with signatures that may denote the period, and isolated signs on other rocks.

"Here in the north-west of Ethiopia lived the ancient Macrobian Ethiopians, whose country possessed vast quantities of gold," said Herodotus.

Cambyses, the Persian monarch and conqueror of Egypt, fought the Ethiopians in these mountains, as well as Ptolemy Eugetes and the Roman general Gallus, all in search of the fabulous gold mines of Ophir. After twenty centuries of silence, the whites followed, seeking the source of the Blue Nile and the Djebel el Gomara: the Mountain of the Moon.

The region was known to all the ancients, including Herodotus, Aristophanes, Strabo, Ptolemy, Dio, Cosmos, and Pliny.

Our carrier mules had been sent to the upper plateau to find pasture, which meant that the caravan took time to assemble; but then we began to climb, helping the animals as much as was possible, for the cliff was almost perpendicular in places and, far in the distance, we could see the mountains of Kurmuk in their purple haze. In the valley, the Mamur's son and his escort were making for the frontier post, hell for leather. Ghogoli was no joke, to him or to us.

We climbed like a caravan of ants along awe-inspiring precipices, in a temperature that rose to 105 degrees Fahrenheit, and
plodded on to the top, where, on a vantage point, we could see
Pastolini, regarding us through his glasses and gesticulating
wildly, wondering what had been keeping us.

Finally we were on the top of the ridge, and the world
changed suddenly as we passed from canyon to plateau. The
upland was jungle-clad, with streams and valleys. The air was
cool. Our trail had trees and alpine flowers on either side, like
the Austrian Tyrol, and the fresher atmosphere made life a joy.

Pastolini was standing on a rock, his arms folded. We rested
the caravan and went into committee, since it had been discovered that there was a Customs post in the next village on our
trail, which we could not avoid by detour. It might be necessary
to rush the post, which we could face with less apprehension
now that we were all armed.

This was the first true Abyssinian village we had encountered; the others, so far, had been peopled by negroes. We
advanced as quietly as possible, and half the caravan had got
beyond the village in safety when six or seven white figures
came out of the huts and gazed in stupefaction at us.

Before they could collect their thoughts, Pastolini and I
rushed at them, with Derissa to interpret, and began to talk as
quickly as we could, instructing the others to keep steadily on,
and to stop for nothing.

The leading Abyssinian was a fiery and proud-looking fellow, who immediately countermanded our orders. The caravan
must stop. He had had no information of our arrival. He wanted
to see our passports.

Pastolini then produced a flamboyant document, written in
Amharic, which he thrust beneath the nose of the guard. It was
really some official concession that he held, and we thought for
a moment that the trick would work, and, seeing that the others
had successfully stampeded their mules and were getting well
away, I suggested that we should try to get a picture of the occasion, and push on ourselves.

The Abyssinians, seeing that nothing was going to stop us, and unused to this lack of reverence for authority, called out their companions; but Pastolini snatched his document back again, crying "Let's go!" and off we went, satisfied by the comforting sounds of our caravan banging and rattling its way through the valley.

We moved slowly, with our guns ready, to see that we were not attacked from the rear.

No active molestation was offered, and we kept on the march till we reached a river. During the night, the guards passed us; but ignored our presence, as they hurried on their way to lay information before Ghogoli.

We were having a certain amount of fun; but knew that rocks were looming ahead. Camp was actually made on little islands in the river, among fine trees, in surroundings that were very like the highlands of Southern Mexico and Peru. The mountains were of the same volcanic origin, and their lower slopes were shrouded in palms and cactus and intensely colourful trees. The peaks themselves seemed to walk straight up to the sky in ascending reaches covered with brilliant brush of aloes, thorny cactus, and intermixed canes and bamboo. The beds of torrential rivers of this savage paradise of the Bani Shanqul were flanked on either side by rack trees *(Racka ovata),* giant wild fig, eucalyptus, capers, and tamarinds, among which were great sycamores which sometimes measured between twenty and twenty-five feet in circumference.

Up on a summit were circular ruins, like those of a watchtower, which we photographed: ancient remains overlooking the river of gold, such as I had seen mentioned in an old document which said that the "trail of the Shebans was lined with watchtowers." But we failed to find any inscriptions on or round them. These we examined while camp was being made, and then returned to our tents on the edge of the topaz waters before the whole caravan took its welcome bathe: the whites upstream and the porters and animals down below, after which the pack animals were turned loose to graze the luxuriant grass, and Said, the cook, began his nightly screams for wood, while he skinned the antelope we had bagged.

I watched the animated scene, thinking how different these people were from my mute Indians of a few months ago.

Several tall natives appeared from the bamboo, carrying long spears, and stopped to gaze at the improvised water-polo match that was going on, with an inflated cushion for ball.

On a convenient rock, our phonograph was providing music in midstream: every few minutes one of the swimmers would wind it up and change the record. Nothing less like an exploring party ever played in Abyssinia, and upstream I saw a group of dark women, peering at the whites in the water.

To catch the effect, I shouted a warning; and as though they were bashful schoolboys, our people dived and covered themselves in the kindly, but rather cold, folds of the stream.

The ladies were less bashful, and crept nearer, waiting for the swimmers to rise again. So I got Derissa to take them off to the camp, for they were as curious as monkeys and not at all shy, and, since the light was quite favourable, Pastolini rounded up the ladies and persuaded them to pose for their photographs.

The next morning, when we should have been ready to start, it was discovered that the mules had wandered. Quite probably the caravan-leaders had made no effort to restrain them, since they were tired. It took a good eight hours to round them up; which time we could ill-afford to lose on account of Ghogoli, but employed in the exploration of the village on the heights above the river, finding it surrounded by boulders which formed a sort of natural fort, with the *tukuls* all in the centre.

The natives, of fine physique, proved to be part Abyssinian, part Semitic, and two parts negro, and we were delighted to find rock-drawings of prehistoric times on their little fortress, mostly of hunting scenes, with one battle-scene cut deep into the face of the rock showing, under the patina, thin spears and shields.

Higher up, we found other inscriptions, which seemed to be rough hieroglyphics, with Egyptian superposed on Sheban.

The next day we were able to get under way; the animals were not only recovered, they were rested, and on a hill-top at a distance of a few miles we came upon a number of skeletons which one of the caravan-leaders said belonged to a recent battle between the Bani Shanqul and the Chankallas, who had probably come over the border, hunting for women.

While we were examining this battlefield, the major part of the expedition went ahead, and either one of the members dropped a cigarette, or some spark had caught the grass, for shortly afterwards, as we were trying to make up the leeway, we were cut off by fire. A cigarette end in the dry elephant grass, fanned by the light breeze, was quite enough to have done the trick; but we had no time to consider how it happened, for the blaze came racing up the hill of skeletons, roaring like a waterfall, and we were confronted by a wall of fire, soon to be racing neck and neck with wild game in the direction of the river, while kites and vultures followed the track of the stampede, anticipating a meal to follow.

It is strange how they follow a jungle fire, and even in our own haste, when a moment allowed, photographs were taken of them, the fire, and the gazelles who crashed through on their way.

Our worst job was to keep the mules and the Abyssinians steady, for we had a part of the caravan with us; but everything seemed to be going well until a gust of wind more powerful than usual carried sparks ahead, to begin another fire through which we had to force our way.

We were horrified by this new menace, and were hard put to it to save the cameras and the animals. The sun was quite obscured by a cloud of smoke, and it was with difficulty that we made our line ahead, ultimately to be separated as we moved north-east through smoke and flame.

It is quite true that such things should not happen on a well-conducted expedition; but occasionally they do. Luckily, we reached the river and safety. The fire passed, and we began searching for one another. Three mules were never recovered.

We could only hope that they had not perished; but had found new owners. Practically every one of us had been singed. We were without eyelashes for a considerable time.

Making a large detour to rejoin our companions, we came on two ruined cities, which were fortified, and which we gained by cutting our way through with the machetes we had brought from the Mexican expedition.

One of our machetes, incidentally, had been bought from me by the Greeks, who intended introducing the implement to the people of Abyssinia.

That by the way, however. We cut our path to a point where vast stones made a fortified circle on the hill-side, inside which stood the ruins of round buildings, including temples, where we were lucky enough to collect numbers of potsherds and a few beads; but what was more important was that we were able to copy rough inscriptions, and photograph what appeared to be an obelisk with phallic symbols. The inscriptions were in a language unknown to me; but have since proved to be closely allied to archaic Sheban. I found also some fine grinders, several arrow heads, and three magnificent stone hatchets.

Continuing, after a few hours we climbed a trail to the top of another hill, where we came upon a scene that gave us a thorough shock. We had cut our way through bamboo canes, and were examining the ground, when we found that about two hundred baboons had made their home among the ruins.

They are said to be dangerous to one man alone; but we were quite a sizable group, and the mothers grabbed for their children while the fathers snarled and chattered, lumbering among the rocks. It must have been a colony and, since we had our portable machine with us, we were able to film their undignified exit, after which we spent another hour collecting flints and several bronze implements.

Our only regret was that we could not climb down to what were obviously rock-tombs in the slopes below, since we needed to overtake the rest of the caravan and make the last rush for the Dabous river and safety in the bordering province of Wallega.

We joined up with the others, and found them in great excitement on the banks of a river. A runner had been sent ahead to see if there were any signs of Ghogoli, and he had just returned to report that Ghogoli was making for Abu Moil and that it was likely to develop into a race between him and us. As soon as we were sufficiently rested we pulled up stakes, well before daybreak, and collected at the base of a hill, beyond which we saw Abu Moti.

The place looked silent enough for us to believe that luck was again with us, so we got into battle array and made as impressive a display as we could, climbing the hill, with gun-bearers leading, and flying every flag we could muster, to add to our seeming importance. I had a flag-bearer with the flag of the Explorers' Club. Hayman and the rest got out all their college banners. The Stars and Stripes, the Union Jack, and Pastolini's Italian flag were grouped in state.

Before reaching Abu Moti, we passed a number of outlying villages on the plateau, most of which were absolutely abandoned and looked as though they had recently been occupied.

In one we found a few very ancient inhabitants, who explained that a year ago Ghogoli's men had made raids through the villages, seeking women and slaves; consequently all the able-bodied inhabitants had fled, some to the jungle, others to the frontier and liberty under the British flag.

It was pathetic to see the abandoned homes, with the pottery, looms, cloth, and implements lying around, falling to pieces for want of attention; but it was significant of the strength of the old Sultan.

Reaching Abu Moti, we had little trouble. It was still the heat of the day, and we were hoping to repeat our tactics at the frontier, and to make the Dabous river without hindrance.

We had actually passed through what seemed to be a dead town, trying hard all the time to give the appearance of being in no haste whatever, and had reached a hill at some distance when, in a cloud of dust that seemed to come from nowhere, the Crown

Prince arrived, and demanded our passports, which were to be presented at headquarters without delay.

Ghogoli had reached the village an hour before, and was waiting for us.

I gave orders to make camp on the brow of the hill; but the Crown Prince, who was a particularly villainous specimen, said there was nothing doing. We must return, every last one of us, and, sitting like a malevolent statue on his horse, he made a gesture which was obviously habitual, drawing his finger across his throat and gurgling. He was Ghogoli's military commander.

Remembering that the British had advised me never to give an inch to the scoundrel, I decided to make a show of force, and put the camp in a defensive position on the top of the hill, disbanding the mules as quickly as possible, and piling our cases in a circle.

But, just at that moment, I followed the gaze of the Crown Prince to two posts that stood there, and what was dangling from them. Corpses, and the evidences of mutilation! It is a pretty custom of the Abyssinians when they kill a man, or even before he dies, to mutilate him and to treat the removed sections of his body in a manner likely to strike terror into the hearts of all who would transgress their laws.

Bits of the human body, obviously masculine, had been so dealt with, cured, stuffed, and hung on cords.

The Crown Prince knew that I had seen, and smiled, repeating his earlier gesture and adding another, equally significant, to it. By some ill chance we had lighted on Execution Hill. Abu Moti is "The Hill of Death"; but still we affected unconcern and continued to arrange camp, until I decided to go back with Derissa and interview the Sultan.

Giving instructions to the rest of the party that they were to hold on, and not to yield an inch of ground, but to bury the money and ammunition boxes, I went with the stolid, silent Crown Prince, taking Derissa as interpreter.

Derissa, in an aside as we approached, said that all the people of the town were *chiftas,* or brigands; and they looked it. Their guns, daggers, revolvers, and lances gave them a certain warlike appearance. They were downright savages, fit men for Ghogoli's slave-raids; by race, a mixture of Abyssinian and negro, with a touch of Arab, which combined to make them the perfect Abyssinian gangsters, so that it was with certain qualms that I went forward to meet Ghogoli himself.

There was a blazing noon sun outside, with fierce white light everywhere, and I was shown into a great *tukul,* his headquarters. The only ray of light came from the half-open door, and, as soon as I could focus my eyes in the semi-darkness, I saw to my surprise a wizened old man sitting on the floor, a cross between Gandhi and a fat Turk, surrounded by half a dozen fat little boys.

To my amazement, a push from behind hastened my approach, and I looked into the fiery, brilliant eyes of the Sultan; eyes which revealed the secret of his virility and command.

Putting up as fair a front as might be, I shook the dry paw of the Sultan which was casually extended, and felt the grip of his claws: the nails sank into my flesh as he sat calmly on his tripod.

A hundred years old, I thought: and he looked it, although there was a strength and power about him not to be denied. His voice was between a snarl and a bark.

Derissa began to translate.

"The Sultan asks what you do here in his country."

I refused to answer, until due courtesy had been paid. It was only playing for time; but I thought I might as well start early, and Pastolini had been preparing for this sort of thing for some time. He had impressed on the Abyssinians that I was an important personage, of great power. To Derissa, I was nothing less than the Crown Prince of seven European kingdoms.

I was silent, save to demand to be seated, or that the Sultan rose, before I replied.

So I won the first inch. I was duly seated, and I noticed that the old fox was eyeing the decorations that I had put on especially for that purpose.

"Tell the old scoundrel that I am on a visit to the King of Kings," I said to Derissa.

Old Solomon Ghogoli gave a snort as my reply was translated. I imagined that his words meant "not of this king!" and I
was right.

"He wish to tell you," continued Derissa, "that Haila Sillasiei
is king only in Addis Ababa."

"Tell the Sultan that I shall be only too glad to convey that
information to the Emperor!"

Derissa translated. The parched old rogue looked at me
through half-closed eyes.

"What makes you so sure you will get to Addis Ababa?" said
he, and just then one of the boys pinched his companion, who let
out an unearthly yell. The Sultan, with a speed that was incredible, picked up his knotty stick and gave the offender a solid rap
over the skull. I have never known such lightning and stinging
repartee.

"Are these his sons?" I asked Derissa, trying to change the
conversation.

"Yes," was the proud reply. "All Abu Moti his sons, grand-
sons, great-grandsons or great-great-grandsons. Big fantasia to-
morrow, because a new son is born in the harem."

Shades of Voronof, I thought; but asked Derissa to convey
my congratulations, which he did with alacrity.

"Sultan pleased," he chirped. "Wishes to know how many
wives you have."

"One," I replied, and there was a snort from the old rout, who
grunted the Abyssinian equivalent of "Now let me tell one!"

"Then ask him how many wives he has," I said to Derissa;
but Derissa demurred, saying that Ghogoli was very sensitive on
the point of his harem, although I knew very well that he had a
Government-controlled seraglio in each major village of his
province.

Incidentally, it was most of a year since he had been in this
village, Derissa told me. Hence the new arrival.

I could see the fox debating in his mind, while the conversation continued.

"He wants to know how many bottles cognac you have with you," said Derissa. "And he wants to know if you are hunting women or gold."

"Tell him I don't care for his women or for gold; but that I have cognac enough for the fantasia!"

"...Sultan pleased!" laughed Derissa. "I tell him you only interested antikas."

For a moment, the snake-like old eyes gleamed, and then Ghogoli gave a sharp order, and, after an interval, asked me if it were true that an escort was on its way to meet me. He seemed half inclined to accept its reality, after I had entered into a long and somewhat impromptu account of the delays attendant on its arrival. Then he gave another shrill command, which Derissa translated, and which threw me into a greater apprehension than I cared to show. The Sultan was sending messengers to the river, to see if the escort was a myth.

"And," concluded Derissa, "he says you will remain his prisoners until the runners return..."

I was about to expostulate when, with a cunning that I had hardly suspected, a box was placed before me, carried by a huge, nude negro, at the command of the Sultan. From it several small bags were removed, and he dug with his claws into one of them, bringing to light two small bronze statuettes and two coins.

If it were his intention to catch me off my guard, he nearly succeeded: the two statuettes were Egyptian, and the coins Roman!

"Ask his Majesty quietly where he found them," I whispered to Derissa.

"Sultan says you give a thousand thalers and he show you place in mountains where there are many such things."

"Five hundred thalers and six bottles of cognac!"

When my reply was translated the Sultan laughed a gay, cackling, triumphant laugh.

"Very fine joke," said Derissa. "Sultan says things found here in Abu Moti, and he will show you place to-morrow. He wishes now to go to your camp..."

A few words, as sharp as machine-gun fire, followed, and the place was in an uproar. In a few moments, horses and an escort appeared, and I saw the old man mount in a flash, and it was all I could do to keep pace with this Massinissa of the Bani Shanqul. His horse, caparisoned with bells and fine harness, moved easily, with the Sultan in a saddle decorated with gold and silver. And he could ride! How he could ride!

Very soon the Sultan, his escort, and his murderous-looking Crown Prince infested the camp.

The Prince still played with his fantastic gesture, and I had the creeps all right just then; but continued to make as big a bluff as could be. For one thing, we were not at all sure of our promised escort. It might be there; or it might not.

Fearing treachery, we kept our hands on our revolvers, and I explained to the company that we were prisoners until the return of the runners, adding that they had better keep their tongues quiet and their heads cool. Incidentally, I looked round to see if there remained any trace of the treasure chests. They were safely buried.

In a few moments, the Sultan and his immediate circle were sampling the fiery Greek cognac, and feelings became less strained for the moment. They knew they had us, and were of a mind to make the most of the opportunity; their eyes roved enviously, and not without malice, over our property.

The guns intrigued them most, and in the excitement of the encounter, a shooting match was arranged between our company and the Sultan's best shots, to take place on the following day, when also I was to be shown the place of the discovery of the antiques, by the Crown Prince in person.

Anything to gain time, was our idea, and we offered presents to our guests; but nothing satisfied them, and we began to feel that if the escort did not arrive on time we could expect anything from the hands of these savages.

When nearly a dozen bottles of our precious reserve of spirits had disappeared down the throats of the brigands, the Sultan took his leave, after giving one last glance around, to see how many men we were, and how well supplied with guns.

Instantly he had disappeared, I gave orders that the camp was closed, and that no individual, white or native, was to attempt to enter the village. I was afraid of what might happen if Ghogoli heard that we had indulged in a little private speculation among his foremen on the Werka Warka.

Almost before I had made the rule, I had to break it, for the Crown Prince returned in high glee, and this time omitted the gesture intended to show that throats were easily cut. He was seeking my company!

I left the camp in a state of siege and followed him, wondering what he intended. He, making a large detour round the village, made for a stockaded house, traveling with what I thought was exaggerated stealth. Arrived at the house, he posted one of his own men as a watchman, and introduced me to...the Sultan's harem!

A large room, lit by an old hurricane lamp, revealed a group of giggling females. This was the seraglio of His Majesty Sultan Ghogoli, and we sat on a carpet, opening my flask of brandy, from which I took a stiff dose before passing it round, since I felt a little uncomfortable in this room of naked women who were not exactly the property of my hilarious host.

His purpose, obviously, was to show off his conquests and his real contempt for the Sultan, for one or two of the dark Venuses were paraded for my inspection.

Giggling, and somewhat disquieted, he put them through their paces; and after the flask had been passed among the ladies, he was about to begin a private display of his own, when a low whistle came from the guard outside.

"Hell!" muttered the Crown Prince, or something to that effect, and snatched the flask, while the nude company pushed me in terror out of the back door. Papa, who also had had a livener, was on his way across!

Chapter 5

We got into the brush just in time, and my only prayer was that the old rogue would be too drunk himself to notice the suspicious aroma on the breath of his favourites.

The Crown Prince, however, was not through. He wanted to make a night of it, and dragged me, somewhat reluctant though I was, to his own abode, stumbling and cursing in disappointment.

His collection was inferior to Papa's in size and quality. It was easy to see that the old man had first choice in such matters. Still, two of the buxom, steatopygic wenches were soon on his knees, and I saw that he was too tipsy to bother about me. Certainly, nothing that was his was offered to me; but what did interest me were the massive gold ornaments two of the favourites wore. They looked to be of ancient make, in the shape of entwining serpents. Pretending to admire the ladies' arms, I studied them carefully; but the Crown Prince was not so drunk as all that, and by signs indicated that they, too, came from the neighbourhood.

There were several strange symbols on the bracelets which I copied down, and tried to make the Crown Prince understand that there would be more cognac to-morrow; but that I must now return to my camp.

He made no objection, save, for the hundredth time, to grin mysteriously and draw his hand across his throat. It was his idea of a joke.

That night we spent in apprehensive watchfulness, looking up to the swaying Abyssinian relics in the pale moonlight, and listening to the sound of the drums rising from the village, while the sentinels kept an unfailing watch at the four corners of the camp.

At dawn, one of the lieutenants of the Crown Prince came, and led me off towards the ruins, about two miles north of Abu Moti, where, in the bed of a dried mountain torrent, large mounds could be seen; obviously the remains of an ancient site.

Higher up on the mountain-side were tomb-like caverns, which seemed to indicate the burial-place of a lost civilization, of the same epoch as those in the Bani Shanqul, with the same masonry marks, the same circular construction, and the same types of potsherds. Everything, of course, had been well ransacked.

The tombs were similar to those of the Djebel Moya, Meroe, and Axum, and the light was just growing strong enough to begin photography when the guide hauled me out of the place, to indicate that the Crown Prince had arrived in the valley below, with his escort, and was wildly shouting to me to come down.

Then I really wished that some civilized power would clean up this archaeological site and let the explorer and scientist work in peace.

The tombs, it seemed, were sacred, and must not be touched – by any other than Ghogoli!

The Crown Prince was in a terrible humour, and obviously had a terrific hangover, and I felt like hitting him over the head with my alpenstock; but there was no use in argument, so I made an attempt to photograph the mounds, after leaving him under a rock with some cognac. About ten gaunt brigands followed me around, and each time that I tried to pick up a stone or piece of pottery they jumped at me, until I gave up my quest in disgust and rode back to camp, where I found another row in progress.

The shooting competition had turned out badly, since every one of my companions was a crack shot, and they were only too glad to show their proficiency with the revolver. The lightning Western drop shot was a revelation to the brigands. Besides, our guns were all of the latest pattern, and the Abyssinians were insulted by the ease with which they were beaten.

We had to appease the crestfallen chiefs, and restore their dignity, after which we went over to the fantasia which was beginning on the opposite hill, in honour of the eight hundredth (or so) official child of the Sultan.

There, thanks to their sensibilities, we fell again into trouble, for, having taken enough presents, and having Derissa with us interpreter, we had found the Crown Prince in better humour.

He, after sufficient prompting, had persuaded the ladies to pose for their photographs, and one of them was doing her best, when someone must have told Ghogoli in his *tukul* what was going on.

He arrived like a cloudburst, in a tearing rage, and we decided that the time was quite opportune to make our way back to camp, and to leave the Crown Prince, in turn, to do his best. Anyway, we had our film and our stills, and the scene between the Crown Prince and Ghogoli we could not photograph.

Just as we were nearing camp, runners went by at speed, their *shammas* streaming in the wind, and we halted anxiously, to await our fate.

Shortly, Ghogoli appeared, and our guards were exultant. They knew. Our escort was there! Ghogoli's ring of men melted away; we were no longer prisoners, so we gave the fox a chair and listened to him, by the mouth of Derissa, explaining that he had not realized we were of such an importance.

Derissa had listened very carefully, and explained that the escort was a strong army, detached by the Emperor himself, which accounted for Ghogoli's change of front, who now thought his best move was to barter for some antiquities that he had had brought from the village.

Our camp was immediately broken. The cases were dug up, and the mules loaded, and while a few of us stayed to bargain with Ghogoli, the main body started off at a good pace downhill to the river, and the last thing that Browne did as he rode off was to turn round in his saddle with a bow to the Crown Prince, and a perfect imitation of that blackguard's favourite gesture: a finger drawn across the throat and a croak in it, followed by a roar of deep-chested laughter.

Ghogoli, now intent on peace and his good repute, made me a present of some antique bracelets and little bronze vases, saying that if we came back he would be glad to give us more from the emerald mountains; but he wanted too much for his other specimens.

Derissa said that the old man was not too anxious to sell, as he could always get his price from the Greeks on the frontier.

The Sultan threw in some leopard skins as good measure, making up for his errors, knowing that we were on our way to that Emperor who was certainly king in Addis Ababa. Then we took the trail, following our companions; but, before reaching the Dabous, we saw Ghogoli's last gruesome sign on a hill overlooking the river: bodies in chains in the trees, with kites and buzzards flying overhead. They were victims taken for some offence or other, and, as usual, grimly mutilated and ornamented.

Muffling our faces because of the stench, we took photographs of this last evidence of the rule we were escaping, asking Derissa if it always happened so.

"It is Abyssinian custom," he replied.

"Are they dead before they are mutilated?"

"Generally!" was the laconic reply.

Late that night, we camped on the near side of the river, to spend our last hours in the land of Ophir, all of us pretty well shattered. We had kept up a decent front; but we were glad to be out of that maniac's hand.

Towards dawn, I heard Derissa calling, and, waking reluctantly, I asked him what was the matter.

"Emperor's representative has arrived," he announced.

"Tell him it's too early. I can't receive him yet. I must have time to make a formal appearance..."

I was unshaven, and very weary; but Derissa was adamant. "Here is message from His Imperial Majesty, King of Kings, who has sent you his Fitaurari Barata (Commander) to escort you into the next province...

"...To Byron de Prorok," I heard. "Greetings! His Imperial Majesty..."

Just then there was an interruption Derissa answered and explained.

"The General's aide-de-camp asks if you are really Byron de Prorok, the leader of the expedition..."

"And who else?" I replied. "Does he take me for a *chifta*, or for Mussolini in disguise?"

"No, I assure him not..."

"Not what?"

"Not Mussolini in disguise..."

"Read me the letter!" I shouted.

"...His Imperial Majesty hopes you are well. He himself is well, thank God! He, the Emperor of Ethiopia, the King of Kings, descendant of Solomon, Conqueror of the Lion of Judah..."

Lion of Judah! Lion of Judah! I lost the rest, as I went off to sleep again. Splendid.

At dawn, we crossed as best we could, to be ready for the meeting and the proper photography of the ceremony.

I was a little ahead, so that at least one of us should be shaved and dressed before the importunate messengers demanded an entry; but even then it was difficult, for the animals had to be forded across and it took the whole company to attend to the mules, who were not docile in the stream. The current was strong, and the crocodiles near. Each detachment that crossed meant that the rest lined the two banks, shooting guns into the stream or heaving such rocks as we could find at the ugly snouts.

Besides, it was a real jungle river; a slow, swirling flood of great force, enclosed on either side by great forests, whose immense trees, flower-garlanded, were reflected in the water. Some way down were rapids, which we could hear roaring as they shot over the rocks, and as we looked across the stream we saw a company of baboons, who had taken possession of our proposed landing-place; huge fellows who played until the last moment.

Naturally, Browne, who was our jester, pointed out that our escort had arrived.

After I had crossed with the first detachment, it was a thing of real beauty to see the rest coming across, with the lovely white monkeys (those with the splendid fringe of hair) flying through the trees, chattering like excited old women, and birds of brilliant plumage traveling up and down the river in search of breakfast.

I shaved; it was the thing to do; and then went to see to the erection of my tent while the others made the crossing. They did not bother too much; they were casual, hardy people, from the ends of the earth, and now we were out of Ghogoli's hands they seemed to pay little enough attention to formalities.

The only man to be conciliated, according to them, was the man who could "do them dirt," and they were still in their pyjamas, some beginning to shave, when Derissa came flying to my tent to say that the escort was moving down to us.

I finished dressing as quickly as I could, as a mighty array wound over the hill. It was not at all difficult then to see why Ghogoli had changed his tune. This was a real army.

"Hurry!" I said to Derissa. "Tell the feringhe to come, particularly the camera-man..."

"Yes, sir!" he said, and stood perfectly still.

The advance guard had now reached the spot chosen for the meeting; but luckily the operator put nothing before duty, and was there in his pyjamas, since nobody had troubled to dress before crossing the river.

The baboons, of course, had gone, and in their place were the aide-de-camp and the guard, waiting for the advent of the Governor, making an avenue for him to pass through.

Shortly afterwards, in full regalia, he appeared on a magnificent white horse, and a couple of hundred hats were swept to the ground as we shook hands.

"The General," said Derissa, "greets you and your companions, in the name of the Emperor."

Just then the flap of a tent opened, and somebody shouted, "What about breakfast?" to retire instantly, while I tried to explain, through Derissa, that we were sorry not to be in order, but it was just a little early.

"Please find seats," said Derissa. "His Excellency has brought gifts and many fine horses..."

I bowed low, and started suddenly, as one of the attendants let loose a great blast on a buffalo horn, after which another procession started, led by a fat zebu, followed by eight horses in rich trappings, with saddles decorated in gold and silver; about thirty sheep and goats, and as many women carrying baskets on their heads. I rubbed my eyes, wondering if they had taken me for Solomon by mistake.

A seat was found for the Fitaurari; that it was a poorly-disguised packing-case did not matter. His interpreter stood on his right. A gun was carried by another attendant – still in its case decorated with gold and silver fringe.

Behind him, a great Abyssinian held a green umbrella, though the sun was not yet strong. A beautiful leopard skin was unrolled and laid before me. Then a huge buffalo horn, containing *tej*, the national beer, was proffered, after which came a great, ancient, and desiccated crocodile.

"Why the croc?" I asked Derissa.

"Excellency says you are interested in ancient things. This is for your museum."

I bowed. It was very thoughtful of him, and I wondered how he had dragged this useless, repulsive, toothless carcase over half the landscape of Abyssinia.

The little horde of women were carrying vases of *tej* and Abyssinian bread piled high, while others presented baskets of eggs: there were three hundred eggs that first morning.

The movie-man, still in his pyjamas, was turning away at the handle of his machine. The others had also appeared, some likewise in pyjamas, and they were brilliant as to colour: real Sing Sing stripes.

His Excellency, through the interpreter, remarked that he liked the uniforms of my attendants; was it possible that I had a spare sample.

Said announced breakfast, and we fell to, while his Excellency, who was observing some religious fast or other, looked on. The marmalade particularly piqued him; but I dared not press him to partake, since he was accompanied by his priest.

Later, we got under way. First went the military guard on foot, all in white, with the toga-like uniform of the country, and then came the General with his green umbrella. Next, the members of the expedition fell into line, and behind rode the notabilities, followed by an army of slaves and servants.

After these came the army of unwilling givers of gifts, and our joint equipment, now augmented to about two hundred mules strong, followed in the far distance by our canteen and Said the cook.

Of course, we felt somewhat important, riding at the head of such an army; but, as time wore on, and we had filmed the reception in each village through which we passed for a few days, it became rather monotonous.

At Mendi we had our first touch of Abyssinian justice. Said had accused two of our porters of stealing the game which had been hung in his quarters for the notables. As soon as the crime was fixed on them they had turned to accuse each other, which necessitated a formal trial.

To discourage any other thieves (of which, the cook said, the expedition was exclusively composed), the Fitaurari of Mendi was called upon to judge the dispute and the culprits were promptly put into chains and carried off to be tried in the usual Abyssinian fashion, under a tree in the centre of the town. where benches had been placed for the guests of honour.

Since the accused demanded the right to be legally represented, they were allowed to draw their pay to the time of the theft, and with it paid their lawyers in advance, who explained the case to a timid-looking judge, who sat on his little platform, accompanied by his recorder.

The whole town congregated to hear and to learn, and utterly ignored the cries for silence, which were frequent in the beginning; but soon dropped.

The opposing lawyers laid hold of the other's client, dragging him hither and thither as the heat of argument rose; and they felt, or assumed, a choler that was astounding, jumping almost on to the judge, and flashing their fists in his face, missing him by the merest fraction of an inch.

Yet he sat unmoved, only flinching occasionally when the blow came too near. He had seen this thing before, and he would return the verdict that pleased him.

The pantomime, for that is what it really was, continued in loud-voiced, bullying fashion, until each lawyer, dragging his opponent's client with him, had sprung like a goat, to come to a dead stop in front of the judge, his free arm flailing the air (and nearly the judge) to cry, "By Menilik I swear my man is innocent..."

Justice was ultimately done by the porters being condemned to pay one thaler each for the crime, which the judge handed over to me, and I made an error by suggesting that I had no use for the dollars; but that they should be given to the poor of the village. When this was translated the whole company rose in a huge roar of laughter. Never in Abyssinian justice had anybody ever given anything to anybody, willingly, rich or poor.

But the poor fellows received also a month's imprisonment and were condemned to be suspended by their thumbs for one hour.

Against that we protested: it was too severe a punishment for so small a thing; but justice was Abyssinian justice and the men went off to prison.

So it continued. At every village, gifts were presented. It was a sort of tax, and we could not use all that was brought. Neither could we return the gifts; consequently our servants, and all the caravan, became gorged. The attendants passed their afternoons in getting rid of the *tej* and their evenings and nights in getting rid of the effects.

The trail was not broad enough to allow us to travel more than two abreast, consequently progress was slow, and what began as a pageant ended as a long line of stragglers stretching almost half-way across the province.

Along the route, I had been constantly worming myself into the confidence of the General's aide, and one day he made a fortunate slip, saying that I might be interested in a sacred mountain, and diplomatically 1 asked Derissa where and what that mountain could be, to learn that the General did not know exactly; but that he had heard that there were pictures on it, according to the Minister of Education, and that it was located not very far from Kakka, to be reached by way of Goddam, Damdam, and Peepee. But, whispered Derissa in my ear, the Fitaurari there is a bad man.

It took me all the next day to persuade the General to leave the main trail and take that to the sacred mountain.

It was far, it was holy, and it was well away from the protected trail to Addis Ababa.

Ultimately, however, by using persuasion and authority, with a distant hint at future conversations with the King of Kings, we were on a rough trail south, and I was quietly excited, for we were proceeding in a direction in which I had reason to believe lay the Mountain of the Moon.

We had three days' travel on that roughest of trails, and on the way encountered that serious pest of the country when, in the distance, from a height, we saw a grey haze moving up the valley at almost unbelievable speed, while above the haze a cloud of birds flew.

The mass was coming our way, and before we knew it we were in a fog of flying locusts. There must have been billions of the creatures – which was a lucky chance for our cameraman, who, in spite of the inconvenience, swung his machine into position and filmed the expedition fighting its way through the plague.

The locusts, intent only on the straight line of their flight, beat in our faces and crashed on cases and harness, rained on the General's umbrella, and attempted to settle on the foliage, whence they were driven by the porters and escort, who knew that, once the cloud had settled, it was only a matter of moments before everything would be stripped clean.

The accompanying priest began to say his prayers, calling on all the saints from Saint John to some unknown and probably uncanonized people to see that the pest passed over their province, and settled in the Sudan, or preferably in the province of that unmitigated rascal Ghogoli; which sentiments seemed to coincide with those of the General, who said that he did not mind the British or Ghogoli being visited; but his province was specially important in the world's affairs.

Meanwhile, above the locusts flew the cloud of birds, with beaks open, diving and swooping, taking their gorge of easy food.

So great was the flight, and so many were killed on the trail, that it became slippery from their crushed bodies.

That night, we camped on the edge of a great, fairy-like canyon, below which was a delicate oasis of graceful palms and multicoloured trees, all draped in jungle flowers which fell away in streamers from the foliage, like red and blue and yellow garlands on Christmas trees for a children's party. Scores of baboons and monkeys could be seen swinging from tree to tree, while blue and gold and green birds flew up and down the valley; bright splashes of colour against the grey, castle-like walls of the canyon.

It looked to me to be a unique place for prehistoric man, except for the brilliant trappings of the Abyssinian camp; for the General had a number of huge tents in his equipment, each of which was nightly pitched, staked, and corded as thoroughly as the big top of a circus, making our serviceable but plain canvas tents look like poor relations: they were colourless, inoffensive, retiring things, and his were bright, rich, and highly decorative.

Our camp being at a little distance from the General's, I resolved, if I could, to slip away in the morning and avoid the steady formulae of greetings. (It took us half an hour every day to discover how each other was, and if he had slept well.)

So I slipped down the side of the canyon among the boulders to make my way to the paradise below, starting well before dawn with the paling African moon casting its ghostly glimmer on trees and crags.

By dawn I was climbing along the lower reaches, on a level with the tallest palms that were beginning to glow in the vivid golden rays. Dark fissures in the overhanging rocks seemed to indicate possible caves, and I was soon scrambling on my stomach, pushing my gun before me, as I wormed my way into the animal-smelling darkness. Smoke-blackened walls, illumined by my torch, indicated that man had lived there, and in a short time my digging was rewarded by the discovery of arrow heads and hatchets, and, to my astonishment, I saw that these old instruments were made of obsidian. Only a few months earlier I had been finding the same typical objects in the jungle fastnesses of Southern Mexico and Guatemala.

Was this yet another link in the chain of Atlantean civilization, which, according to my theory, spread east and west?

Coming out of that gloomy cave, and spreading the objects before me in the quickening light, I found that they consisted of arrow heads, a percuter, and a *coup-de-poing*. Here was the last link in an unbroken chain...but my thoughts were disturbed by a sudden clamour above. For a while, I was at a loss to understand the reason for the din: there were tom-toms drumming, men calling, whistles blowing, and I saw people jumping about on the top of the cliff. Then I understood: the escort was looking for the guest who had slipped out of camp.

Returning, I resolved to get them all to work, and soon had a crowd collecting prehistoric implements; but the General could not understand my interest in the stones, saying that he had walked on them by thousands, all over his province. "Where?" I asked quickly.

"In the Chankalla district," he replied, naming a region to the east. "Near the 'Smoking Mountains' on the edge of the Blue Nile."

Storing this information in the back of my mind, I left the valley of the caves, and the caravan began to form.

"I will have the villagers collect stones for you, and send them on to Nekempti," the complaisant General announced, with a strange look in his eye. I am convinced that he had doubts of my sanity.

On the third day of the trail we reached Kakka. A runner had advised the authorities of our impending arrival, with the result that the local Governor had his troop out to meet us, and, after the customary photography and gifts (which by now had become monotonous), the escort fell in behind, with the result that we became a veritable mob; not so disadvantageous to me, since the two Generals had a great deal to talk over between themselves. Derissa and I, with two guides, slipped away to the circular mountain beyond the village: the sacred Mountain of the Moon, for all I could discover to the contrary.

There is something exultant in arriving at a point of which one has thought, and perhaps dreamed, for years. I might actually be on the sacred site; it coincided well with all the indications, and I went off quickly, knowing well that if I waited there would be complications, and it was better to see what there was to see, before asking permission.

The local Governor looked more like a brigand, to me, surrounded as he was by priests with turbans piled high like a heap of small inner tubes. They would certainly raise objections, if I asked them for permission.

We had to cut our way through a mass of thorny underbrush to get to the "written stones," and I thought for a time that we had come on another wild-goose chase, until one of the guides pointed to a stone in the jungle undergrowth and said "There!"

By cutting and slashing, we removed the moss and foliage from the stone, while my anxiety grew. I wondered what it could be, for the guide said it had not been seen for fifty years, since the stones belonged to the priests, who had forbidden anyone tampering with them.

That meant nothing to me, and I worked steadily on, to find that, deeply engraved in the stone, but worn by time, were symbols and hieroglyphs in a strange language.

"Are there any more?" I asked, for I could at least recognize the link with Egypt and prehistoric times on the same stone.

"Many stones here," muttered the guide. "But not touch – evil spirits here."

"Nonsense!" I replied to Derissa, and we began hurriedly to uncover adjacent rocks and clear a space to make photography possible.

Skulls and mystic symbols appeared, together with many well-defined crescent moons.

On seeing them, Hayman shouted "The Mountain of the Moon," and I hoped he was right, as I filled in the designs with chalk to bring them out for the camera.

The light was bad, due to the thickness of the trees, but our machetes cleared a space, and we worked as fast as was possible, for in the distance the drums were calling us home, and I knew that before long we should have the superstitious priests on our heels, with the villagers following.

One large rock had a battle scene carved on it, including men with spears and shields, similar to the drawings seen in the land of the Tuaregs, the Bushmen, and the Libyans. Another had a distinctly Egyptian figure, with worn cartouche near by. On another was an Amharic inscription and a ram's head. Two others were covered with an inscription in an unknown language.

This might mean four distinct epochs, with Egypt added to primitive man, and the ancient Ethiopians followed by the modern Abyssinians.

The unknown language, according to oriental scholars who studied it later, might be ancient Sheban.

I wished I were able to dig down under the stones: but we were lucky even to get our photographs, for with much crashing and yelling, the town, led by the ignorant priests and monks, surrounded our cameras, and the uncovering of the inscriptions ended.

The Emperor's emissary was sorry for us; but explained that this district was out of his jurisdiction, and the Gallas here were difficult to treat with. For a while, I thought that the fanatical mob, headed by the priests, would smash our cameras; but the escort, fortunately, was strong enough to prevent that.

I asked Derissa why they were all so furious.

"This," he replied, "they claim to be a sacred mountain, the Mountain of the Moon, and the place of the royal tombs of ancient Ethiopians. The priests are angry, and cannot understand how you know about the place. They say that the devil led you here, and that now you will go straight to Gehennab!"

"Tell the Ecagai [head priest] that we have removed nothing and that I will make a gift for his church, that my interest in the stones is only that of a *liq* [student]."

However, for the second time, I was arrested, and carried off, with the faithful Derissa hugging the precious films under his *shamma*.

My first contact with the redoubtable Abyssinian clergy showed me that their power was unlimited. It seems strange now that this empire in the heart of Africa was Christian when Europe was in the grip of a purely pagan worship. They are Christians of the Coptic branch, which originated in Egypt and reached Ethiopia about the end of the third century. There are hundreds of thousands of priests, about one in every four of the male population, and priesthood demands no educational accomplishment, only a sufficiency of money to buy office; and their power, it is said, is greater than that of the Central Government. The priests form a definite class, and all bow down to them: a serious problem, as the mass of the priests are totally ignorant, bigoted, and extortionate. They rule the common people, and keep close contact. One word from them and even the Emperor would be in trouble. More than a third of Ethiopia is independently in their hands: a dangerous state within a state.

The *tukul* allotted to me by the Governor was spacious if not over-clean, although fresh laurel and eucalyptus leaves had been strewn on the floor for me, and the Emperor's representative had sufficiently calmed the fanatical high priest to provide me with safe conduct; but the crowd outside was definitely hostile and sentries were placed at my door.

Chapter 6

Evidently the feringhe is not wanted in the remoter parts of the country, and I was afraid that my money and gifts would be gone long before I reached Addis Ababa; but, after the customary *tej* had been brought to my prison-guest house, I crept into my sleeping-bag for a rest I had earned.

I was, alas! destined to pass a bad night, for I had no sooner tried to settle down than rustling began among the leaves, which sounded like the advance of an army of grasshoppers. Then came the first bite, quickly followed by a dozen more.

I flashed on my light and was amazed to see hordes of fleas: there must have been millions in the *tukul,* on the warpath.

I tried to cover myself; but they attacked in force and I was in real agony, so decided to make for the open. In haste, carrying my bed over my head, I stumbled out of the hut, and walked plump into the stomach of a prone guard, which made me lose my foothold, and I fell among the sleeping forms, who waked and yelled in terror. In a moment, all was in uproar, and Derissa appeared, to ask what was the matter.

"Only fleas!" I shouted, and the Governor next turned out, clad in a purple robe, deeply insulted because nobody had ever complained before.

"That's because no white man has tried to sleep in the place!" I exclaimed, and even Derissa was shocked.

"We are all white people, Abyssinians," said the Governor; but white or not, I refused to sleep in the *tukul,* preferring the stars for canopy. Even so, the fleas had made their home with me, and it was weeks before I was clear of them.

The next day, I left with Derissa, to join the caravan on the banks of the Didessa river, without so much as saying good-bye to the Governor or the ecclesiastical authorities.

The way from the mountains, which I saw were actually in the shape of a crude crescent moon, lay along a plateau succeeded by a hollow to the Didessa: a wild and savage tract of country which took us three days to cross; and as we approached the lowlands bordering the river it was as though we travelled through a zoo, with hundreds of baboons, wild pigs, and deer with fine antlers; while at night, the roar of lions, attracted by the smell of our food, seemed nearly continuous.

The Didessa, a magnificent stream, was surrounded by real primeval forest. Every kind of tree was there, specially noticeable being giant mahoganies and teak. The air was hot and humid, for we had come down from the heights, and the Fitaurari put up camp in great style on a hill overlooking the river. It was unsafe to camp nearer, because we were in the worst of malarial regions, and the mosquitoes were waiting (and noticeably hungry), besides which, there was an uncomfortable number of wild animals using the river, and if we had camped on the banks we should, as likely as not, have been visited by hippopotamus, rhinoceros, and crocodile families.

Using the camp as headquarters, we split into groups, since the neighbourhood was particularly interesting, and we were in a region where game abounded.

Some of the members went north to visit a famous witch-doctor, and I, who had always been interested in lycanthropy since visiting Haiti, several years ago, went off with Derissa to follow up hints and reports of a strange cult in the inner jungle.

There was a Chankalla village not far from camp, a little more civilized than the others, and from this village I was able to obtain a local guide, a great negro, who, with Derissa and four or five of our best porters, accompanied me along the banks of the river, searching for the place where the Chankallas (or "devil people" as the Abyssinians called them) were to hold their ceremonies.

Getting away from the Fitaurari was not so difficult this time, for he was noble, portly, soft, and exhausted, and wanted time in which to recover from the unwonted hardships of the heavy trail and our forced marches.

According to such information as we had, the Buda cult was much influenced by the state of the moon, and I wondered if we should succeed in tracing the source of those African claims to animal transformation.

After two days' march along the river, we heard the usual sounds indicating a village not far away: tom-toms beating, and vague shouts.

Our camp was well concealed among the boulders and brush of the river, and with Derissa and the negro I went slowly forward.

This area is still one of the least explored regions in the world; the jungle is difficult to penetrate, and necessitated our following the river instead of cutting through, although the negro said that he knew a path whereby we could approach the village from behind, should it become necessary.

I, however, did not want to approach openly. I wanted to wait and see, to see without being seen: but, being well away from the village, I did follow the jungle path for a few hundred yards, to prove for myself what the negro had said: that the path would be locked if there were any likelihood of the ceremonies of the cult going forward.

It was as he had said. We wound and twisted along the path, suddenly to come to a woven blanket of thorns which effectively cut off the trail. The only way to advance would have been to cut our way through the screen; but then, the Chankalla told me, we should be faced by other screens, and probably by guards and poison.

I photographed the jungle trail and its barrier, and returned to the river-bed, where we lay in ambush until night, being careful to use what cover there was, and to avoid observation.

When night had fallen we went among the boulders and brush to a point where we could see a small clearing and the *tukuls* of the village facing the wall of the precipice leading to the upper plateau.

It was a magnificent setting for whatever was being staged: the gorgeous canyon and volcanic peaks, the booming of drums and the roar of a distant cataract, the sibilant, unceasing murmur of the jungle, and, as the moon rose, the ebony figures of the villagers preparing for their festival.

Even at our distance, we could smell the ever-present *merissa* as it was wafted on the moist air by a gentle breeze. We could see also that the natives were gorging themselves on great chunks of raw meat, cut from a none-too-fresh hippo on their bank of the river.

An almost constant procession of negroes moved to the carcase, each carrying a knife, and going backwards and forwards from the animal to the spot where the meal was being taken. The meat was eaten raw, and the feast continued almost interminably, so that I thought that that was all there was to be seen, until, after much guzzling and swilling, a painted witch-doctor came from a den at the back of the village and began to make the night hideous by his imitations of the calls of mating jackals.

During the howling, the drinking continued, and as the night wore on we saw the villagers, all completely naked, men and women, groveling on hands and knees, sniffing each other like animals.

The witch-doctor stood in the centre of the orgy, howling at the moon, and abruptly there was a silence, and to my horror I heard the call answered from above, among the heights. My blood turned cold when a young woman offered herself to the medicine man, and it is impossible to describe the realistic animal performance that followed. It was a perfect representation of animals in rut, while all the other females crouched round, howling their jackal calls.

This, it seemed to me, must have been from the same source as the Haitian voodoo cult; but worse was to come, for real jackals came from the forest behind...

I was scared, uneasy. The whole village seemed to be hypnotized. A jackal, passing along the river-bed, stopped and sat on his haunches, raised his snout into the air, and howled in our faces.

I thought it best to be gone, and we stole back along the river. I have certainly witnessed some strange things in this dark continent: the fanatical dance of the Aissaoua, the orgy of the Tuareg *ahal*, the fire-walk of different North African tribes, as well as my recent experience of the Bili cult; but never such an incredible orgy as that scene on the snake-infested borders of the Didessa. Its explanation and significance must be left to specialists.

On the return trip, I had one of the most disagreeable adventures of my life. Looking for game, I had gone ahead of the guides and porters, watching a crocodile in the stream, and wondering whether I should take a pot shot at him, when a couple of very active little yellow bees got under my helmet. I brushed them away, and thought nothing of it; but was stung on the arm, just as I was about to shoot, and in a second felt myself stung again on neck, arms, and face. Then I realized the meaning of the attack – something that Pastolini had told me about, and at which I had rather smiled. Dropping my gun, I ran for the jungle cane-grass, hoping to escape the enemy; but it was too late, they were all over me, stinging everywhere. I rolled through the grass; I covered my head in a mud pool; I fell into a hippo hole in my blindness, and contemplated jumping into the river to wash myself free; but the snout of the crocodile was enough to deter me.

Finally, Derissa and the porters, hearing my shouts, came up and beat off the swarm, although they, too, were badly stung. They carried me back to camp, since I could not see; eyes and mouth had completely lost their shape, and my nose was one with the rest of my face.

Derissa told me later that the swarm continued to attack for another hour on the trail; but when we reached camp I was all in, although, with usual promptitude, I was photographed, to be added to what must be the strangest collection of African photo-graphs any individual possesses.

Yet they did what they could. I was soon sick with colic and ran a high fever. One sting need not be serious; but to be thoroughly and completely stung, as I was, might have had more serious consequences. The torture of the Inquisition missed one of its exquisite moments in omitting bee-stings.

Nor were the others in very much better state when they returned from their trip north. Two came back with dysentery, so we prolonged our stay on the river, hunting and fishing, although the camp looked more like a hospital.

The other members of the expedition had found their village, at a distance of about thirty miles, and had learned something more of the Buda cult.

Ironworkers and potters, it seemed, were taboo: like some native tribes, they are reputed to be able to change themselves into hyænas and other beasts. All convulsions or hysterical disorders (which are common in Abyssinia) are attributed to the evil eye of these unfortunate workmen.

Budas are distinguished from other Abyssinians by a peculiarly worked gold ring, worn by the whole caste, which ring, the witch-doctor explained, is frequently found in the ears of hyænas that have been shot, or speared, or caught in traps.

The inference, of course, is that some unlucky Buda has not had time to change himself back again; but Pastolini had told us that the hyænas were caught young, and branded, to throw the cult into greater relief.

So convinced are the Abyssinians that these potters and blacksmiths rifle caves in their character of hyænas that no one will eat with them, for fear that their dried meat (called *quantar*) is more – or less – than it seems to be.

The party had brought back a number of terra-cotta statuettes, all utterly obscene, which added weight to the evidence of the sexual cults, and they spoke of seeing a sect of Zakaris who performed the same horrible rites as the Aissaoua of North Africa, with the same power of stopping, or coagulating, the blood.

These people called themselves descendants of St. George, and were all flagellants.

The witch-doctor used for divination the mummified hand of his grandfather, which hung on the wall across the room, and when addressed replied "yes" or "no" by different motions.

That some trickery was used was certain; but it was equally certain that the trickery could not be traced. There were no cords attached: the hand was apparently quite free, and would certainly be sufficient to impress the credulous villagers.

Convalescent, we explored the neighbourhood, especially the Chankalla villages, where it was reported that the barber was operating.

His was a unique ceremony. We filmed it.

The head of the client was first washed in cow urine, to get rid of some of the vermin, following which the hair was well plastered with a mixture of gum, cow dung, and urine, and this was worked into the hair until it assumed the shape of a fantastic halo, offering scope for the barber to produce a variety of designs which would endure after being put into the hot sun to dry.

The coiffure is similar to that of the warriors of the southern Sudan: in waves, haloes, flat, or spread fanwise, and is a matter of importance. It must not be caught in the rain or it would be spoiled; but must last for months, for which reason the victims sleep with their necks on uncomfortable rests, so that no damage is done.

The men of the village were blood-drinkers, and we were invited to participate.

The national drink of the Chankallas is obtained by securing a bull and a short spear. The spear serves to make an incision in a vein, from which thick, red, hot blood pours into bowls. After the bowl is filled, a tourniquet is applied and the flow of blood stopped. The wound is dressed with dung and wet clay and the skin brought over the wound. With every semblance of delight, the steaming blood is drunk.

Since returning, I have been asked by amateurs of Ethiopia if I saw the practice of eating animals alive. I heard much of the custom; but saw none of it, although Pastolini, who knows more of Abyssinia, probably, than he ought to, has full documentation and photography of the habit, and he told us a tale which, incredible as it may sound, was fully proved.

One night, nearing Axum, he overtook three people on the trail who were driving a cow along with them, and when they came to the time of the evening meal they threw the animal down and, while one sat across the neck, holding the cow by the horns, another bound the animal and with a knife made a clean incision in the hide of the upper part of the rump. Pastolini, thinking they intended to kill and bleed the animal, asked to be allowed to purchase part of the carcase for his own caravan; but was told that it was not intended to kill the cow, since they were not the sole owners. It belonged to a group.

"Amazed," continued Pastolini, "I sent my caravan ahead and waited to see what happened. And I saw, with some astonishment, that two steaks were cut from the rump most adroitly. These were laid on a shield, and while one man continued to hold the animal's head the others effected repairs by closing the wound. Nor was this done in an ordinary manner. The skin that had covered the flesh had been left entire, and was stretched over the wound, to be secured by two skewers.

"Whether anything had been put under the skin, I do not know; but the third man had gone to the river and prepared a cataplasm of clay, which served as dressing. The cow was then allowed to rise, and was driven slowly along, while the company ate the raw meat."

Other tales Pastolini told us, which were received at first in stony silence; but he was supported not only by incontrovertible evidence, but by the testimony of our guides.

Native banquets, for example, take on a form that is probably unique.

The company is assembled in the chief's *tukul* and a bull is brought, to be tied firmly to the doorpost. The cook selects the most delicate morsels, which are cut from the live animal. Before killing the animal, all the rump is severed, in square sections, without bones or much effusion of blood, and servants offer the meat to the guests on slabs of Abyssinian bread, to be washed down with *tej*.

"All this time," Pastolini continued, "the bull is bleeding and the Abyssinians are so clever that they avoid cutting the arteries..."

After we were all recovered, we passed through an increasing number of villages on our way to Nekempti, and each time there was a procession of gifts, which in time became burdensome.

There was also another procession: the sick who came to see if we could do anything for them, and who depleted our medicine chests without, perhaps, receiving much permanent benefit. The amount of venereal and skin disease was appalling: I have never seen anything like it, and agreed with Pastolini, who had said that about 90 per cent. of the population had skin trouble badly, and the other 10 per cent. had it very badly. Time and again we had to drive the lepers from our camp, for we could do nothing to help them.

Hunting was a free-and-easy sport: game was abundant; food easy to get. The excess we distributed among the villages, where the flesh was invariably eaten raw; the Chankallas had an orgiastic way of eating which was disgusting to us, and unhealthy for them. Moreover, our porters, since food and *tej* were abundant, generally ended the evening's meal in a state of in capacity, and we not only had to treat them for wounds and sickness, crushed toes, and deep thorn-punctures; but also for gluttony.

Many of our two hundred men preferred to treat themselves for wounds by placing hot coals from Said's fire on their injuries, to effect a thorough cauterization, being afraid of gangrene.

Night by night our fight against the ermoli continued – that tick which penetrates, and lays eggs. We could be seen digging away at each other's feet with sterilized needles, extracting the horny-headed little pests. In Mexico it was a battle against the garapatas; here it was the ermoli. Such things, with the fear of poisoning from snakes, ticks, plants, and thorns, are the joys of the explorer.

We continued steadily on the trail, and as we neared Nekempti we began to preen ourselves, for we were coming to the first great Abyssinian centre, and our final entry was amusing, since the Governor possessed a motor-car, which had been sent out in pieces from Addis Ababa, and reconstructed in Nekempti.

The car was sent out to meet us, and as it came along the trail, driven by an Abyssinian chauffeur who had no idea of driving, it was more of a threat than a favour. Our porters fled from the sight of it; but those of us who could find room took our chances, and drove ahead of the procession to the capital of the province, coming to a magnificent town, seemingly set in a forest of eucalyptus.

The Governor was so anxious to see us that we were taken at once to the Royal Palace, which was a collection of tin-roofed buildings on a hill in the heart of the town. It looked like a frontier town of a by-gone Wild West, compact together, that palace; but we drove up to the main entrance and waited for the preliminary meeting with the Dajjazmac, who ranks next to the Royal Princes.

While we were waiting, our ears were assailed by a cry with which we were to become all too familiar during our stay: that of the slaves in the prison yard crying "Mariam, Mariam." Two thousand people asking for pardon and liberty.

The Governor, who wished to read us greetings from the Emperor, received us in a great and showy room; but was himself surprisingly young and fine looking, in a magnificent, formal costume, which incorporated the manes of lions, a golden crown with precious stones, a General's costume with orders and stars of the Crown of Ethiopia, the Lion of Judah, and of Menilik all ablaze on his chest, while a servant stood by holding a cloak made of the manes of lions, which was placed on the Governor's shoulders as we took photographs of the great man and his entourage.

A formal invitation was extended to an official banquet later; meanwhile we were given an encampment on the opposite hill, in tents erected by the military authorities, with an escort circling round, while we went through the usual and now pitiful ceremony of receiving hundreds of eggs, some goats, deer, and milk from the people of the capital of the wealthiest province of the country.

The first person we saw after the formalities was a white-robed gentleman, obviously European and demonstrably Greek, who sought our custom in the matter of stores of cognac and local presents.

Sunset meant that camp was closed, or that if we went out we were necessarily accompanied by a servant carrying a great lamp and a bludgeon; but some members of the expedition, not knowing this, went round the town and to the Greek store, which nearly cost them their freedom, from which danger they were saved only by the forethought of the Governor's escort, who hauled them out of their various places and back to camp. There was no investigation of night-life for them on that night, at least.

Market day brought a crowd. Thousands upon thousands of figures on mules and camels, donkeys and horses were to be seen coming in from the outlying districts bringing their wares, eggs, coffee, and spices; and always the Greeks were at them, doing them in right and left, and two Armenian lawyers.

Everything that Abyssinia produces was brought down to market, including sugar cane, tobacco, chickens, steers – wonderful cattle, these, with great horns – pots and cases of milk, honey, and *tej*.

In the streets, ludicrous little processions moved: dignitaries taking the air, accompanied by escorts of varying size, to indicate social position. It is a craze with the Abyssinians, this possession of an escort. Even beggars will save their alms, so that they may hire a slave for a day or two, and take a rise in the social scale.

The hills were white with people coming to market. There must have been fifteen thousand people there when trade began soon after sunrise. All over the hills were the long lines of white-robed countrymen approaching the great market-places, where a terrific hubbub was soon in progress.

The vendors sat in parallel lines, leaving a wide avenue between, with their goods on the ground. Nearly everybody carried a parasol, made of straw, gaily coloured and of bell shape.

Between the rows walked the buyers, and among them I had my first glimpse of the nice Abyssinian custom of the creditor hauling his debtor along, chained to his wrist; held until the debt was liquidated.

The town itself was laid out in the usual Abyssinian style, and seemed particularly beautiful, since all the houses were surrounded by eucalyptus trees. The houses themselves were really only *tukuls* of wood and straw, a little more stable, perhaps, than those of the jungle; while the houses of the Greeks and Armenians rose to two stories and had tin roofs.

The air was fragrant with the smell of eucalyptus; but the streets were labyrinthine, broad, and winding, with houses standing well away from the roadway, and frequently we were lost, when our only hope was to look for the Royal Palace and then to find our way across to the camp.

Hearing that there was a telephone in the town, we tried to send messages through; but an Abyssinian telephone is a phenomenon of the first order, attended by four clerks, who listen in relays for messages to come through, sitting like idols in their little hut.

Gimbo was the point of relay for Addis Ababa, and as messages were few and far between most of the time was spent in idle contemplation, until suddenly one of the clerks roused from his semi-coma, gave a little scream, and snatched a pencil. After a long wait, we received a bland announcement: "American Minister!"

An hour later, another phrase was added:

"French Minister inquiring..."

Inquiring what, didn't matter! That was a conversation, as relayed in Amharic by the operators. I tried to let the authorities in Addis Ababa know that we had travelled safely so far, and left it at that, since we were due to visit the church and see the Temkett (high priest).

We had heard that the priests still danced before the tabernacle; but had our doubts. A Greek guide, however, assured us that it was so and took us to the church on the top of a hill: a great, wooden edifice (cathedrals have tin roofs).

Generally, the tombs of notable people are arranged in mounds around the church, and to enter we went round a circular passage to a great door, which led to a spacious room with an altar at one end, with the tabernacle. Behind was another room, containing the tables of sacrifice and the Laws of Moses: the holy of holies.

Enormous paintings, realistic beyond credence, ornamented the walls, mostly of Solomon being vamped by the Queen of Sheba (no doubt who was the aggressor in the matter), and the past history of the Abyssinians. St. George and the Dragon were also there; but the great scenes were those of the Queen leaving her capital with caravans of gold and precious stones, followed by an intimate, domestic picture of the bed chamber with Solomon and the Queen couched together.

The next was of Menilik, as a consequence of this union. Some prominence was given to historical scenes: the mutilation of the Italians at Adua, in which huge Abyssinians with knives performed the tragic operation.

One picture showed the siege of Magdala by the British, and the King committing suicide, while many others were pages from the life-story of Menilik; mostly of his conquest of the recalcitrant tribes, and the inevitable treatment of prisoners.

The priests were wearing their spiral turbans, and drew up in two lines. Drums began to beat on either side, antiphonally, and the priests, standing before the tabernacle, began a sort of slow minuet, pirouetting from time to time as the music hurried along, to end finally in a mad, dervish-like caper. They were in real ecstasy, their robes and turbans swirling.

The sight of these ignorant, almost uncouth figures performing their tricks was almost too much for us. Some of the party began to develop hysterics. We made for the door.

"And that," said one, "is the oldest Christian religion in the world!"

Returning, we passed a number of prisoners, past and present, some manacled and wearing leg-chains, others trudging along with the familiar gait of the chain-gang.

The Government does not feed its prisoners; either the family provides the food, or the prisoner is allowed to earn it. Failing such provision, he starves. Punishments are varied and severe. The false witness has his left leg amputated. The thief has his right hand severed. The blasphemer loses his tongue. But the removed part is duly returned to the victim, so that it may be buried with the rest of his body in due course, and simplify the matter of resurrection.

These punishments are now more or less confined to the outlying places, for the Emperor is rapidly wiping out this form of justice; but Pastolini assured me that he had himself seen with his own eyes hands being cut off, not so long ago. The local butcher was the executioner.

Chapter 7

Market day was drawing to a close, with the usual crop of minor lawsuits and the habitual harvest for the lawyers. No market closes without such happenings.

Whosoever thinks he has been cheated during the trading lodges a complaint, and the judge, sitting on his platform in the market, listens to the raucous, blustering, violent lawyers, gives his verdict, and then waits for the ensuing free-for-all fight to cease before he continues.

We were lucky enough to get a full-dress film of the occurrence, and it seemed to me that the judge was in greater danger than the culprits; but it was amusing. The successful litigant seemed invariably to lose, for there appeared to be hired assassins to take the part of the defeated, and to take out of the skin of the complainant what had passed to his pocket. *Shammas* flowing, the throng would surge and swell, crash here and there, all to the accompaniment of screams and curses, until the local police brushed that case aside, and made way for the next.

More important was a trial for murder that was being held, in which a man was accused of the murder of his brother, and we heard him adjudged guilty; but, as the punishment was bloody and gruesome, we were not present at the execution.

We were not sure, when the prisoner appeared in chains, whether he was to suffer death by knifing, hanging, or shooting: but the law was "an eye for an eye."

Retribution, it seems, follows exactly the footsteps of the crime. For so long as the victim suffered, so does the criminal. In what manner he killed, he dies. As much of his blood is spilled as he spilled in his crime, and the nearest relative of the dead man, even though it be a child of tender years, strikes the first blow.

My own interest was to worm out of the people any news that might, even remotely, be connected with things archaeological in the region, and information was scarce, or nonexistent. The feringhe was not to be shown caves, inscriptions, or ruins; but, as usual, one of the Greeks was amenable to bargaining, and told me of caves a few miles south of the capital, the secret of which had been betrayed by one of the servants of the Dajjazmac, and who agreed to show me the entrance to an underground fortress.

The boy spoke mission French, and I asked him how he knew about the caves.

As a child, he said, he had been told that if he were not good he would be sent to these holes in the earth, and on a hunting trip had seen the entrance; but dared not go inside, because no man had been there for generations, since it was the haunt of jackals and killing birds.

In the morning, while the others prepared for a hunting excursion as guests of the Governor, I went with the boy and my Greek to a particularly wild spot about two hours' ride away.

Here, on the terraces leading to the upper levels, holes in the walls were pointed out to me, and I suggested that we should all climb up.

The Greek, however, considered the horses too valuable to be left, so I went on, loading my shot-gun and loosening my revolver as I went, and climbed to the mouth of the nearest cave.

Looking down, it seemed to be just such a spot as prehistoric man would have welcomed: the caves faced south, with a fine river below and jungle round about. It offered food and an impregnable position.

I noticed that the entrance to the caves had been roughly blocked by great stones, and could recognize man's defensive work. This I indicated to the boy; but he only shook his head.

"Devils or *chiftas* move the rocks!" he said.

Inside the cave I was surprised to find a vast grotto, which my torch illumined none too well. The stench was terrible, and a wail from outside made me return. It was my boy, asking me to leave the caves alone, as his master would be angry. He seemed to think that, having shown me the entrance, that ought to suffice; but I returned, and began to examine the walls for rock-drawings, and to dig for flints with my alpenstock.

When, as I calculated, I was about thirty yards from the entrance, I discovered two well-cut passages leading, one to the right and the other to the left, towards the rear of the grotto, which appeared to be the work of ancient man.

From the depths came a most agonizing noise. Something was coming out. I stood back, holding my gun ready, and the rays of my torch concentrated on a bend in the rock corridor. There was an increasing pattering of feet, and a group of hyænas tore headlong past me. I emptied both barrels as they went, without being sure that I had done any damage, and they were gone, into the open, to the surprise of my guide, who let out a yell that would have roused half the city, had he been nearer. I followed, and found him jabbering with fear; but not so frightened but that he was stoning a wounded jackal with the great rocks of the canyon.

His scream, and my shots, had roused the echoes, and I was surprised to see two tattered and evil-looking individuals approaching from a narrow trail. They were the thinnest, most emaciated specimens that Abyssinia could boast of, and I asked who they were when they drew near and tried to prevent my return to the cave.

"Governor's goat-herds, *ras!*" said my guide. "Say no go back. There are death-birds in the caves."

I learned that he was not speaking of eagles, kites, or vultures. Then it must be bats again, and I had had experience of them in Mexico. There was no real need to worry about them whatever the natives might believe, so I went back to continue my examination, and, to give the birds something to think about, I emptied two cartridges into the roof of the far chamber.

The consequence was frankly startling. There was the sound of the whirring of wings as steady as the roar of water over a weir, and the birds flew around in fright, flapping me in the face, and knocking my helmet to the ground. Then there was dead silence, and I was left with only the smell, and my torch blazing, in whose rays I saw the remains of the prey of bats and hyænas on the ground, and their terribly foul carpet of filth; but I got to the end of the passage, and found a stone altar at the farthest point.

The altar was a sort of stone table, which had been roughly chipped to shape and size, and in the centre was a well-carved depression, with a channel leading over the edge.

Covering my face with my handkerchief, I roughly copied the drawings, which depicted a battle scene, similar to those of the Mountain of the Moon, and, note-book in hand, went back to the open, gasping for breath, and covered with the droppings of bats and hyænas. As I had had to work in the noisome stuff, my boots were covered with it, and incidentally I had released puffs of disgusting gas.

The attendants were returning, and I asked them why they were so afraid, to which they replied in good faith that they *were* afraid, because the birds were bloodsuckers, and preyed on men in the night. I laughed, and the two goat-herds said they would show me if it was anything to laugh at, leading the way up the side of the canyon by a path which must have been of ancient construction, and was cut in well-spaced steps out of the face of the rock.

The frailty of the goat-herds became more apparent as we climbed. They were so weak that their legs could hardly bear their weight; but, after half an hour's sweltering climb, I saw what they intended. Their *tukul* was open, and on the floor was a third man, covered with rags, obviously in sore straits.

He, I was told, was a victim of the birds. And they showed me punctures in his arm, and also in their own arms, which they attributed to the bats.

"Well, why not keep them out?" I asked.

They led me round, and showed me that every possible hole had been sealed with clay.

"Why not leave?"

They could not leave because they were tending the Governor's goats.

I turned, intending to quit the *tukul,* and walked straight into the headman of a nearby village, who had heard the commotion, seen us arrive, and had come to see what it was all about.

"Say nothing about the sick man," whispered my boy, and rather than incur any further complications I left them to it for the time being, and signaled across the valley to the Greek to go ahead and meet me at the point where the two paths joined.

The mission boy, who trotted along at my side, suddenly pulled out the tail of the dead hyæna from under his *sharama* and began to use it as a fly whisk. It is impossible ever to get into the mentality of these people.

That night, when the escort came to take us to the palace for the banquet, the private secretary came to my tent – news of my intended appeal to the Governor on behalf of the sick man having reached him through the agency of the guide, I suppose, and he, trying to forestall me, said that the Governor would be bitterly annoyed that I had gone to the caves without his permission.

"And what about the sick man?" I demanded. "Is nothing to be done for him?"

"There are many sick men in Wallega," he replied, "and they are none of your business. You cause trouble!"

For some time we kept it up, and finally he promised to take money and medicines to the man himself, provided that I kept quiet. I have often wondered if he did.

The "state" motor came for us. We dressed as well as we could, and, to make a showing, pooled our decorations, then drove over to the palace, where we were ushered into a sumptuous room, to await the moment when everyone was ready and due formality could be observed.

We were a fairly sorry lot, although we had got rid of our beards; but we thought it wouldn't matter too much, since after all this was an "up-state" capital. And then, just as we were complimenting ourselves, the door opened, and a servant in spotless and elegant uniform entered, bearing a silver tray on which were delicate glasses, filled with...an assortment of cocktails!

Almost immediately the Prince followed, in full evening dress of exquisite cut, and the Princess in a Paris gown, making one concession to Ethiopian decorum: her coiffure, which was done in traditional fashion, piled high and away from the forehead. She was one of the most beautiful women I have seen, with a skin that had a golden texture, fine and regular features, and large, expressive, almost Oriental eyes.

Dinner, which was prepared by a Russian chef, with three French assistants, was as formal and superb as could have been desired in any of the world's greatest capitals; the wines were in accordance with the courses, and of fine vintage; conversation was in French, and in my ears sounded the plaint of a man who wanted to get abroad again, or he would die of ennui. The Prince wanted particularly to go to Carlsbad for a cure, and the Princess would have been delighted to spend a little time in Paris!

I think, for contrast, that that dinner was the most unusual, unexpected thing that happened to us throughout Ethiopia!

The next morning, the Prince and Princess and their bodyguard posed for us in traditional costume, so that a film could be taken. Presents were exchanged, and we started again on the last stretch of trail, and happily with a greatly diminished escort.

While we had been banqueting with the Prince, the caravan had been feasting and drinking in a fashion perhaps less fastidious.

When it was time to start, we had to restore some of the porters, who had been on a drunk, and get others out of jail.

We left Nekempti with a mutual hang-over, loaded down with gifts of every kind, including many with which we parted on the way: they were so heavy that they could not be transported.

Our first stop was at a small Swedish mission on the way to Ambo, where, as if to remind us that we were once more nearing civilization, we learned of the riots in Paris and the death of

King Albert of Belgium. The missionary had a wireless that
worked.

These isolated missionaries are perhaps the most heroic people in the country, fighting a hopeless battle, because they are so
few, against disease. Our friend was as pale as death, almost
worn out in his fight against leprosy and venereal diseases.
Heroic; but defeated. It needs not one or two, but thousands,
properly to deal with the situation.

Leaving the mission, we approached the great mountains of
the central range, and enormous forests, covering wild canyons
and picturesque valleys, which made the country seem to be
more like a tourist-less Switzerland, or an African Tibet: a country of beauty and, as we soon saw, of secret terror.

Several days out from Nekempti, we came upon our first
sight of the secret slave traffic. Our camp lay among giant boab-
dids: massive trees of considerable beauty, giving excellent
shade. In the branches were baskets which the natives had hung
there for the wild bees, to facilitate the collection of honey.
There was also a dead *chifta,* in chains, mutilated and left to rot
or dry in the open.

We were near an old caravan ground, favourably placed on
the cross-roads of the Sudan, Eritrea, and Red Sea trails, so that
it was not so surprising to hear the muffled approach of a company travelling, towards midnight.

Nor did that approach worry us, even with our reduced
escort: we were well armed and guarded, and feared no attack.

What did increase our anxiety was the silence with which the
new-comers moved, for the Abyssinian on the trail is as noisy as
a travelling circus. These were moving with stealth, and we
could hear the distinct sound of chains.

I got to Derissa, and roused him, to ask what was passing on
the other side of the stream. He listened for a few moments and
gave his verdict. It was probably a slave caravan, trying to get
through to the Red Sea.

"What can we do about it?"

"Nothing, to-night," he replied. "Wait till to-morrow. They will march and hide. During the night, they would fight. During the day, talk."

As is well known, Ethiopia is now a member of the League of Nations, and slavery is officially abolished in consequence; but it is quite impossible to exterminate a centuries-old custom in five minutes. There are between three and four millions of unofficial slaves in Abyssinia to-day, and, just as in the days before the American Civil War, the slaves try to escape by the underground route, hiding in holes during the day, and at night making a dash for free territory.

Those who cannot escape are transported from time to time by secret trails, travelling at night in the direction of distant provinces and the shores of the Red Sea, where they are sold like cattle to the slave markets of Arabia and the east.

Not quite willing to accept Derissa's warning, we crept silently among the trees and watched, with hearts beating too noisily, the approach of the ancient curse of Africa.

First came an armed escort, carrying lances and guns, looming fantastically in the dim light, followed by a procession of foot-weary prisoners who seemed more like ghosts than human beings. Not a sound was heard beyond the shuffling of dragging feet and the dull clank of chains. It was a scene that almost drove us to challenge the caravan then and there; but we had to let the sorrowful company pass, Derissa saying that it would be better to lay information at Ambo when we arrived, and have a force sent out strong enough to deal with the Arabs, who would still be in the province of Shoa.

The mournful procession was soon swallowed in the night, bent on some hiding-place where they would lie low in the daytime.

For hours I lay awake, haunted by the silent phantoms, and the next day, after holding a council, we tried to find some means of overtaking the caravan, and, if possible, of taking photographs, not only for documentation, but for identification.

The result was that Derissa and one of the guides went on, to
search for the caravan, taking with them food and drink as presents, and later we collected the cameras and equipment, waiting
until they returned.

By what means I could never learn, they succeeded in persuading the leaders to permit us to visit them, on the solemn
promise that there should be no attack, and the bald statement
that my throat, among others, would be slit if there were any
trouble. So we followed, taking only our whistles, and leaving
our guard behind; but not too far behind.

We were met by a tall Arab, with a greying black beard and a
hawk-like face, whose piercing black eyes looked us over suspi-
ciously. Evidently he was satisfied that we had nothing to do
with the Abyssinian authorities, and Derissa explained that we
were a party of scientists.

At first we saw nobody but the Arabs who were carrying on
the slave trade; but baksheesh and a drink had the required
effect. Derissa with a gesture indicated the line of our search,
and we wandered until we came upon a group of famished individuals eating some of the corn we had sent.

They were a pitiful lot, and we chose one woman to question
while Derissa translated. She was evidently worn by suffering,
old before her time, and we learned that she came from the
extreme south of Wallega, and that slave raids and razzias are
still common among the Chankallas, as well as in Oualamo,
Sidamo, and the Bani Shanqul; at the cross-roads for which
provinces we then were.

The villages, she said, were raided repeatedly and she could
not remember her father or her mother, only that she was in her
village as a little girl when there was a raid by horsemen, and a
hand lifted her on to a saddle. In her life she had frequently been
in the beds of different people; but her children had all been
taken from her. She had travelled long distances by trail, from
place to place, punctuated only by frequent rape.

Derissa interpreted our question, "Had she now come to
accept her life?" and she grunted "Life!" All her faculties

seemed to be dead. She was always working, always being made love to, always being sold from one master to another. Often beaten. And she showed us the weals of the lash.

Repeating her slow words, Derissa said, "The children in our bodies never belong to us, but to the Arab merchants."

We were not allowed to stay. And we feared she would suffer more; but we got photographs of the groups, devouring their food like wild animals; of the slave-runners with their whips of raw hide, and of the encampment.

The flesh we had carried was eaten raw; but even that brought the slaves no pleasure; their expression was dull and glazed. There was not even the flash of a smile; they were too weary.

"What would happen if they escaped?" I asked.

Derissa knew the answer.

"If they were caught again, they would be hung upside down over a fire."

I should have been willing to see the Arabs shot on the spot, as we went back to our camp and took the trail again, a melancholy group.

Two days later, two of the slaves, having seen their chance, made their escape and caught up with us. We took them as far as Addis Ababa, where we tried to get them jobs as hotel porters.

Even our own company was not without the predatory spirit. One of the caravan leaders, seeing a boy of about fourteen years of age working alone in a bit of pasture, descended on him and would have (literally) bagged him, to become his own servant, had we not interfered. There was a fight before we could make him see our point of view; but he cursed us roundly, and told us that we were no Christians.

On arrival at Ambo, we informed the authorities that we had seen the slave caravan going through the mountains, and the official reply was that information would be sent through to the Central Government at Addis Ababa, asking for a military escort to cut them off; but it seemed to me that before Addis Ababa could act (even if such a request were forwarded), the poor devils would finish their journey without hindrance, to end some-where in a country where slavery had no official significance.

Unfortunately, on the way to Ambo, due entirely to my own carelessness, I was badly bitten by a horned viper, and the rest of my journey was as painful as it was unadventurous.

Game had been seen in different directions, and some of us went one way, some another. I had not stopped to put on my boots, going after a deer with only light canvas shoes on my feet. Treading quietly, as I tried to get near enough for a shot, I felt something soft give underfoot, and the next moment received a blow that sent an electric current up my leg, and, looking down, saw the snake just disappearing.

I ran back to camp, and a serum was injected; but we were not quite certain what snake it was. The others went to see if they could find it or its mate on the trail; but failed. So we pushed on, sending our fastest horses to Bilo, where there was a telephone station. From Bilo a message was sent to Addis Ababa, asking for a car to be sent out to pick me up.

At Guedalla we had our last battle with the officials. It is well named the "place of thieves," and the boy (he was little more) who held us up for baksheesh in the name of authority was a true son of the place. We were refused passage. Our passports and the letters of Governors and Ministers meant nothing to him, although by that time we were not so very far from Addis Ababa.

I was full of whisky and serum and pain, and I simply drew a revolver and pushed it in the youngster's face. My companions did the same, while Derissa translated our last message to the bandit.

"There is no question of baksheesh, and we are going through. In twenty-four hours you will have the Emperor's troops here, and I hope they string you up!"

It worked. It generally happens in Abyssinia that, if you make a sufficient show of force, and don't retract an inch, you get your way.

At Ambo, I remember the kindness of the Italian Mission, and the arrival of a car, sent by the French Minister from Addis Ababa, in which I was taken to the capital, laid on the operating table, cut about a bit, and cauterized. Then we waited to see what would follow. Gangrene meant a foot; but nothing developed, and several days later a message was received from the Minister of Foreign Affairs that His Majesty the Emperor would receive the expedition at the Jhibi, or Royal Palace, at four o'clock on the following afternoon.

I paid my round of courtesy visits, returning honest thanks for everything that had been done to make the expedition a success. We had succeeded in getting through the back door, and everything had turned out well, including some worthwhile discoveries.

Incidentally, we borrowed fitting clothes for the reception; our own having been lost somewhere in transit, and, full of anti-toxin, we proceeded to the palace on the hill.

There, amid the magnificent gardens that surround the palace, we saw the supplicants waiting their turn. Evidently, many had no appointment; for they had waited, and might wait still, for weeks. Or so we were told.

In the royal enclosures, something like two thousand people were housed, including officials, priests, ministers and generals, political leaders and courtiers.

I was on crutches, but they helped me down the long corridors and through rooms full of white-clad dignitaries, who passed us along until we stood in the throne room, where the members of the expedition were presented, one by one, to a tired-looking, noble figure who smiled us a friendly greeting.

Through his interpreter, for court procedure demanded classic Amharic, he asked us frankly about the expedition, since we had come through a little-known region, concerning which even the authorities were anxious to learn. He wanted to know if his representatives had done all they should: had our escorts been sufficient and efficient; and for an hour and a half we told the

Emperor in detail of our discoveries, which he considered important enough to have published.

Then he turned to the question of Ophir, the gold and emerald mines, and the rock-inscriptions.

"It has been a long trail, Alexandria to Addis Ababa," he smiled. "I am sorry you were wounded at the end."

A subject that interested him was the reported discovery by a French aviator of the capital of the Queen of Sheba, and he discussed the probability of its authenticity, since the Emperor is supposed to be the direct descendant of that Queen and Solomon.

When he gave us a kindly farewell, he suggested that it might be within my programme to take an expedition by land to reach what had been seen from the air. His mind was still on the famous Queen. So is mine! It is not out of the realm of possibilities that my next trail will be on the way to just that place.

The End

THE NARRATIVE PRESS

TRUE FIRST PERSON ACCOUNTS OF HIGH ADVENTURE

The Narrative Press prints only true, first-person accounts of adventures — explorations, circumnavigations, shipwrecks, jungle treks, safaris, mountain climbing, spelunking, treasure hunts, espionage, polar expeditions, and a lot more.

Some of the authors are famous (Ernest Shackleton, Kit Carson, Sir Richard Burton, Francis Chichester, Henry Stanley, T. E. Lawrence, Buffalo Bill). Some of the adventures are scientifically or historically important. Every one of these stories is fascinating.

All of our books are available as high-quality, lifetime softcover paper books. Each is also available as an electronic ebook, ready for viewing on your desktop, laptop, or handheld computer.

Visit our on-line catalog today, or call or write to us for a free copy of our printed catalog.

THE NARRATIVE PRESS
P.O.Box 2487, Santa Barbara, California 93120 U.S.A.
(800) 315-9005
www.narrativepress.com